VISUAL METHODS of Inquiry

Visual Methods of Inquiry: Images as Research presents qualitative researchers in the social sciences with the benefits, applications, and forms of visual research methods. It includes a wide variety of images to illustrate the many uses of visual methods for social research.

Contemporary visual culture theory and practice offers wide-ranging opportunities for methodological advancement in the social sciences. This book covers the basics of image use in visual research methods and explores how these methods can be used effectively in social science research by surveying the conditions of visual forms, materials, and concepts, and the ways these represent and influence social conditions, phenomena, beliefs, and actions. It examines the roles and processes of interpretation in visual research and discusses ethical considerations that arise when using visual research methods.

Students of social science and the visual arts will find this book useful in expanding and improving their methods of inquiry. Artists and researchers already familiar with visual methods will find that this book clarifies the ways the visual works in various research contexts and provides helpful language to describe and explain those methods.

Kerry Freedman is a professor and coordinator of Doctoral Programs in Art and Design Education at Northern Illinois University, USA. She is the author and editor of several books and many articles, and has won numerous awards for her work.

Richard Siegesmund is a professor of art and design education at Northern Illinois University, USA. He is the co-author (with Melisa Cahnmann-Taylor) of *Arts-Based Research in Education: Foundations for Practice*, second edition (Routledge, 2018).

"In this book, Kerry Freedman and Richard Siegesmund brilliantly demonstrate the benefits, applications and forms of critical visual research methods in the humanities and social sciences. It is a must read. Visual research comes of age with this book. It challenges artists and inquirers to embrace uncertainty, to organize disruption, to empower resistance, to work without the guardrails of methodology, to find that cliff where they fly to new horizons."
— **Norman K. Denzin,** *Emeritus Professor of Sociology, Communications, and Cinema Studies, University of Illinois*

"Visual Methods of Inquiry: Images as Research is a must-read. This comprehensive, accessible text is a theoretically informed introduction to the increasingly popular domain of visual research. Offering striking imagery and wide-ranging practical strategies with ethical considerations, this cross-disciplinary book will be highly influential for researchers, and students alike, who wish to enhance their knowledge and understanding of qualitative visual research methodologies."
— **Wanda B. Knight,** *Ph.D., Professor of Art Education, African American Studies, and Women's, Gender, and Sexuality Studies, and Bioethics, Penn State University, United States. President of the National Art Education Association*

"From images as data records to images as reports: this book covers it all, with respect for the diversity in epistemological positions taken in different disciplines. It makes a convincing case for how visual evidence can be produced, processed, interpreted and judged for quality in relation to other types of research data. How can one not recognize the value of images to capture and transfer complex layers of information that language struggles to reveal? Consider this book a purposeful invitation to move from intertextuality to intergraphicality."
— **Karin Hannes,** *Ph.D. Professor, Urban Studies Institute, Faculty of Social Sciences, KU Leuven, Belgium. Chair, European Network of Qualitative Inquiry*

"Visual Methods of Inquiry: Images as Research is a groundbreaking book that explores and critically analyzes visual research methods, offering an innovative perspective for students and researchers across disciplines. As an excellent introductory text, it expertly draws connections between the visual arts and social sciences with its lucid writing and rich visuals. It is an indispensable resource providing students and researchers with the knowledge and tools to better understand how visuals work in research."
— **Juan Carlos Castro,** *Ph.D., Professor, Art Education, Concordia University, Canada*

VISUAL METHODS of Inquiry

Images as Research

Kerry Freedman and Richard Siegesmund

LONDON AND NEW YORK

Designed cover image: Aboriginal painting, c. 2014, Esther 1721

First published 2024
by Routledge
4 Park Square, Milton Park, Abingdon, Oxon OX14 4RN

and by Routledge
605 Third Avenue, New York, NY 10158

Routledge is an imprint of the Taylor & Francis Group, an informa business

© 2024 Kerry Freedman and Richard Siegesmund

The right of Kerry Freedman and Richard Siegesmund to be identified as authors of this work has been asserted in accordance with sections 77 and 78 of the Copyright, Designs and Patents Act 1988.

All rights reserved. No part of this book may be reprinted or reproduced or utilised in any form or by any electronic, mechanical, or other means, now known or hereafter invented, including photocopying and recording, or in any information storage or retrieval system, without permission in writing from the publishers.

Trademark notice: Product or corporate names may be trademarks or registered trademarks, and are used only for identification and explanation without intent to infringe.

British Library Cataloguing-in-Publication Data
A catalogue record for this book is available from the British Library

ISBN: 978-0-367-25049-2 (hbk)
ISBN: 978-0-367-25048-5 (pbk)
ISBN: 978-0-429-28572-1 (ebk)

DOI: 10.4324/9780429285721

Typeset in Warnock Pro
by KnowledgeWorks Global Ltd.

Contents

Acknowledgements		vii
Introduction:	Why Visual Research Methods?	1
	Why Is This Book Needed Now? 4	
	References 5	
Chapter 1	Visual Research Methods Across the Disciplines	7
	A Brief History of Visual Investigation 7	
	The Influence of Visual Culture on Social Life 18	
	Foundations of the Book 21	
	Four Major Problems of the Visual in Research 24	
	Overview of the Book 30	
	Conclusion 32	
	References 33	
Chapter 2	Visual Perception and Conceptions of Visual Research	35
	The Science of Visual Perception 37	
	The Philosophy of Vision and Perception 48	
	Conclusion 54	
	Note 55	
	References 55	
Chapter 3	Visual Qualities and the Functions of Images in Research	59
	Visual Literacy and the Power of the Image 61	
	Formal Visual Qualities: The Elements and Principles of Design 65	
	Empirical Evidence: Visual Qualities and New Materialism 69	
	Four Sources of Evidence for Visual Interpretation 71	
	How Images Function in Research 76	

Contents

Thinking with Materials in and Through Qualities 79
Conclusion 80
References 81

Chapter 4 Visuality in Social Science Research — 85

The Influence of Aesthetic Modernism on Contemporary Images 86
Research as Visual Criticism: The Connection of Knowledge to Emotion 90
The Phenomenological Flexibility of Visual Methodologies 93
Disciplinary Approaches to the Use of Visual Research Methods 98
Conclusion 110
References 111

Chapter 5 Description of Visual Methods: The Research Image Framework — 117

Building an Iconic Store to Support Visual Evidence 119
Choosing the Right Visual Research Method 121
The Research Image Framework 123
Expanding the Research Image Framework 125
Conclusion 141
References 141

Chapter 6 Making Judgments: Analyzing the Visual as Evidence — 147

Quantitative and Qualitative Analyses from Visual Sources 148
Making Reliable Judgments: The Concept and Practices of Provenance 153
Establishing Criteria and the Zone of Image Interpretation 155
Approaches to an Analysis of Research Images 156
The Image Analysis Matrix 172
Conclusion 193
References 193

Chapter 7 Ethics of Practice for Visual Research Methods — 197

Responsibility in Social Science Research 198
Images and Truth 203
The Agency of Imagery 205
Interpretation and Rationality 209
The Moral Obligation of Creation 211
Conclusion 213
References 214

Index — 217

Acknowledgements

The authors are eternally grateful to Norm Denzin, who first invited us to conduct a workshop on visual research methods at the International Congress of Qualitative Inquiry at the University of Illinois, Champaign-Urbana, and asked us back again and again. We also thank Karin Hannes for inviting us to conduct workshops at the European Congress of Qualitative Inquiry. Many thanks to the participants who filled those workshops and asked the questions that lead to writing this book. We are appreciative of Allan Edmunds of the Brandywine Workshop and Archives in Philadelphia for permissions to reproduce visual images from its collection, as well as the other scholars and artists who supported this effort by allowing us to publish their work. We are indebted to the scholarship of Elliot Eisner, which opened the door for us to explore methodological relationships between the visual arts and the social sciences.

We thank our first Senior Editor at Routledge, Hannah Shakespeare, for her faith in this project. We are grateful for the support of Northern Illinois University for this work.

We thank our current and former doctoral students who contributed to and made comments about this project. Many thanks to Johnson Wor and Meng-Jung Yang for their graphic design work and to Eva Coker, Kathryn Sowinski, and Johnson Wor for their help with editing and indexing.

Finally, we express our deepest gratitude to our spouses, Doug Boughton and Brigitta Hangartner, who have continually supported us through the highs and lows of this project and often acted as sounding boards. Without their care, this project would not have been accomplished.

Introduction

Why Visual Research Methods?

This book introduces qualitative researchers in the social sciences to the benefits, applications, and forms of visual research methods. We hope that both artists and researchers who are already familiar with arts-based methods will find that this book clarifies the ways the visual works in various research contexts and provides helpful language to describe and explain those methods.

While the forms and conditions of visual culture are increasingly recognized as topics of research, relatively little has changed with regards to education about visual research methods. Contemporary visual culture offers wide-ranging opportunities for methodological advancement, including through the uses of personal enhancements (such as mobile phones), creative computer graphics, robot design, and innovations in virtual reality. Just a few years ago, the technology to produce a Hollywood movie would have cost many thousands of dollars to obtain and years of training to master. Now, researchers hold it in their hands, opening up new opportunities for inquiry.

Nevertheless, little or no formal training exists in the application and analysis of visual images in many academic social science programs. Visual methods are treated in an auxiliary manner, sometimes merely mentioned in qualitative research methods education, sometimes ignored all together. It is high time for all social science and arts-based researchers to be educated in the effects of visual culture, not only as a topic of research, but also in terms of the many visual methods used to conduct research. A range of basic visual research methods exists that are successfully applied across multiple disciplines, which should be included in any contemporary social researcher's toolbox of research strategies. In this book, we have added and delineated more. Visual methods can aid researchers in their investigations of many types of questions and should be considered foundational to any social science research methods course, not only limited to researchers who self-identify as visual researchers or whose research questions specifically pertain to the visual.

The authors draw on their academic and professional training in both the social sciences and the visual arts. This includes decades of experience in conducting empirical and philosophical research concerning visual information, learning, and making. We have conducted and published the results of those analyses; used and taught multiple courses in collecting, analyzing, and reporting visual data; and critiqued the use of such methods as members of doctoral dissertation and scientific committees, editorial boards, and book editors.

Over several years, the authors of this book have conducted many workshops about visual research methods for professional art and social science researchers in various venues, particularly the International Congress of Qualitative Inquiry (ICQI) and the European Congress of Qualitative Inquiry (ECQI). In part, this book is a response to the challenges our ICQI and ECQI workshop participants have faced in their research that we hope we have helped them to address.

We have been asked many questions by workshop participants, such as: "I have collected a bunch of pictures from the participants in my study — what should I do with them?" How can I use imagery to represent my results?" "I think some type of images should be used in this study, but I don't know anything about art — what should I do?" This book answers those questions and much more. It introduces new qualitative researchers in the arts and social sciences to the benefits, applications, and forms of visual research methods. The book adds clarity to subtle differences in the ways images function and are analyzed in different research contexts for researchers already familiar with visual research methods. We hope that it will help experienced social scientists who have not used visual research methods to become comfortable with the use of images in their work.

Visual research methods are a set of techniques and approaches used to gather, analyze, and interpret data through the use of newer and traditional visual media. These methods can provide unique insights into the social world, by revealing and helping to construct knowledge related to complex social phenomena and behaviors in ways that traditional research methods cannot. In this book, we cover the basics of image use in visual research methods and explore how these methods can be used effectively in social science research. We examine the conditions of visual form, different types of visual media (such as photography, digital imagery, and traditional art materials), and the ways these can be used to represent social conditions, phenomena, beliefs, and

Introduction

actions. We will also examine the roles and processes of interpretation in visual research and explore the ethical considerations that arise when using visual research methods.

For decades, professionals across disciplines in the arts and social science have begun to recognize the ways images can be fundamental to contemporary research by inscribing complex information that language struggles to reveal. However, full acceptance of the visual in social science research has been slow. For some researchers, images are an afterthought or perhaps merely an illustration of text and numbers. Yet, images are so much more as they emphasize knowledge that cannot be put into words and carry complex associative meanings that defy simple declarative sentences.

Images can disrupt semiotic analysis and actively resist the textual interpretation a researcher attempts to drape over them because they do not have fixed meanings. The interpretation of an image changes through the influence of the maker, the image itself, and the audiences who view it. Thus, the authentic power of the visual lies beyond illustration—it may even expose failures of semiotic systems. Images push beyond symbolic communication to what has been left unsaid. These mercurial characteristics of visuality are dealt within the discipline of visual art.

Social scientists should consider using images in their research for several broad reasons. First, images can provide valuable insights and perspectives not apparent through traditional research methods, such as surveys or interviews. Through images, researchers can gain greater access to social phenomena and behaviors shaped by cultural, historical, and social contexts. Social science research, in a sense, literally and figuratively slows down phenomena so people can see it better. For example, researchers have learned how humans and animals run by slowing down their motions with a camera so that each part of the movement can be seen. This is one of many advantages of the use of images in research — they help people see.

Second, images are useful tools for engaging and communicating research findings to multiple audiences. Visual media can be an effective way to convey complex ideas and information in an accessible and engaging way. This can be particularly useful for researchers working in fields such as sociology, anthropology, education, and cultural studies, where the use of visual media can help to bring research findings to life and make them relevant and relatable to different groups of people.

Third, the use of images in research can also help to challenge and complicate traditional ways of thinking and understanding social phenomena, often enabling a more complex representation or explanation than words alone. By using visual media, researchers can bring attention to underrepresented or marginalized perspectives and help to expand and diversify the ways in which social phenomena are studied and understood. Whether you are new to visual research methods, or an experienced researcher intending to expand your methods knowledge and skills, this book will provide you with an understanding of the power of visual images in social science research.

Why Is This Book Needed Now?

At least three aspects of visual culture have changed in recent decades, which now requires researchers to both adopt visual methods and be skeptical about a solely semiotic approach as a foundation for designing visual research, applying visual methods, and interpreting visual data. First, new brain and cognition research on human responses to imagery is at the heart of the ontological and epistemological debate concerning ways that meaning is made (e.g. Klein, 2010; Poldrack & Yarkoni, 2015; Shulman, 2013). Epistemology rests on coming to know through symbols. Ontology suggests the shaping of meaning and responsive actions based on experience: what we sense before we have words to say. The processes of the brain that lead to concept building prior to making meaning are still unclear to brain researchers, and they have been working to find a first step. Regardless, the evidence is clear that viewers make selections and decisions about the images they see to make meaning (Spelke & Kinzler, 2007).

Second, imagery has come to underpin all social behavior and influence all sociological substructures and superstructures. The superstructure is easy to find; it is the art, media, and other visual culture people see every day. The substructure of visual culture may be less easy to see, but it has become critical to understanding contemporary human behavior. It includes the human desires and capacities to make something visible, to create using visual tools, and to view these creations daily. This process can be long-lasting and have far-reaching effects. It follows the accepted process of visual perception: visual reception, transduction, transmission, organization, and interpretation. However, the authors of this book add the process of *integration* following *interpretation,* where a person absorbs and integrates selected interpretations of the image, applies them to conscious thought and carries them in memory. Integration involves the adoption of visual creations as schema, and the use of small and large-scale effects of schema to re-shape one's ideas, actions, and beliefs over time. The psychological integration of images changes a person, including their identities, the person then may create (or recreate) new visual forms, which feed back to the creator, as well as their intended and unintended audiences. It is through this integration cycle that one has the possibility of seeing and being seen, creating and re-creating oneself — and culture at large — in and through images.

Third, visual research methods have developed as part of visual culture, which has increased in complexity, clarity, and applicability. As a result, visual methods of research and analyses now have the capacity to enable researchers to investigate social behaviors that words and numbers cannot reveal, increasing the possibilities of inquiry in the social sciences. Although such research methods are just being introduced in some social sciences, other disciplines have developed and used these methods long enough for them to have been theorized, challenged, and improved.

Anyone in the social sciences can come to know and use visual research methods; however, as is the case with other research methods, this knowledge requires learning. Visual culture has played expanding roles in advanced cultures and economies through its many forms of production, interpretation, and criticism, which require both an expanding pool of creators and a visually literate population of viewers. In this book, we will discuss why and how the use of visual research methods requires researchers to develop specifically visual literacies and what those literacies entail.

References

Klein, C. (2010). Images are not the evidence in neuroimaging. *The British Journal for the Philosophy of Science*, 61(2), 265–278.

Poldrack, R. A. &, Yarkoni, T. (2015). From brain maps to cognitive ontologies: Informatics and the search for mental structure. *Annual Review of Psychology*, 67, 587–612. https://doi.org/10.1146/annurev-psych-122414-033729

Shulman, R. G. (2013). *Brain imaging: What it can (and cannot) tell us about consciousness.* Oxford University Press.

Spelke, E. S., & Kinzler, K. D. (2007). Core knowledge. *Developmental Science*, 10(1), 89–96. https://doi.org/10.1111/j.1467-7687.2007.00569.x

CHAPTER 1

Visual Research Methods Across the Disciplines

Visual forms of expression and communication have become deeply embedded in all world cultures, and vast amounts of knowledge and experience are mediated by humanly created visual forms. From the creation of a painting or photograph to the mass distribution of visual content through digital media, humanly made visual information, communication, and investigation have become essential parts of contemporary daily life. As a result, researchers across disciplines need a new level of visual literacy, which accurately relates to the impact of the visual on all forms of human interaction and knowledge. In this chapter, we briefly present a summary of the history of visual research methods, discuss the influence of the visual on social life, present the theoretical foundations of the book, and finally delineate four major problems of visual research methods. Visual research methods are a group of processes and strategies that depend on visuality for inquiry through the use of drawing, photography, video, and other traditionally and digitally made visual culture forms. In this book, we focus primarily on the benefits, theories, and methods of including imagery in qualitative research.

A Brief History of Visual Investigation

Visual images have always had far-reaching implications for the acquisition and representation of human knowledge. Beginning at least 65,000 years ago

Visual Methods of Inquiry

Figure 1.1 Bunjil Shelter, Australia: Koori Aboriginal rock painting. Courtesy Michael Barnett, CC BY-SA 3.0 via Wikimedia Common.

with early European cave paintings, 45,000-year-old Indonesian cave paintings, and 40,000-year-old Australian Aboriginal rock art paintings (Figure 1.1), humans have had a long history of creating images and artifacts as part of our search for remembrance and knowledge. Before letter-based alphabets, people learned through the use of visual symbol systems. Ancient empires used images to convey political messages and demonstrate and consolidate power. In Africa and South and Central America, early calendars and other visual devises reveal mathematical, phenological, and astronomical research. People began to illustrate their studies of the world around them in China in the Eastern Zhou period (770–256 BC). Paper-making is believed to have been invented in China in 105 A.D., making not only writing, but drawing and painting, cheaply transportable (Figure 1.2). The earliest surviving Western botanical illustrations are in a copy of the Roman *Dioscoride's Materia Medica* made in 512.

In the European Middle Ages and Renaissance, as writing advanced, but few could read, images were critical sources of information. Illustrated religious manuscripts and precious devotional objects were carefully maintained by clergy and elite social classes to preserve knowledge. Visual representations of important social messages were placed in selected locations, such as places of worship and public spaces. People learned Bible stories, and the morals they carried, by viewing frescos, bas-reliefs, paintings, free-standing sculptures, and stained-glass windows in churches; even the architecture had a message. One of the authors of this book recalls first visiting European, Medieval cathedrals as an undergraduate, and coming to understand how their immense grandeur must have helped convince people living in local hovels to believe that only the hand of a supernatural being could hold them up (Figure 1.3).

Visual Research Methods Across the Disciplines

Figure 1.2 *Fish Swimming Amid Falling Flowers*, Liu Cai, c.1080–1120.
Saint Louis Art Museum, Public domain, via Wikimedia Commons.

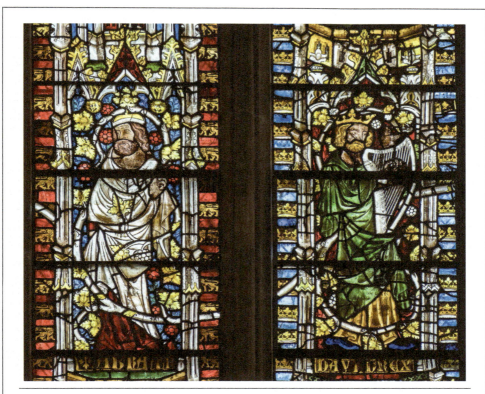

Figure 1.3 Abraham and King David, Jesse Window detail, Wells Cathedral Somerset, England, c. 1340.
Courtesy Jules and Jenny from Lincoln, UK, CC BY 2.0 via Wikimedia Commons.

Visual Methods of Inquiry

Figure 1.4 Angkor Wat, Cambodia, 12th century.
Courtesy Diego Delso, delso.photo, License CC-BY-SA via Wikimedia Commons.

Similarly, Buddhist temple sculpture also attempted to alter the viewer's reality as they walked through carefully designed visual spaces. At Angkor Wat, built in the 12th century in Cambodia, the rooms and artwork encountered while meandering through pathways and climbing the temple steps were intended to instruct the viewer in how to obtain enlightenment (Figure 1.4).

Early in the history of elite art across cultures, artists and patrons realized that images of people could flatter, and images of events could exaggerate and otherwise alter the historical record. Increasingly over time, powerful Europeans leveraged the visual arts to display their individual grandeur and consolidate political power. As exemplified by the 15th-century the *Très Riches Heures,* many royal and aristocratic owners over centuries paid artists to complete, enhance, and augment the images in order to glorify owners' significance. Sometimes owners' figures were even added to the work several centuries after the work's initial painting. Whether for religious, political, or other purposes, images have long been used for social control (Figure 1.5).

As fine art evolved as a means to document people and events, art also projected an *impression* of reality. For example, through court artists (starting in Europe by the mid-13th century), royalty could be presented as wealthier and more powerful than they were, instead of "warts and all." Artists began to develop subtle perceptual tricks to aggrandize the subject. Hans Holbein's 16th-century portrait of the English King Henry VIII is a classic example. Holbein captures the king's elaborate costuming: the padding that makes

Figure 1.5 *Très Riches Heures du duc de Berry*, Folio 5, verso: May, Limbourg brothers, c. 1412.
Public domain, via Wikimedia Commons.

Henry's shoulders extend like bulging muscles and the jewelry to denote wealth and authority. All of these contribute to sense of the King as a kind of superhero (Figure 1.6).

At the same time, the desire to see and create imagery that accurately records seems to be hardwired into the human brain. This could be called the Rumpelstiltskin effect. In the fairytale, to speak the name of the evil spirit destroys its mystical influence; the speaker has the power to control the subject. Drawing something as it appears does the same thing; the image, in a sense, allows the artist control over the subject—or at least control over how it is seen. Once an individual is bronze casted as a heroic general on horseback, the historical record is set; it becomes difficult to unsee such an image. It is difficult to rewrite in text the message projected from cast bronze, carved marble, or other monumental materials. The image becomes the fact. The early 20th-century rush to fill city squares in the American South with heroic statues of generals and soldiers from the American Civil War was an attempt to control the future by establishing a narrative that would secure a continuing social order, which had

Visual Methods of Inquiry

Figure 1.6 *Henry VIII at 49*, 1540, by Hans Holbein the Younger, Gallerie Nazionali d'arte antica, Palazzo Barberini, Rome.
Public domain, via Wikimedia Commons.

been lost on the battlefield and repudiated in national legislation. The visual gambit worked for over 100 years.

The desire to render and map the world as a permanent record appears across cultures. Maps take many forms. For example, early European cartographers mapped the known world beautifully with sea monsters and treacherous mermaids. In contrast, Australia Aboriginal paintings made of dots are not abstractions in the French Impressionist sense. They are dreamtime paintings, which are literal maps of co-current realities (Figure 1.7).

Different cultures produce diversity in conceptions of what is important to record in regard to time and space. An early 20th-century railroad map from Japan provides a strikingly different conception from Western map making conventions as to the importance of explanatory contextual information that a traveler would find helpful (Figures 1.8 and 1.9).

One aspect of the history of European fine art is the continued effort to increase human capabilities for visual realism through representational skills and technologies. A hallmark of the transition between the Middle Ages and the Renaissance in Europe depended on efforts to discover (and re-discover) realistic methods of visual representation. European artists and scientists

Visual Research Methods Across the Disciplines

Figure 1.7 Aboriginal dreamtime painting, 2014.
Courtesy Esther 1721 https://pixabay.com/nl/users/esther1721-534895/, CC0, via Wikimedia Commons.

began to investigate the visual from a scientific perspective, using careful analyses to figure out ways to show three-dimensional objects and space on a two-dimensional surface. This ability to accurately represent the world enabled people to use drawing as a tool to advance the study of natural forms, such as human anatomy and plant species. Artists such as Leonardo Da Vinci and his

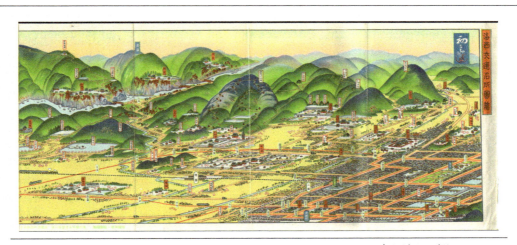

Figure 1.8 *Kyoto Rail Guide* (detail), Hatsusaburō Yoshida (吉田初三郎), 1928. Public domain, via Wikimedia Commons.

13

Visual Methods of Inquiry

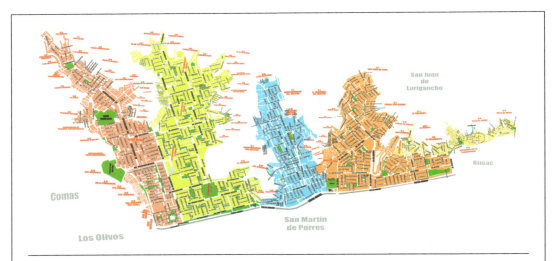

Figure 1.9 Map of Independencia, Lima, Peru, 2001.
Courtesy Dunkwadie, CC BY-SA 4.0 via Wikimedia Commons.

contemporary Albrecht Dürer considered drawing a mechanism for scientific, as well as aesthetic, investigation. In Italy, Da Vinci wrote that new ideas often arise through deep analysis of the visual (Isaacson, 2017). He looked for visual patterns and forms in nature, then drew them to come to know their intricacies. Juxtaposing dissimilar images sparked creativity. Da Vinci found information in the visual, then studied it through drawing so as to construct new knowledge—he used drawing as a method of research. In Germany, Dürer did visual research to clarify principles of measurement and body proportion, which he described in two published books. He created a drawing technology that enabled him to study perspective and established the basic principle of ray tracing, a rendering technique foundational to contemporary computer graphic software (Figure 1.10). In the Netherlands, the techniques for manufacturing high-quality reflective lenses—key to producing precise images through a camera obscura—were closely guarded state secrets.

Close to a century after Da Vinci and Dürer, Renaissance scientists used images to communicate ideas to large populations. For example, in the early 1600s when Galileo sought to publish his research into the rotation of the sun, his publisher wanted to reproduce his drawings with woodcuts. However, woodcuts produce ragged, irregular lines. Galileo feared that the scruffy line quality would not convey the illusion of sequential movement, so he personally paid to have his drawings engraved in metal to produce an extraordinary level of precision and detail critical for the reader seeing, and understanding, his sequential drawings as an animation. Not any kind of illustration would do; Galileo recognized that different *qualities* of visual information produce

Visual Research Methods Across the Disciplines

Figure 1.10 Renaissance perspective grid, n.d.
CC BY 4.0 via Wikimedia Commons.

different understandings. Galileo's final illustrations produced a kind of flip book that allowed the reader to clearly grasp that the sun rotated. John Amos Comenius, who also lived in the late 16th and early 17th centuries, remembered in the discipline of education for creating the first educational textbooks with engraved plates to support learning, demonstrated that pictures aid comprehension. Words could not fully replace visual information.

Although Chinese artists' interest in precise, accurate drawings of the natural world had begun as early as 900 A.D., the European "golden age" of scientific illustration was not until the 18th century when artists and scientists became highly skilled at showing plants and animals in extreme detail. Many of the nature artists of the period were women, such as Sarah Drake in England. The German-born artist, Maria Sibylla Merian, was one of the earliest naturalists to observe and document insects, discovering that caterpillars turn to butterflies. She also drew detailed, scientific images of flora, fauna, and sea life (Figure 1.11).

In the early days of Western social science research during the 19th century, much of the visual character of the culture we have today had not been imagined. Cameras were a new technology, clothes and other cultural products were not mass produced for worldwide distribution, and publications did not

Visual Methods of Inquiry

Figure 1.11 Maria Sibylla Merian, *Metamorphosis insectorum Surinamensium*, Plate LX, 1705.
Public domain, via Wikimedia Commons.

include color. By the mid-19th century, art education was proposed for schools in the United States as a means of improving handwriting legibility (Efland, 1990). However, drawing education quickly became a means to prepare students for industrial work and school curriculum required the children to make precise copies of geometric forms and patterns. As children got older, they were to copy adult landscape and moral story drawings. Children did not see mass produced images in U.S. public schools until the late 19th century. Although the adult artists' crayon was introduced in 1644, and the concept of a color stick is even older, the Crayola crayons most children now grow up with were only introduced into schools in 1903, quickly popularizing the concept that image making was something everyone could do.

The camera evolved from being regarded as a highly specialized novelty for producing a historical record, to an innovative global tool for popular creative exploration. When the technology capable of recording a fixed, light-sensitive image was widely introduced in the early 19th century, some people believed that the camera's images represented "real life," and therefore did not show the photographer's hand. At the same time, art was expected to illustrate the natural world. This prompted a widespread, cultural discussion suggesting that photography would end art because representations of reality had finally been achieved. Ironically, this debate unleashed painting and sculpture to new expressive and interpretive possibilities. Rather than being elevated to the epitome of art, photography was relegated to the role of a mechanical tool that passively recorded non-biased information. Even the highly manipulated spirit photographs of the latter 19th century, which superimposed ghostly images of a deceased loved one around the living sitter, were peddled as more mysteriously true (since they were photographs) than works of imaginative art (Figure 1.12). The concept that photography itself was creative did not gain mainstream acceptance until the mid-20th century as benchmarked by the Museum of Modern Art's (1940) recognition of two new art forms: motion pictures in 1936 and photography in 1940. As it became more apparent that photography was highly selective, framed, posed, and manipulated, the long-standing search for reality on a two-dimensional surface continued in newer, digital technologies through investigations of computer graphics, leading to images that are hyper-real.

Today, most people experience life through mass-produced, distributed, and redistributed images and artifacts. Widespread images and artifacts can influence how we feel, how we look, what we believe, how we vote, what we eat,

Figure 1.12 Spirit photograph portrait of John K. Hallowell, surrounded by faces of the dead, 1901.
Fallis, S. W., photographer, Public domain, via Wikimedia Commons.

Visual Methods of Inquiry

and so on. Humanly created visual forms not only influence what we think, but also *how* we think, and they have changed the ways people interact, conduct business, and come to know.

The Influence of Visual Culture on Social Life

Research has illustrated the effects of contemporary imagery on the ways people see themselves and others, even at a young age (Reavey, 2020). For example, extensive research has demonstrated that the visual qualities of advertising influence youth identity, but the range of popular culture has the same potential. Images in international, popular culture, such as games, comics, and videos, influence youth group identities through social, intellectual, and aesthetic learning (e.g., Freedman et al., 2013). Young people learn and socialize through their use and production of such popular imagery (e.g., Karpati et al., 2016). Those who grow up in postindustrial countries are likely to experience this pervasive popular, visual context as a fish in water, often being unaware of the profound effects of the image rich milieu (Figure 1.13).

As a result, the range of visual forms and their conditions are now referred to as visual culture. Visual culture is the variety of humanly made forms and

Figure 1.13 Comic-Con 2013, San Diego.
Courtesy Pat Loika, CC BY 2.0, via Wikimedia Commons.

practices, including historical and contemporary visual and media arts, which represent and transform individuals and cultural groups, influencing through their visual impact (Freedman, 2003). As part of this cultural transformation, social scientists are investigating the ramifications of visual culture on human behavior and the implications of making for both creators and their audiences.

In the past, a distinction was made between creators and audience; creators were primarily those who made art for a living, assumed to be artists or designers and thought to have special talents, whereas audiences were viewers. In contrast, contemporary technologies enable anyone to play the role of both creator and audience, as they use their phones to take and view photographs, make and watch videos, and create and see digital images. The immense power of such creator/audience imagery is seen in videos of Black men being killed by police officers, such as the death of George Floyd on May 25, 2020. The emotional outpouring in response to those powerful videos added fuel to the Black Lives Matter movement and sparked demonstrations in the United States and around the world. The demonstrations were then seen on television and online, which not only informed viewers, but also prompted discussion of police reform. The videos have now become icons of many issues of race, institutions, and visual culture, representing and influencing human behavior on a large scale.

Early Social Science Investigation Involving Visual Culture

The social science investigation of visual culture first began in the late 19th century, and then, only some types of visual culture were considered of interest. For example, up until this point, children's drawings were dismissed as failed attempts to represent life realistically. An early, pivotal social science reflection on children's drawings by educator Ebenezer Cooke (1885), entitled "Our Art Teaching and Child Nature," openly challenged the dominant British and American regimented curricular methods for copied line drawing in public schools. He called for revisions that recognized the unique quality of mind in the young. Successively, interest rose in the psychological study of children's drawing. In the late 19th century and into the early 20th century, European and American social scientists conducted several large-scale studies. Carrado Ricci's 1887 study involved 1,250 examples of Italian children's art. Georg Kerschensteiner's 1895 study in Germany involved approximately 1000,000 children's drawings, and Georges-Henri Luquet's 1912 study in France consisted of 1,500 children's drawings.

More recent studies of children's drawings have demonstrated important aspects of cognitive and physical growth (Arnheim, 1954/1974). In 1966, David Chambers (1983) began a collection of almost 5,000 children's drawings to see how children visualized scientists. His Draw-a-Scientist Test was based on Florence Goodenough's initial 1926 Draw-a-Man Test, which was later extended to the Goodenough–Harris Drawing Test (Harris, 1963). The results of Chambers' study using the Draw-a-Scientist Test indicated several visual stereotypes of scientists, not the least of which was that only 6% of the drawings represented a woman scientist. When David Miller et al. (2018) did a meta-analysis of five decades of Draw-a-Scientist studies, involving 78 studies and 20,000 drawings, it showed that the percentage had increased to an average of 28% of drawings of women scientists since the 1980s. The majority of that change could be found in girls' drawings; boys' drawings of women scientists continued to be at only 5%. Girls draw scientists as women more often when they are younger. As they enter late elementary school, and through junior high school and high school, girls are more likely to draw scientists as men. Images made by children can be a window into the unconscious in ways that are more accurate and unfiltered than simply asking a child to talk about a topic in words. Through these changing conceptions of children's drawings, researchers' ideas of what data might be, and what questions might be asked, evolved.

Early social science research into the visual was not limited to children's drawing. However, it was through children's drawings and other ways of making and playing with materials that theories began to be developed about the importance of learning through such entanglements. Friedrich Froebel's (1826/1885) theory, which became the original premise for kindergarten and eventually influenced all levels of education, was that children learn through both their opportunistic manipulations of objects and the limitations objects place on them.

A wide range of social science research dependent on visual stimuli has been prevalent since the mid-1800s as visual technologies became increasingly available. For example, the tachistoscope, a machine that briefly flashes an image in a research participant's eye, first described by German scientist A. W. Volkman in 1859, was used for psychological and other studies requiring the display of visual information until the use of computers became prevalent. Tachistoscopes were critical during World War II in training pilots and anti-aircraft gunners in shape recognition of enemy and ally aircraft. Throughout the 20th century, a range of visual research methods were developed for studies where language or numbers could not be used, for example with sight-impaired or infant participants. And, visual means of data analysis increased, as in the case of big data, which helps scientists to understand behavioral patterns as Da Vinci's drawings helped him to understand patterns in nature (Tufte, 1983). Indeed, without the capacity for visualization, many scientific discoveries would not have taken place. The range of visual methods has expanded even more in the 21st century.

The Contemporary Importance of Visual Culture to Inquiry

From the perspective of the authors of this book, visual communication and the construction of meaning in and through visual sources of information have become essential considerations to all forms of social science and arts-based research. Newer social science disciplines and sub-disciplines have emerged as a result of the increasing impact of the visual, such as visual anthropology, visual sociology, and media studies, all reflecting an awareness of the central location of visual culture in human societies. Visual culture can reveal information otherwise unavailable or ignored, such as characteristics of people previously erased in research by words and numbers. Also, arts-based research has expanded to include the study of a wide range of human and environmental conditions. As a result of this growing awareness of the impact of visual culture, attention to visual research methods has increased. Just as a basic knowledge of numerical analysis is considered foundational to most research training, so should a basic knowledge of visual data collection and analysis be considered core knowledge for all researchers.

Foundations of the Book

Regardless of research topic, visual methods have the potential to improve social science research processes and techniques. Using visual methods, researchers can enable new types of inquiry, answer research questions that could not be investigated before, and study conditions and occurrences that cannot be studied adequately through the use of other methods. For example, the method referred to as *photo elicitation* is the use of photographs and visual artifacts to elicit comments from research participants and a key strategy for the qualitative research method of interviewing.

In this book, we build our argument and examples on a foundation of multiple forms, conditions, and concepts of the aesthetic character of visual culture, which can support social science investigations. These include both the easily seen and the highly problematic issues of the visual related to empirical, social research. It also includes theoretical constructs related to visual culture, such as knowledge of the visual that has developed in the disciplines of art and design, the perceptual and cognitive study of visual processing and interpretation, and the agency of the visual suggested by the new materialisms (Coole & Frost, 2010), which we illustrate and explain.

The Theoretical Framework: Semiotic Versus Aesthetic Approaches to Imagery

The application of visual culture theories we use in this book differs from the standard approach taken in most visual research methods textbooks. Our analysis indicates that most visual methods books rely on a semiotic approach to their arguments for why and how visual methods can be used. A semiotic approach depends on a theory of text-based literacy, concepts, and symbolism. From this perspective, thinking is assumed to be a matter of reading symbols, and images are merely symbols to be "read." As a result of semiotic literary theories, such as Nelson Goodman's *Languages of Art* (1968), images are commonly referred to as a type of text and not considered essentially different from it. Philosopher Markus Lannenranta (1992) observed that Goodman's semiotic approach holds that there is nothing more in an image than the symbols that we see and choose to manipulate.

> Traditionally, the aim of a theory of art has been to capture the essence of art, to describe what is common to all works of art and at the same time distinguishes them from everything else. As a nominalist, Goodman does not, however, believe that there is any essence of art that we can discover.
> (Lammenranta, 339)

A semiotic approach to images undervalues the unique characteristics of the visual by separating form from content. In this context, the concept of "reading" the visual is incomplete; it ignores the seductive character of aesthetic qualities (e.g., the intensity of hue, the delicacy of vapory translucence). This reduction of the complexity of visual aspects of form—dismissing them as merely decorative functions of composition—has caused critical problems to emerge in education and elsewhere. In texts such as Nelson Goodman's (1968), the highly complex somatic character of the visual per se is left unanalyzed, and by suggestion, made magical. Goodman's work is part of an analytic tradition that emphasizes the metaphorical use of language and isolates symbols, detracting from other essential aspects of visual form. In contrast, we contend that images are more than symbols to be interpreted, they are material objects and our interactions with them are felt. Our bodies encounter the form of an image. A drip of paint is not a symbol of drip. It is a drip. It has weight and length. We feel drippiness—a running, an elongation. Rather than a symbol, it is the thing-in-itself that we sense.

For example, consider the work of arts-based researcher James Rolling Jr. In his image, *Where Do We Go from Here?* (Figure 1.14) one can identify that a

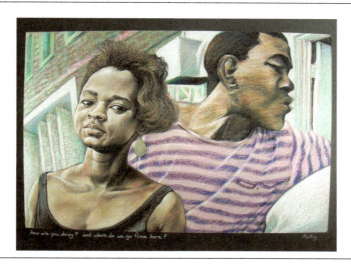

Figure 1.14 *Where Do We Go From Here?*, James Haywood Rolling, Jr., 1997. Courtesy of the creator.

woman and a man are portrayed: her glance looks out, but avoids the viewer; he looks to the side. Further attention to visual qualities in the picture renders additional information. Details that emerge include that the woman's face is in sharp focus; the man's face—connected to a bodily gesture that suggests movement and pulling away—blurs. The figures are presented as together, but there are visual clues of disconnection. Behind these two individuals the building is composed of complementary colors, red and green. Optically, complementary colors generate visual tension. One does not need to know color theory to feel this; one senses it. Color theory merely explains what one feels.

Mentally processing visual information is different from processing texts. For example, unlike reading lines of text, we process an image through a series of eye movements, which take a searching path, settling on locations from which we can make meaning. This takes a much shorter time than reading a page of text and depends on the image as a whole.

Images function as gestalts (Arnheim, 1954/1974). Gestalts suggest meaning as a result of their immediate, holistic effects, which are greater than sums of their parts. Text-based theories cannot capture these effects, not just because text is perceived differently from images, but also because people tend to be psychobiologically attracted to images more than texts. People are naturally drawn to images—we must learn to read text. Cognitive psychological research shows that infants, who have not yet developed a capacity to understand spoken language, construct expectations of the world around them through visual gestalts (Spelke & Kinzler, 2007). We develop complex forms of visual thinking before we acquire language. This mode of thinking does not disappear when we master written and spoken language. Visual thinking stays with us throughout our lives, and with training, it develops, improves and expands.

The research evidence that concludes images should be considered differently from text that includes studies of the brain. Such studies have shown that we have a dual coding system in our brains, which processes text and images differently (e.g., Paivio, 2007). Dual coding research has demonstrated that people learn best when they use images and words together. This suggests that images and words contribute different, but mutually supportive types of information, which can be stored and accessed to help navigate experience. These conditions illustrate some of the reasons that visual methods need to be included as part of social science research processes and techniques.

This book extends the concept of intertextuality to *intergraphicality* in order to explain not only semiotic connections, overlaps, and infusions of meaning, but also meanings outside of the textual that have to do with the visual characteristics of formal qualities (the visual qualities of form) and the structures and codes of visual creative practice. As Estelle Barrett argues "creative practice allows us to access such codes via the aesthetic image and to make visual knowledge that everyday use of language and discourse hide" (Barrett & Bolt, 2010, p. 66). In this book, we include—but extend beyond—the boundaries of semiotics and return to the characteristics and application of the seductive, tacit power of aesthetics.

In the following sections of this chapter, we explain the unique contributions of visual methods and their relationship to the broad range of visual culture. In particular, we seek to move beyond "linguistic imperialism" (Deleuze & Guattari, 1980/1987) and speak to knowing in and through the visual and illustrate how this can expand knowledge of the social world. Without a serious consideration of the power of the visual to represent, suggest, communicate, and express, social science and even non-visual, arts-based research is only showing us part of the picture. We now turn to four major problems of visual research methods, which have caused some resistance in social research, following by a brief summary of the ways this book addresses these problems. We then close with an overview of the book.

Four Major Problems of the Visual in Research

Several major problems exist with regard to attitudes about the visual in research, which have caused a reluctance to use imagery in social science studies. A few technical problems exist, such as working with publishers through a range of issues to include images in articles and books. The problems we refer to have more to do with misconceptions in social science fields that result in pervasive attitudes concerning issues of mediation, intention, and the agency of visual culture and visual methods.

Historically, social science has depended upon translations of the concepts that made the physical sciences believable, such as validity, reliability, and representationality. In qualitative research, which relies heavily on language, these concepts had to be translated for appropriate use with qualitative methods and the particular types of evidence they could reveal. For example, credibility (accuracy of participant perspective portrayal), dependability (researcher position and self-monitoring), confirmability (triangulation and capacity of the data to be tested), and transferability (detail of research context presentation and application to similar contexts) have been used to determine the quality of a research report (Denzin & Lincoln, 2018).

Social scientists have had enduring problems related to visual methods and we aim to address four of these problems. We describe these problems in the following sections and address them throughout the book: verifying tacit knowledge, the divergence of meaning enabled by the visual, taste versus judgments of visual quality, and determinations of quality.

Problem 1: The Visual as Verifiable, Tacit Knowledge

Traditional quantitative and qualitative research have maintained a commitment to verifiable, factual knowledge and the research methods that provide such information. Often, traditional language methods, such as text content analyses, are presented as verifiable information, but images are not. Even when images are used in data collection, their interpretation is often subsumed or at least dependent upon numbers or texts, such as transcripts, which are considered more verifiable than imagery. This presents a strange conundrum of the contemporary visual, particularly the photographic. Photographs can be very close to literal documentation and can present more verifiable information than language, but they can also be manipulated, changing and distorting information. Artificial intelligence can produce deep fakes. Yet text and numbers have all these same problems. They too are always selected and can be manipulated easily. The problem of manipulation does invalidate visual sources, but just like text and numbers, one must be adept at understanding the context of images in order to use them as research information.

Recognizing the context of an image requires recognition of the visual's tacit dimension, which means that attaching language to images is not only difficult, but it can sometimes be impossible. Images can retain an element of shapeshifting. They can resist definitive categorization. As a result, viewers may look at the use of imagery as data with suspicion. Researchers must know enough about images and the language that can reasonably surround a given image to be able to help viewers understand what they see in the context of research.

As discussed earlier, images are processed differently than text and numbers, which are intended to be read sequentially in rows. An image acts as a gestalt; the whole is more than the sum of its parts. Although we use eye movements to move around an image, our eyes take in information extremely quickly and our brain processes the information with virtual immediacy, which can result in a wide perceptual process range, from superficial looking to deep study. When looking at an image, we tend to search for information. We spend the most time looking at faces, then we travel around the image trying to find a way to make meaning. The eye darts over the surface, looking for clues to meaning. Visual image creators frequently know this and build images designed to reward sustained searching. They can tightly direct this search and lead us to a meaning they intend, or they can deliberately disrupt the search for meaning and make meaning unclear. Either way, the viewer, in a sense, completes an image by constructing meaning from the information it provides.

Human visual perception enables us to seek patterns, contrasts, and colors. Within the physiology of the eye, human cones and rods lead us to search for edges and particular colors on the blue, yellow, and magenta light continuum (Palmer, 1999). This perceptual system both enables and restricts our use of imagery (Kosslyn & Osherson, 1995). Sighted people and animals select visual information on a continual basis from a very young age. Visual memory must be selective because if people consciously attended to everything we see, we would become overwhelmed. As a result, visual information, even important visual information, can easily be ignored or deliberately dismissed.

Humans have a large capacity for visual memory. In fact, some perceptual scientists speculate that this is our largest memory capacity, which adds to the power of imagery. However, that large capacity of image memory can be frightening. We expect that every reader of this book has had at least one experience they saw and wish to forget but find that the image stays in their mind.

Problem 2: Divergence of Meaning in Interpretations of the Visual

The ability of the visual to promote a divergence of meaning can cause problems when visual methods are used in research. In the visual methods workshops we teach for professors and graduate students, we have found that this apparent contradiction between the intended convergence of meaning in research and intended divergent meanings in the visual arts causes stress among researchers trying to use visual methods.

Although the products of visual methods can be interpreted with the same flexibility that all qualitative methods have, they have some limitations of interpretation, which can be discerned through viewing experience and visual learning. Perception is a quest; viewers who not visually dig into an image will not see as much as the person who continues to engage with the image. The quest requires moving beyond snap judgments and assumptions and opening oneself up to new—possibly pre-conceptualized—information. Although our brains require us to make sudden judgments about many things that we see, images require continuing probing between the general and the specific, as is the case with other research methods.

Visual arts professionals have theorized that artist intention is not important because viewers interpret. However, intention is always revealed in the visual. In the visual arts, form is created deliberately to converge on a single meaning or diverge to multiple meanings. That is, artists sometimes limit interpretation, as in the case of a medical illustration or a book cover, whereas other images are intended to broaden interpretation, as in the case with some contemporary fine art. In the case of contemporary fine art, artists may be deliberately suggestive, intending viewers to construct their own meanings, thus broadening the appeal of their work. However, this does not mean that intention is unavailable to viewers.

Furthermore, artist intent is only one piece of evidence to consider in the analysis of an image. An image may be made with intent, and the tacit information contained within work may support the creator's intention, or the tacit information might work against or even negate the creator's intention. An image may be made without an avowed intention, yet the tacit information could be so compelling that an unspoken intention is clear. Or, an image may be made without intention and the tacit information may be equally ambiguous.

While there are situations where an image prompts speculation and projection, in contrast, there are also many images that have agreed upon meanings. To argue that all images lack agreed upon meanings and are inferior to text and numbers is based on an illusion. The meaning of images can be influenced by the context in which they are placed and seen, which is no less the case for text and numbers. In scholarship, the acceptance of a form of representation of data depends on peer review within a qualified community. For example, it is of little importance to interpretation whether one reads the same textual, quantitative, or visual research data article in a library or a museum. It could be important to the interpretation of an image whether it is hung in a library or a museum, but it is just as important whether one reads an unpublished manuscript, or a book published after a professional process of layers of peer review.

Problem 3: Taste Versus Judgments of Visual Quality

Viewers may know what they like when it comes to images; that is a matter of taste, but not necessarily a reasoned judgment. As is the case with other reasoned judgments, reasoned judgments about images require evidence. Visual evidence is found primarily in the work itself embodied in its visual qualities. Visual qualities are the qualities of visual form, such as line, shape, color, texture, pattern, and so on, and the ways in which these are arranged. We will discuss these in greater detail in Chapter 3. To make any reasoned judgments of quality, one needs to have knowledge of those qualities and their possibilities. This is the case with visual qualities as well. Most people can recognize and judge a familiar object within 100 milliseconds. However, people generally take longer than that to make a high-stakes decision, unless they are in dire circumstances. Making reasoned judgments about the qualities of everyday objects and images also comes quickly because we are hardwired to attend to those qualities; they make us want to look.

As a result of human brain hardwiring, most people have a basic visual literacy. A basic visual literacy provides humans with the ability to recognize people and objects, understand how to interact with images on a surface level based on the visual information they provide, and respond to images in terms of likes and preferences. Those who have had art education through secondary school will have a higher level of visual literacy. However, even that level of literacy may not be good enough to conduct research using visual methods and evidence because images have many complex, aesthetic entanglements with human and non-human agencies. For example, images that can be used for research are also always connected to past and future images; they are entangled with historical, social, political, and economic conditions. Our constructions of meaning through images are influenced by other, related images we have seen, and these in turn will influence our constructions of meaning in the future. The ways in which imagery acts on humans and non-humans must be taken into account when considering the use of visual research methods. Images often cluster in similarity and are always of a type. An avant-garde artist will work to escape this clustering across time and space by working to make their images different from previous images, but similar to each other (indicating the artist's style), the characteristics of which are used as evidence of the image being made by that artist.

Visual literacy has something in common with textual literacy; both involve coming to know and use a symbolic form. However, the visual and its practices are quite different from those of texts. In the following chapters, we will discuss the need for increased visual literacy among researchers, new discoveries and applications of knowledge gained from visual methods, and the construction of meaning mediated by visual forms. We will also lead readers through the process of gaining visual literacy to aid in the use of visual research methods.

Problem 4: Compatibility of Social Research and the Visual Arts

The fourth problem commonly raised about the use of visual methods is concern that the visual arts cannot be applied to other areas of inquiry. It is true that visual arts images can have unique qualities, but they also depend on histories of similarity, such as commonalities among images within a particular style or treatment of a particular subject matter. For example, consider a realistic landscape painting. The painting may be unique in the way the subject is handled, reveal the particular style of an individual artist, and show artistic license in composition. However, in order to be classified as a landscape painting, the image will have commonalities with other landscape paintings done over centuries and across cultures. They will all be related to color theory, aesthetics, nature studies and sciences, landscape design, and so on. It is those commonalities that enable analyses of the visual arts.

Researchers are educated to interpret words and numbers both deductively (general to specific) and inductively (specific to general). However, images are sometimes thought to be unique in their cognitive integration, as well as their form, and assumed to be interpreted neither deductively or inductively. In other words, the assumption is that their meanings can only exist in relation to themselves, so any interpretation is as valid as any other. If this were true, images would not only exist outside history, but they could also not be compared against a reality (Feldman, 1992). However, as we have discussed, images do exist within history and are constantly compared to reality.

Visual methods help to reveal the seductive and immediate character of visual information, mediation, and agency. As a result, any particular visual study has the capacity of applications beyond the specifics of the case. In part, these applications are enabled as a result of common aspects of visual forms and their interpretation, as research methods do in the case of other qualitative studies. But visual methods of research can provide unique looks at personal and cultural issues, conditions, and responses of social research that text- and number-dependent methods cannot.

In this book, we tackle these four problems partly by attending to the ways they have been addressed in the visual arts, but also through the ways they have been addressed in the social sciences. We discuss ways to take advantage of the visual characteristics noted in these four problems when conducting research. In response to Problem 1, we highlight the importance of visual information, and explain how it can be accessed to benefit researchers. With regard to Problem 2, we explain specific ways to use this information in data collection and analysis. Pertaining to Problem 3, we explore the entanglement of aesthetic and semiotic approaches to images and appropriate conceptual locations of text in visual research. In response to Problem 4, we discuss ways that analyzing imagery involves both qualitative and quantitative knowledge, which builds viewers' abilities to make judgments about imagery in the use of research methods. The process of research method triangulation is designed to dovetail or confront different types of data collected through the use of several methods and we provide various visual methods that can be used as part of this process.

This book also contributes criteria for judgments of quality when using visual materials and methods in research. Most qualitative methods have agreed upon sets of criteria for enabling journal and book manuscript reviewers, dissertation committees, and grant funders to determine whether qualitative methods are being used appropriately and with rigor. However, at the time of the writing of this book, no agreed upon criteria exist for the use of visual research methods. This text will contribute to discussions of quality, and hopefully, help move these discussions toward communal agreement, by presenting several conditions of quality and criteria that can be applied to visual methods.

Overview of the Book

This book surveys and critiques the current range of visual frameworks and methods, as well as offering criteria for their use, which could support the development of such a community. We provide examples of projects, analyses, and the academic language necessary for accurate descriptions of this and other visual methods. Throughout the book, specific research project examples are discussed to aid readers in establishing whether a particular project should include visual research methods.

The following is a summary of the coming chapters. Chapter 2 is intended to help readers come to know how visual research methods function based on the psychology and philosophy of visual perception. Several theories of visual perception are explored to discuss ways that the sensory, pre-linguistic, embodied empirical evidence in the visual becomes accessible to analysis. We also describe the field of empirical aesthetics and suggest ways that field can aid research in other disciplines. Visual methods are based to some extent on the didactic power of visual form, so this chapter explains how images and forms communicate visually in terms of psychobiology and cultural context. We discuss examples to show that new knowledge is constructed through visual imagery, including the types of tacit and overt information that can be gleaned from visual research methods, through the ideas of new materialism and current theories of making.

Chapter 3 focuses on the character and interpretation of visual information, which lead to the construction of visual knowledge in a research context. This chapter picks up the psychobiological thread from the previous chapter and explores the concept of an iconic store, which is the set of images we have seen and remember. As an increasing number of researchers are taught visual methods, their iconic stores will increase and become part of their expertise. This chapter discusses the idea of a community of visual researchers, which has been difficult to create because of boundaries between disciplines and the relatively independent work of people in the visual arts. We lay out the problem of creator intention versus researcher intention and illustrate ways to use these to broaden research questions. A major criterion for the determination of quality in research has long been the generation of new knowledge. In Chapter 3, issues related to validity and reliability will be discussed in terms of communities of agreement, which are the contexts and processes by which visual culture is judged and valued. With regard to visual culture, the concepts of objectivity and subjectivity are complex theoretical constructs that exist on a relational scale. Interpretation concerning "objective" visual sources and "subjective" meaning are addressed.

Chapter 4 examines the conceptual structures that frame the visual within well-known visual culture and research methodologies. This chapter starts with a discussion of methodological changes, which have occurred in the visual arts since Modernism began, as they have reconceptualized the ways that images are made and interpreted. Then, we survey visual methodologies across art and social science disciplines, illustrating that many of the visual methods currently used originated in the visual arts or a particular social science discipline, and now influence all of the social sciences. Chapter 4 finishes with a discussion of common themes of visual inquiry that apply to all social science fields.

In Chapter 5, we introduce our Research Image Framework (RIF), of *Image as Record, Image as Data, Image as Investigation, Image as Theorizing, and Image as Reporting*, and explain how it applies to virtually any research methodology that incorporates visual sources. The chapter also explains two additional levels of image use in research. The RIF is not intended to put images in a box, but rather to help researchers reflect on image use patterns and projects and suggest language for describing, interpreting, and analyzing images.

Chapter 6 surveys multiple processes and techniques of visual data analysis and presents an Image Analysis Matrix (IAM). We understand the visual by looking at images. This chapter includes a taxonomical framework of research methods with visual examples. Each image is accompanied by ways the image can engage inquiry to convey tacit information and suggests ways that information can be analyzed. The IAM can be used for visual benchmarking to analyze images in research. Strategies introduced earlier in the text, such as interpretation techniques and formal, critical analysis, are applied using examples of analytical rubrics and other useful tools. We discuss ways to quantitatively score images using rubrics, checklists, and semantic differentials.

Chapter 7 concludes the book with an emphasis on issues of ethics. Since the 18th century, when aesthetics was conceptualized as its own realm unburdened by the constraints of morality and ethics, many have considered the visual arts to function autonomously. In part, as a result of this condition, the use of visual imagery in the arts and social sciences is replete with ethical tensions. While there are no easy resolutions to these tensions, we work toward an easing of them. The social sciences have traditionally emphasized problem solving, whereas contemporary visual art has often been about conscious disruption. The scientific paradigm is about circle forming; the artistic paradigm is about box breaking. Science pushes toward resolution; fine art pushes toward dissidence. Debate concerning these tensions can enrich dialogue about what it means to engage with images and accelerate the robust contributions of visual research methods across the visual arts and social sciences.

Conclusion

Our objective is to help social researchers broaden their research questions, deepen their analyses, bridge disciplines, communicate clearly, and otherwise enhance their inquiry and publication. We have strived for language in this book so that it is both accessible and cross disciplinary. The primary audience for this book is students and instructors in the visual arts and social sciences. This book can be included in courses across the social sciences, including Introduction to Research Methods, Qualitative Research Methods, Arts-based Research, and Data Visualization. Courses in the visual arts, and in art and design education, include Research Methods in the Visual Arts, Curriculum Methods in Art and Design Education. In addition, with the move to the Ph.D. in Visual Arts studio practice, this book can serve as a textbook for socially engaged studio practice.

Our aim is to explain the different roles the visual can play in research. The researcher does not always control how a visual image is working—a visual image may not be doing what the researcher wants it to do. However, the researcher should always identify how the visual is functioning. The research needs to identify the agency of the image. We stress that an image is a creative provocateur that works through empirical evidence. These two factors, the generative and the pragmatic, work in tandem. While these two dynamics run throughout research, increasing attention to their vibrant tension places the visual at the center of post-structural, post-qualitative research and opens new possibilities for social science inquiry.

References

Arnheim, R. (1974). *Art and visual perception: A psychology of the creative eye.* University of California Press. (Original work published 1954)

Barrett, E., & Bolt, B. (2010). *Practice as research: Approaches to creative arts enquiry.* I.B. Tauris.

Chambers, D. W. (1983). Stereotypical images of the scientist: The draw-a-scientist test. *Science Education, 67*(2), 255–265. https://doi.org/10.1002/sce.3730670213

Cooke, E. (1885). Our art teaching and child nature. *Journal of Education, 7* (Dec 1), 462–465.

Coole, D., & Frost, S. (2010). *New materialisms: Ontology, agency, and politics.* Duke University Press.

Deleuze, G., & Guattari, F. (1987). *A thousand plateaus: Capitalism and schizophrenia* (B. Massumi, Trans.). University of Minnesota Press. (Original work published 1980)

Denzin, N. K., & Lincoln, Y. S. (Eds.) (2018). *The SAGE handbook of qualitative research* (5th ed.). SAGE.

Efland, A. (1990). *A history of art education: Intellectual and social currents in teaching the visual arts.* Teachers College Press.

Feldman, E. B. (1992). *Varieties of visual experience* (4th ed.). H.N. Abrams.

Freedman, K. J. (2003). *Teaching visual culture: Curriculum, aesthetics, and the social life of art.* Teachers College Press & National Art Education Association.

Freedman, K., Heijnen, E., Kallio-Tavin, M., Karpati, A., & Papp, L. (2013). Visual culture learning communities: How and what students come to know in informal art groups. *Studies in Art Education, 53*(2), 103–115. https://doi.org/10.1080/00393541.2013.11518886

Froebel, F. (1826/1885). *The education of man.* A. Lovell and Co. Translated by J. Jarvis.

Goodenough, F. (1926). *Measurement of intelligence by drawings.* World Book.

Goodman, N. (1968). *Languages of art: an approach to a theory of symbols.* Bobbs-Merrill.

Harris, D. B. (1963). *Children's drawings as measures of intellectual maturity.* Harcourt, Brace, & World.

Isaacson, W. (2017). *Leonardo da Vinci.* Simon & Schuster.

Karpati, A., Freedman, K., Kallio-Tavin, M. Heijnen, E., & Castro, J. C. (2016). Collaboration in visual culture learning communities: Towards a synergy of individual and collective creative practice. *International Journal of Art and Design Education, 36*(2), 164–175. https://doi.org/10.1111/jade.12099

Kosslyn, S. M., & Osherson, D. N. (Eds.) (1995). *An invitation to cognitive science: Visual cognition* (2nd ed., Vol. 2). MIT Press.

Lammenranta, M. (1993). Goodman's semiotic theory of art. *Canadian Journal of Philosophy, 22*(3), 339–351. https://doi.org/10.1080/00455091.1992.10717284

Miller, D. I., Nolla, K. M., Eagly, A. H., & Uttal, D. H. (2018). The development of children's gender-science stereotypes: A meta-analysis of 5 decades of U.S. draw-a-scientist studies. *Child Development, 89*(6), 1943–1955. https://doi.org/10.1111/cdev.13039

Museum of Modern Art (December 31, 1940). *Museum of Modern Art establishes new department of photography* [Press release]. https://www.moma.org/docs/press_archives/661/releases/MOMA_1940_0092_1940-12-24_401224-83.pdf

Paivio, A. (2007). *Mind and its evolution: A dual coding theoretical approach.* Lawrence Erlbaum.

Palmer, S. E. (1999). *Vision science: Photons to phenomenology.* MIT Press.

Reavey, P. (Ed.). (2020). *A handbook of visual methods in psychology: Using and interpreting images in qualitative research* (2nd ed.). Routledge.

Spelke, E. S., & Kinzler, K. D. (2007). Core knowledge. *Developmental Science, 10*(1), 89–96. https://doi.org/10.1111/j.1467-7687.2007.00569.x

Tufte, E. R. (1983). *The visual display of quantitative information.* Graphics Press.

CHAPTER 2

Visual Perception and Conceptions of Visual Research

Occasionally, science provokes a disruption in cultural understandings and triggers a reconfiguration of how we perceive visually. Feminist physicist Karen Barad (2007) points to Niels Bohr's experiments with light as a moment when science forced such a reconfiguration. Empirical evidence—evidence that one can see—is usually conclusive, but in this case, seeing produced contradictory findings. Not only did these experiments change a concept of the physical universe, they also opened philosophical questions about the role of humans as active mediators in the ways we perceive and record the world. Based on the results of Bohr's experiments, it turned out that the physics of light adapted to the experimental contexts. The outcomes in each context were true, but contradictory when compared. Bohr's conclusion was that light is a permanent element, but reacts in relation to the contexts in which humans attempt to document it. This conclusion changed our philosophical understanding of human agency as affecting seemingly objective empirical matter. Bohr not only made us rethink how we see the world, but who we are in the world, and how our very presence affects the way we see and understand images.

This chapter focuses on psychological and philosophical views of visual perception. Like any human sense, visual perception is selective. Without the ability to selectively attend to the vast amount of stimuli people encounter every day, humans would not be able to focus our thoughts and actions. People make unconscious, as well as conscious, choices when we look. Unconscious choices are made as a result of psychobiological, sociological, and other abilities and habits, which act as foundations for conceptual frameworks that influence attention. These conceptual frameworks are important to consider when discussing research methods because, to some extent, humans see what our conceptual frameworks allow us to see. For example, commercial advertisers know that culturally loaded visual cues can subconsciously drive a consumer to make the purchase the advertiser desires (Packard, 1958). Yet, most viewers do not critique our own vision in a reflexive manner; we tend to believe what we see. Psychological concepts inform the philosophical speculation that results in conceptual frameworks, which act as lenses through which to look at imagery. Different lenses can produce different outcomes, so the more a researcher knows about visual perception, the better that researcher will be able to make reasonable judgments in their use of visual research methods.

In this book, we use multiple lenses to view, interpret, and analyze images and their roles in research. We include visual representations of four of the lenses we discuss, adding one of these lenses to each of Chapters 2–5. Any image material is embedded in and influences context. The lens in Figure 2.1 points to their entanglement, which influences creation and viewing. The two colors of this lens demonstrate an entanglement: the look of a color will change based on the colors that surround it. Cut a small hole in a piece of paper near its edge and hold the paper up to the lens so that you can see both the purple color through the hole and the orange and purple together next to the paper—you will see that the purple looks different through the hole than it does next to the orange. Researchers can focus analysis of an image, but human perceptions of

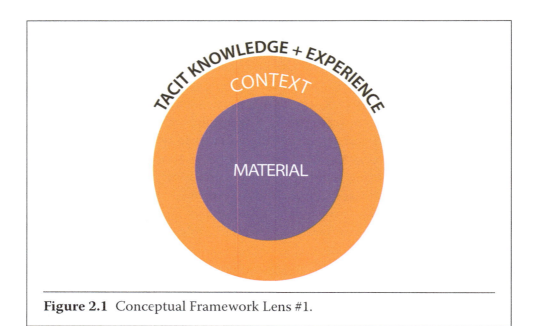

Figure 2.1 Conceptual Framework Lens #1.

images exist within contexts, including the context of bodies, their common and unique perceptions, memories, and so on. In the following sections, we discuss the tacit character of perceptual knowledge and experience.

The Science of Visual Perception

Scientists work to adhere closely to the world as it appears to be. Since the Renaissance, Western traditions of scientific knowledge have generally valued models that claim to accurately mirror nature (Rorty, 1980). Visual imagery was no exception. The world was conceived as a passive diorama waiting for both the scientist and the artist to faithfully record it. This belief that the world is out there waiting to be captured through vision resulted in the "eye is a camera" metaphor.

For an individual whose vision falls within a wide spectrum of what might be considered biological normality, it is easy to accept the eye-is-camera metaphor as a description of perception. Therefore, it is not surprising that in the late 19th century, scientific explorations about vision in the discipline of psychology began with the eye-is-camera metaphor as a conceptual framework called structuralism. Since then, three additional frameworks for understanding visual perception have emerged: Gestalt psychology, ecological optics, and constructivism (Palmer, 1999). In this section, we will discuss how these four different scientific frameworks and the ways that each framework influenced psychological, empirical aesthetics (also called cognitive aesthetics), which developed in parallel to the general field of vision science. Empirical aesthetics followed its own evolutionary path with the changing paradigms of vision science and became a foundation of visual research methods.[1]

Structuralism: Vision as Linked Chain of Individual Moments

The earliest psychological theory of perception, structuralism, is closest to the "eye is a camera" metaphor. It is attributed to Wilhelm Wundt, a founder of modern scientific psychology. Structuralism is based on an empiricist interpretation of perception as the product of a tightly linked chain of minute sense impressions. From this perspective, the brain builds up rich, complex meanings through repeated exposure to distinctive sense impressions. In its suggestion that the whole is the product of small parts, structuralism used chemistry as an analogy for understanding perception.

However, visual experience is far more complex than the eye-is-camera metaphor suggests, in part, because sight works on conscious and unconscious levels. Simultaneously, humans can be critically reflective of our perceptual array through slow, controlled processing while at the same time we are acting rapidly on automatic, unconscious tacit information (Bauer & Schwan, 2018). Human eyes take in information even when we are not mindful of the act of viewing. This works in multiple ways. For example, we can walk through a familiar room without "looking" where we are going. Perhaps even more disconcerting is our ability to drive a car along a familiar itinerary and not remember "seeing" anything enroute. When our world starts conforming to our expectations of how it should be ordered, our perceptual system begins to ignore unnecessary information to avoid troubling the conscious brain. Undoing and reshaping these unconscious perceptual editing systems is a specific goal of some visual research methods. It is necessary to tear down unconscious perception in order to rebuild conscious, critical perception.

Gestalt Psychology I: The Whole Is More Than the Sum of Its Parts

In response to structuralism, Gestalt psychologists recognized a tacit level of cognitive vision (Koffka, 1935). Gestalt vision theory points out that perception operates on an unconscious level that produces recognition and conscious meaning. As Gestalt psychologist Michael Polanyi (1967) claimed, we know more than we can say. Through specific graphic designs that could be easily adapted for scientific experiments, Gestalt psychologists successfully refuted the structuralist claim that the whole is simply a layering of individual perceptual snippets. For example, through a theory of emergent properties, Gestalt psychologists demonstrated that the whole form can take on unpredictable visual properties. The context in which visual parts work together produce unanticipated meanings. In other words, the whole is more than the sum of its parts.

Gestalt concepts were important not only as the foundation of a scientific theory of perception, but also highly influential in training people to make and interpret visual images. In art and design education, students learn how parts of an image work together and influence each other to generate meaning. As an example, data visualization advocate Edward Tufte (1990) provided a classic Gestalt example from the teachings of Bauhaus artists/designer Josef Albers of what Albers called 1+1=3 (Figure 2.2).

On the left of the equal sign are two black bars. To the right, the position of the black bars generates an equal sized white bar that now appears between them. This is a play of the Gestalt principle of positive and negative space. The black bars on the left are positive, they draw our attention, but when placed in a specific relationship, they activate the negative white space between them, turning the negative space into a positive shape: 1+1=3. An outside border can

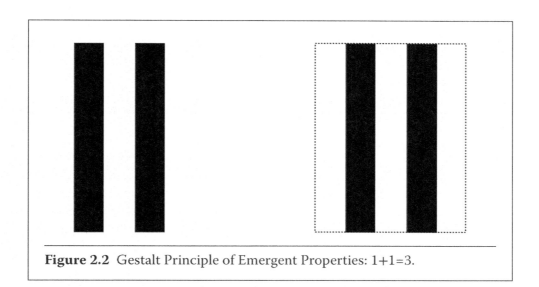

Figure 2.2 Gestalt Principle of Emergent Properties: 1+1=3.

further activate the external white space as bars. This produces five felt forms: 1+1=3 or more.

In another example, on the left in Figure 2.3, one sees a circle. On the right, eight circles of the same circumference and value are presented. The individual properties of each circle are identical, and yet the circles themselves do not suggest the visual pattern (a square) that is immediately recognizable. Eight circles transform into the new emergent property of a single square. There is nothing in the individual circular shapes that can predict this. The Gestalt principle of continuity demonstrates that the eye seizes opportunities for a potential path of smooth continuous motion. Through eye movement, the mind

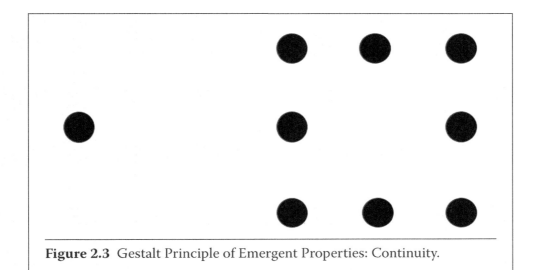

Figure 2.3 Gestalt Principle of Emergent Properties: Continuity.

creates form. Because of a sense of emerging, interactive forces, Gestaltists analogized their theory to physics.

Gestalt Psychology II: Knowing More Than We Can Say

Michael Polanyi was especially interested in how gestalt experiences could nurture idiosyncratic, individual vision that in turn would both critique authoritarianism and promote social progress. He argued that humans have *tacit knowledge* (Polanyi, 1967), the ability to perceptually sense "more than we can tell" (p. 4). By this, Polanyi was not arguing that all forms of tacit knowledge reside irredeemably beyond human understanding, but that sensed understandings of rational structure often precede human ability to be fully articulate with language. For Polanyi, clever social, political manipulators understand how people can be controlled through the use of tacit knowledge. Polanyi argued that learning how to critically analyze visual tacit information was essential for the general population to resist propaganda. From the perspective of applying visual research methods, learning to analyze the tacit knowledge captured by visual images can enable researchers to use images as information and communication.

Although tacit understanding can sometimes serve as a road to language, Polanyi demonstrated that language often falls short of some forms of tacit knowledge. This idea was given greater prominence later in the 20th century in the philosophical reflections of Jacques Derrida (1967/1976) and Gilles Deleuze (1969/1990). A gap between linguistic or numeric explanation and the intuitive sense of a pervasive gestalt may always exist, but a skilled embrace of the effort to describe the tacit dimension—to produce what anthropologist Clifford Gertz (1973) called *thick description*—can shorten the distance between the visual and the linguistic and numeric. This exercise of constantly moving closer, although never arriving at the final destination of putting tacit knowledge into words, is a distinctive quality of the visual. For example, it is the hallmark of professional art criticism (see Berger, 1977). Polanyi's tacit dimension is critical to understanding how visual images work, and we will return throughout the book to demonstrate points of tacit understanding.

Without directly referencing Polanyi, the psychologist Rudolph Arnheim (1969) furthered the Gestalt claim that perceptual experience is not merely a visualization of categorical quantities, but rather its own synthetic, analytic tool that works in a tacit dimension. Perception itself is cognitive. Arnheim claimed the following:

> Cognitive operations called thinking are not the privilege of mental processes above and beyond perception but the essential

ingredients of perception itself. I am referring to such operations as active exploration, selection, grasping of essentials, simplification, abstraction, analysis and synthesis, completion, correction, comparison, problem solving, as well as combining, separating, putting in context. These operations are not the prerogative of any one mental function.... There is no basic difference in this respect between what happens when a person looks at the world directly and when he sits with his eyes closed and "thinks."

(p. 13)

Our perceptual world is more than we can name and quantify. We both see an image and think an image—imbuing that image with meaning through comparisons with our personal bank of mental images. Perception is a dynamic process, shaped by our physical bodies moving in space. Gestalt experiences are layered, equivocal, and resist a single propositional description.

This process works in at least two ways: pattern recognition and matching. First, gestalt perception promotes schematic ordering, which is literally a process of making sense. Humans make and find patterns. We can experience a fixed image unfolding in front of us. We dwell with the picture, and the picture reveals differing possibilities for making order. We can get the feel of different pattern combinations. We can toggle among these permutations, trying them on and feeling them out.

However, the creator of an image narrows the range of interpretation. For example, consider the classic photograph that sociologist Lewis Hine took in a textile mill in the American South in 1908 (Figure 2.4). Hine sought to expose the exploitation of children as laborers. In the picture, we see the young girl, Sadie Pfeifer—whom Hine documented as 48 inches tall—at work in the factory. However, we also feel the girl dwarfed by the dangerous spinning machines. She is virtually alone in swirling monotonous repetitive motion, except for the watchful surveillance of an adult at the end of the corridor. Sadie stands in the middle distance: away from us, just outside of our immediate reach, beyond our ability to protect her. The sense of isolation, dread, and imminent danger are tacit levels of meaning that may evolve as we commit our time to looking closely and analyzing the formal details of the picture.

Second, from our exploration of this palette of details, speculative interpretations emerge as we try to construct meaning. These possible interpretations allow us to compare the visual patterns in the image to those we know and decide which of these comparisons are the best rightness of fit (Goodman, 1978). Although a single right answer to the question of meaning is never possible with any image, study of the evidence in an image provides pattern recognition that focuses and narrows the range of interpretation.

Visual Methods of Inquiry

Figure 2.4 *Sadie Pfeifer*, by Lewis Hine, 1908.
National Child Labor Committee Collection, Public domain, via Wikimedia Commons.

Creators use this capacity to direct interpretation. In Figure 2.5, we see Hine explore a portrait of another young girl in a North Carolina mill. However, this picture is a close-up. The child confronts the camera confidently with her hand assuredly handling the machine beside her. She is so close to us that she seems in control of her surroundings. This is not what Hine wanted to communicate about child labor, and so he composed the image of the child in the previous photograph in the middle ground where the textile machine looms above her. He used the large scale of the machines to dwarf the child, but the child needs to be in the middle distance to achieve this visual effect. Placing the child further back in space would achieve this contrast of scale as well, but if the child was too far away, we would lose a sense of personal connection to her. Also, placing the child in the middle distance allowed Hine to include the adult in the distance whose panopticonic vision is another form of control over the child (Figure 2.4).

Ecological Optics: Context Determines What We See

Psychologist James J. Gibson (1950; 1979) broke with both the structuralists and the Gestaltists by changing the focus of perception from speculation on what happened between the eye and the brain to attention to the environment

Visual Perception and Conceptions of Visual Research

Figure 2.5 *Spinner, Whitnel Cotton Mill, NC,* by Lewis Hine, 1908. Public domain, via Wikimedia Commons.

that presented itself to the eye. This is referred to as the theory of *ecological optics*. Gibson challenged the paradigm of the Gestalt psychologists by suggesting that humans do not only see carefully rendered graphic designs displayed in antiseptic laboratories under flat, uniform, florescent lighting. Vision takes place in complex environments in which an individual is actively scanning as well as physically moving. The brain does not attempt to extract inferences from a single image but compares and contrasts a flow of changing optical information. The information that the retina can code and send to the brain already exists in meaningful relationships within the environment. Gibson calls these visual relationships *affordances*. Through affordances, the brain has direct, nonlinguistic, access to information. For example, the cognitive designer Don Norman (1988) observed that a doorknob is a rather unremarkable form. However, when mounted on a vertical surface at 36 inches from the floor line, it is intuitively apparent that the form fits comfortably into the human hand, and it immediately invites being grasped. The shape and its surrounding context offer affordances into the device's operation. No one needs instruction as to how to properly hold a standard doorknob: through its design and context, it tacitly communicates how the hand is to be placed. Typically, children learn to use doorknobs at about two and a half years through observation. No intervening manipulations of data, such as might occur through language, are necessary.

Gibson is sympathetic to the Gestalt analogy to physics for understanding perception; however, he used the more specific metaphor of a tuning fork to articulate his concept of perception as a process of locating resonance. Art educator Donal O'Donoghue (2019) searches for places of educational resonance for his research participants through imagery so that educators "might learn about how some boys negotiate and articulate their gendered and sexed subjectivities (always incomplete and ever-emerging) by considering how they perceive and experience place in school, while they produce it simultaneously" (p. 5). To explore this question, he employed a photo-voice methodology of allowing his participants to photograph spaces and then talk about the significance of these places.

Figure 2.6, in many ways, is a record of nothing: a bleak building. It is the imaginative context of the space that is important—and possibly the viewer's own personal history with such spaces that activates the image. Here the emptiness of the white-washed concrete corner creates a blank screen on which the student projects a memory of his past trauma of being bullied at school. The viewer may do the same bringing similar visual memories that add complexity to the image.

Ecological optics acknowledges a nuanced visual experience of the world that rarely occurs in the stark black and white drawings favored by Gestalt

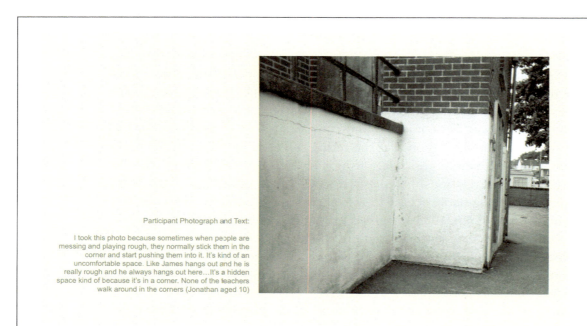

Figure 2.6 *James always hangs out here*, Jonathan aged 10.
Courtesy Donal O'Donoghue.

psychologists (see Figures 2.1 and 2.2). Ecological optics focuses on the ways perception works in the equivocal conditions of the real world. Cognitive philosopher Fred Dretske (1995) observed that a challenge to the construction of a commercially successful personal laundry robot would be to develop an effective perceptual system for the robot so that at dusk as it whirled through the living room, it would reliably distinguish between a crumbled sweater and a sleeping cat. Nuanced qualitative distinctions make all the difference in perception. If the robot does not know what it is looking at, it will put the cat in the washer. Daily cognitive perception is a relentless exercise of judgment. No bright dividing line exists between what is clear and what is ambiguous. Learning to sort enigmatic visual information with analytic precision requires learning to perceive and judge. Learning to identify, sort, and correct visually ambiguous information is fundamental to the use of visual research methods.

Contemporary Perceptual Constructivism: Vision as a Process of Bricolage

Cognitive psychologist Stephen Palmer (1999) recognizes a fourth major theory of perception: Constructivism. Nineteenth-century physiologist Herman Helmholtz carefully observed the mechanics of vision to show that there are gaps in the information that the retina sends to the brain. Yet, the brain fills in these gaps; rather than having black holes in our perceptual field, the brain supplies missing data. Thus, Helmholtz argued vision is an active construction and achievement of mind, and not just the simple cataloging of signs and symbols. Today, constructivists continue to agree with Helmholtz's concept of vision as an active mental process of bricolage. However, to develop these ideas, modern constructivists have borrowed freely from the other three theoretical areas: structuralism, Gestalt psychology, and ecological optics. Contemporary constructivist theory sees vision as immensely complex, and the issue is not whether the structuralists, or the Gestalt psychologists, or the followers of ecological optics are right, but rather *when* they are right, and how humans apply these different modes of vision as we move through our daily lives.

A fundamental problem for psychologists has been to distinguish between where perception provides the conscious brain with pictures to think about and where perception itself is a form of pre-linguistic thinking. To help answer this question, the early research by cognitive vision scientist Elizabeth Spelke investigated how pre-verbal infants visually analyze their environments, form judgments, and build hypotheses without access to semiotic systems. She drew on Gibson's ideas of an active, searching perception and Gestalt concepts of object recognition to explore how, through perception, children begin the construction of meaning (Spelke et al., 1995).

Spelke found that an infant's ability to recognize objects is a function of motion. The way an object moves—or, if the object is static, the way an infant moves around it—is how humans begin to learn about our world. Gestalt psychologists used force and weight as metaphors for perception and the ecologists favored the tuning fork metaphor. Spelke's metaphor for perception was a pendulum, which involves a process of movement through space. We do not merely see things. Perception is a projection of patterns occurring within space and over time.

Like Figure 2.2, vision is constantly searching to establish lines and speeds of continuous motion that allow humans to navigate our environment. We actively construct hypotheses and conceptual understandings of how the forms around us are moving in space. We constantly tacitly calculate these relationships, even for stationary objects tacitly categorized as motionless. We startle if an object anywhere in our perceptual array that we unconsciously assume is static suddenly moves. Perception assigns roles and functions to everything. Spelke called these constructs conceptual precursors to language (Hespos & Spelke, 2004). Tacit knowledge precedes words and establishes the paradigms in which language eventually operates.

However, Spelke did not see this movement from the tacit to the linguistic as developmental, which is critically important in the use of visual research methods. Tacit visual knowing is not a stage that we pass through and abandon once we have gained access to linguistic and numeric symbol systems. The tacit is, and may remain, its own realm of *core knowledge* (Spelke & Kinzler, 2007). However, this core knowledge does not continue to develop automatically with growth. It requires education and effort, otherwise it remains a separate realm of knowing that may atrophy. A child who does not suffer from visual impairment will almost immediately after birth begin to build visual tacit learning skills based on the somatic exploration of objects, movement, and space. Yet, these skills may slip back into an inaccessible unconscious if an effort is not made to exercise these mental abilities.

This is exemplified by a century of children's drawing development research. From the time a child first begins to draw, the tacit knowledge required for visual representation increases. With training through pre K-12 school, most people can learn to draw with a modest accuracy. However, formal education requirements in art usually stop at the end of elementary school. As a result, most adults can only draw at about a fifth-grade level.

The lack of continual visual training was not greatly missed until recent decades when the prevalence of visual communication led to new questions about essential learning. For example, cognitive vision scientists refer to the exploration of concrete problems of recognition and categorization of problems as *high vision* (Kosslyn, 1995). These tend to be problems of digital processing of information, surveillance, and robotics. However, "high" vision carries with it an implicit suggestion of superiority. Spelke's research pointed out that while earlier research dismissed the tacit function of vision as "low" it may be more helpful to think of tacit learning as "core."

A second important message of Spelke's research is that core knowledge does not develop on its own. It requires experience and practice. In Chapter 3, we argue that we educate ourselves in tacit knowledge of the visual in two ways: (1) an understanding of how visual form functions, and (2) an understanding of how we make visual judgments.

Perceptual Constructivism and Cognitive Development

Spelke's research points to the need for educational development of visual perception; however, a substantial body of psychological research shows that basic drawing skills are learned auto-didactically. Given the opportunity to draw, a "normal" child will progress through predictable stages of vision development and mark making that records the child's visual experience. (Arnheim, 1954/1974; Golomb, 1992; Goodenough, 1926; Harris, 1963; Kellogg, 1959). Art educators (Lowenfeld, 1947; Parsons, 1988; Wilson, 2019) have further studied children's drawing and aesthetic responses to art to better understand how much of children's making and interpreting of images is an organic process of cognitive and motor skill maturation as distinct from cultural observation, didactic instruction, or intentional pedagogical intervention. A common finding by these researchers is that when making images, young children are not struggling to express themselves due to underdeveloped hand motor skills as assumed by early psychologists. Instead, they are intentionally exploring meaningful constructions of worlds both perceived and imagined (Arnheim, 1954/1974; Golomb, 1992; Schulte, 2015). Furthermore, perception is not so much what a child sees. Rather, experiences influence a child's perception. From our earliest moments, visual making is an attempt to capture and communicate tacit dimensions of experience that exceed the immediately visible.

Implications for Empirical Aesthetics: Constructing Tacit Meaning

Constructivist empirical aesthetics reflects an expanding attention in the field, which goes beyond investigations of visual preference, to measuring empirical qualities of aesthetic experience as well as teasing out empirical dimensions of aesthetic consciousness and higher order thinking (Bullot & Reber, 2013). Physicists and computer scientists have demonstrated mathematically that emergent meanings are not only meaning connections, but quantum entanglements (e.g., Arguëlles, 2018; Arguëlles & Sozzo, 2020), and that associative meanings can be so powerful as to violate numerical probabilities. Researchers, such as educational psychologists and art educators (Housen, 1983; Parsons, 1988), have articulated non-developmental taxonomies of higher order thinking that adolescents and adults engage in when viewing art. Thinking through the visual is not something that develops as a result of maturation, rather it is a cognitive skill that withers if ignored or grows from a novice level to an expert level with instruction (Freedman, 1997).

The Philosophy of Vision and Perception

Philosophers can imagine aspects of human experience that science has not been able to scrutinize. They can consider anomalies in scientific findings and reimagine ways in which humans can account for these differences. Both disciplines do more than describe the world as it is; they open theoretical realms that allow for consideration of dimensions of experience. Nevertheless, until recently, an anthropocentric attitude has dominated the European philosophical and scientific tradition, which assumes that the human researcher captures, records, and classifies the details of a permanent, passive, external world.

However, a conception of the world as alive and in relationship to humans is a cornerstone of indigenous knowledge systems from around the world. These knowledge systems have long regarded perception as more than just seeing the literal objects in front of one's eyes. Rather, perception is more a process of sensing living networks and tangible energies from a context in which we navigate (Pratt, 2002). We sense these energies and experience them with our bodies. Importantly, this knowledge is not just about what the human sensory system can do with these energies, it is also a recognition of the independent agency of these energies and of how human volition needs to bend to them.

While anthropocentrism has dominated Western thought, there has always been a minority thread that imagined sensory, embodied perception. For example, the early Greeks recognized the empirical world as possessing its own agency, and viewed sensory perception as a dynamic, constructed relationship that challenged a complacent anthropocentrism (Welsch, 1995). The philosophical discipline of aesthetics initially drew on the early Greek words for sensory perception as an active, never settled state of being in relationship, so that it might hypothesize a science of sensuous "poetic cognition" (Baumgarten, 1735/1954, p. 36). Through such a philosophical lens, a photographic image is not really evidence of the world as it is, but rather a negotiated settlement that exists under certain conditions and is valid for only as long as those ephemeral conditions might endure.

Visual Perception and Conceptions of Visual Research

The American Pragmatic philosopher John Dewey (1934/1989) made the audacious claim that symbol systems did not delimit the elaboration of meaning. Indeed, no symbol system (linguistic, numeric, or visual) can capture the scope of human comprehension. Dewey maintained that the full meaning of a work of art was built on interweaving experiential tacit relationships of qualities with formal semiotic analysis (Siegesmund, 2012).

The British art critic John Berger eloquently demonstrated tacit dimensions of imagery in his deconstruction of pictures in the popular 1972 BBC television series, *Ways of Seeing,* and the book of the same title that followed thereafter (Berger, 1977). In the opening to the first program—before the first credits roll—Berger walked up to what appears to be Botticelli's *Venus and Mars* at the National Gallery in London, pulled a box cutter out of his pocket and cut out the female face to vividly illustrate two of his main themes: (a) the influence on perception of decontextualization through image reproduction, and (b) the primary focus of Western fine art on the objectification of women. The context in which a symbol or sign exists is critical to the reading of semiotic code, and an unconscious, predisposed interpretation (e.g., the male gaze) of certain images (e.g., the female nude) obstructs a viewer's understanding of larger contexts. Berger's analysis of the ways in which visual images tacitly communicate is credited with setting the stage for an explosion of interest in the analytic possibilities of visual methods in multiple academic disciplines (Pauwels & Mannay, 2020).

The Ontological Turn: What Humans Might Become

An important philosophical move that marked the beginning of the 21st century was a shift from an epistemological concern with what humans could know to an ontological concern about what we might become. Philosopher Gilles Deleuze and psychoanalyst Félix Guattari (1980/1987) refer to *becoming* as being in liminal states of that which is not yet. Deleuze and Guattari suggest that we never secure an arrival at any destination, we are simply in motion on a trajectory to transfiguring termini. The past echoes into the present, but has not yet faded beyond recognition, and the present itself is not yet fixed, but perseveres in an unending process of imprinting. Together they present evocative possibilities. A summative statement—a definitive form—fails to coalesce, and with no assuredness of culmination, remains constantly elusive. From Deleuze and Guattari's (1980/1987) perspective, all we have are *lines of flight* across the infinite potential of a *plane of immanence.* By challenging our conception of empirical reality, Deleuze and Guattari provoke us to reconsider the meaning of empirical research (St. Pierre, 2017).

From this perspective, research is fundamentally an aesthetic project as aesthetics was initially conceived: a dynamic sense of becoming in relation to the world. In this view, research consists of continuing acts of incomplete devising in an ongoing dialogue with the universe. While traditional social science research attempts to successfully navigate the world as it apparently exists, this approach to research both imagines worlds as they otherwise might be and challenges oppressive narratives through acts of unforming, deconstruction, and subversion.

For Deleuze and Guattari, the researcher does not fully control how a visual image functions because images have their own agency. Like the mythological genie-in-a-bottle, the researcher may set a visual image in motion that will have interactions and consequences imagined and never imagined by the researcher.

Long before Deleuze and Guattari articulated their philosophy, schools of art and design regularly introduced students to the independent autonomy of visual objects. As an illustration, a common art school technique during an individual critique is to challenge a student to see what the image itself—the same image that the student has created—"wants to be." The image now has its own life, its own volition. The student, who made the image, no longer fully controls it in a Frankenstein-like metaphor (Shelley, 1818/2018). But before Deleuze and Guattari, this was just crazy art school talk.

For the visual researcher, the lesson from this art school exercise is to be skeptical of what the producer of an image claims the image to be. The viewer, including a researcher or a research participant, must be able to make meaning from the image for what it is in itself and its context. The researcher needs to understand the image's own agency separate from anthropocentric intent.

Aesthetic Foundations of New Materialisms

New materialism (Alaimo & Hekman, 2008; Barad, 2007; Bennett, 2010) is an interdisciplinary cultural theory that questions the empirical scientific schema of a passive world awaiting human experimental probes. In its place, it offers a vision of the nonhuman, material world as active and agential. The nonhuman possesses force that pushes back in ways that may resist human intent. New materialism theorists argue that this theory provides a different way of thinking about matter in philosophy and the social sciences (Braidotti, 2019). They challenge the dependence on language—as traditionally understood, particularly in qualitative research—in the arguments of postmodern linguistic theorists, critical theorists, and social constructivists, as well as continuing the critique of oppositions that those theorists deconstructed (St. Pierre, 2017). Discussions of matter in the discipline of history and the social sciences emerged as researchers and theorists questioned the reliance on text as a mechanism of institutionalized patriarchy. Feminist researchers and theoreticians have pointed out that the domain of text has excluded material life, historically the domain of women (Alaimo & Hekman, 2008).

New materialism is a transversal theory in which nature and culture are not conceived as opposites; rather, they are considered two sides of the same coin that are necessary and interacting with each other. Previous critical theories have been usurped by theories of new materialism and posthumanism, which seek to move beyond the critical to Barad's (2007) "agential realism," which is a performative ethics that conceptualizes agency, subjectivity, and causality as characteristics of the universe. As Foucault argued, agency is a relationship (Bevir, 1999). New materialist theorists do not privilege matter over meaning. Barad stated this perspective as:

> An epistemological-ontological-ethical framework that provides an understanding of the role of human and nonhuman, material and discursive, and natural and cultural factors in scientific and other social-material practices, thereby moving such considerations beyond the well-worn debates that pit constructivism against realism, agency against structure, and idealism against materialism.
>
> (p. 26)

We agree that the inter- and intra-actions of imagery, their material, and their contexts are important to visual research methods. However, while new materialist theory is a challenge to Marxist historical materialism (Coole & Frost, 2010; St. Pierre et al., 2016), it is important to reiterate that new materialism is not new. First, new materialism is a revisiting of pre-industrial ideas held by various Aboriginal groups, such as Australian Aboriginals and Native Americans, who valued and lived holistically through natural material, including the material of images. Second, the intellectual thread of new materialism theory can also be found internationally in historical visual arts communities. New materialism validates a knowledge that has long existed in the arts that visual qualities not only express meaning, but have an agency that the artist must negotiate. For example, in his letters and poems the artist Michelangelo pointed to ways that the material would act on him. He suggested that he could taste the sensuous qualities of the marble and was convinced that a sculpture, already existing within the stone, would reveal itself through the entanglement of the artistic process (Gayford, 2013).

The implication of new materialism for social research is that it is not enough for a researcher to simply state their intentions; researchers must also recognize how materials themselves act in tacit and potentially unintended ways. Materials and objects, including images, represent and influence societies and cultures; they bring social groups together and push them apart. Even an image seen by only a small group, such as a family photograph, can have wide-ranging effects over time. The effects of materials occur in part through the impact of their aesthetic qualities, which can be unexpected. While conducting research, a researcher may need to acknowledge the unexpected, document the ways they adapted their purposes in response to the visual data, and demonstrate that the visual data itself moved beyond the researcher's intentions.

Deconstructing Visual Making

In our everyday lives, humans routinely take perception for granted. As Dewey observed, we do not distinguish between seeing and perceiving. Vision is primarily a quick recognition system, but as Dewey cautioned, "recognition is perception arrested" (Dewey, 1934/1989, p. 58). It is not uncommon for visual researchers to take an unreflective stance to their visual perception and the ways it records visual moments. Images may be seen as their subject: a rushing river in the park, a favorite pet, a family gathering on a special occasion. Generally, these appear as unremarkable records of stable memories. However, for example, the universal habit of smiling for a camera is an exercise in altering, or even deceiving, that record. As stated at the opening of this chapter, perception is a complex process. It can be conceptualized in different ways.

As cultures are constructed, they are also mutable (Clifford & Marcus, 1986), so social science becomes an *imaginative* endeavor. The person taking the picture is not recording; they are intervening, making, and staging. It is a site of reconstructing the past and projecting the present into the future. In this view, image making or image capturing apparatuses are not neutral, objective recorders. They are instruments that slice and dissect the fabric of reality and extract, at best, a partial rendering of the empirical world, reminding us that the human eye functions in a selective system, allowing some facets of reality to be seen while occluding others.

Research as Acts of Fiction

A traditional approach to research holds that it should replicate the world as it is, and serve as an accurate mirror of nature (Rorty, 1980). In the social sciences, we apply inferential and deductive reasoning to construct models that we believe to be close replications of the world. We test these models for trustworthiness: their validity in relationship to the contexts to which they specifically apply, and their reliability to be replicable in a variety of new situations. An epistemological hazard when basing models on quantitative measures is that a numeric expression of probability may lull the researcher into believing that probability is certainty. In these cases, the good approximation is elevated to the status of truth. Such models are never passive recordings of the external world; they are constructed. Science depends on responsible, but imaginary

Visual Perception and Conceptions of Visual Research

personal and subjective forms of engagement (Holton, 1996). Research is a constructivist process where theoretical models are prosthetic devices to help us successfully navigate the world.

For example, studies in empirical cognitive aesthetics demonstrate that the first description of an image, by someone not trained in the visual arts, will be a listing of the objects that appear to be recorded (Parsons, 1988). Humans immediately categorize representational semiotics (e.g., I see a farmer, a barn, a cow, or a tree). These summative statements are actually instantaneously constructed understandings from multiple sources of differentiated visual evidence. A claim such as "I see a farmer" would be based on an analysis of clothes that the individual is wearing along with other contextual information surrounding the individual, such as tools, equipment, buildings, or the relationship of the figure to the landscape.

However, complex images do more than signify. In Figure 2.7, the image also includes emotional, sensory clues. The washed-out blue in the farmer's denim jeans does more than signify a state of being physically drained. The color *is* washed-out; it is not just a symbol of being washed-out. This is reinforced by the barren landscape. The colors are muted and grayish. The visual qualities communicate directly. Like the trope in the Lewis Hine photographs, the farmer is dwarfed by two mules that seemingly pull him forward. His crisp white shirt and hat are brilliant counterpoints to the dingy environment, but also act with the white on the animals, both tying the man to them and

Figure 2.7 Corn farmer, Guatemala.
Courtesy Tomas Castelazo, CC BY 3.0, via Wikimedia Commons.

drawing our eye through the image. These layered, visual meanings demand the viewer take time with the image to uncover and disclose evidence to support interpretation. In the first moments of perception, a viewer might not identify all the visual semiotic and somatic clues; the viewer is likely to just see a farmer. The implicit subtexts that the context provides may be far more complex and remain on a tacit level. An unexamined visual image runs the risk of reproducing what both researcher and participant expect to see, running the risk of unintentionally oversimplifying an image and its impact.

So far in this chapter, we have introduced psychological and philosophical frameworks for looking at images to assume a reflexive stance toward the images one shapes and the images one views while forming interpretations. The Latin word for shaping and forming in the service of making is *fictio*. This is the etymological root of the English word fiction. While fictio is primarily understood as a process of manifesting something new, there is a sub-meaning that this new thing may contain a quality of deceit. Therefore, in the shaping that goes into the making and interpretation of an image, there is concern for parsing deceitful from authentic forms of making. Dewey (1934/1989) called this a test for an image's sincerity. This idea changes the way we might approach the analysis of the image. Rather than asking what an image is or what it represents, we would ask what does the image do? What is the sincerity of the image to its proposition of doing? How did the image come into existence, and where does this image take us?

Works of fiction may be intentionally calibrated to subvert paradigmatic thinking. As such, they can be important contributors to the work of imagining previously silenced or unseen possibilities. Visual methods are well suited for subversive acts of questioning and exposing tensions and contradictions of theoretical erasures. They hold a promise of providing ways to control the levers of institutional power and production. Identifying fault lines in theory through imagery serves as a site of resistance to totalizing discourses. Such destabilizing acts are not meant to be positive assertive statements; they are meant to be troubling. They challenge certainty by bringing exceptions into focus that falsify the homogeneity of the master narrative (Popper, 1985). The result is greater attention to the modesty of our scientific claims, or what curriculum theorist Tom Barone (2008) calls *epistemological humility*. Such humility is especially critical when dealing with the complex and tacit meanings of the visual.

Conclusion

Psychology and philosophy show us that there is not one simple way to think about visual perception. How we see and how we interpret the visual records of perception are part of systems of visual analysis whose borders are permeable and blurred. However, we can establish initial coordinates through which we can begin to map our conceptual frameworks for human interactions with visual culture, and in turn, shape models based on visual information.

> To determine whether to use imagery in a study, considering a checklist of questions can be helpful. For example, consider the following:
>
> 1. Does the study depend on tacit information?
> 2. What does the image contribute to the study? (Can the researcher acquire the necessary data for the study through numbers and words?)
> 3. Would an image help the researcher to investigate some aspect of the study?
> 4. Would an image help the researcher to theorize about some aspect of the study?
> 5. Would an image help the researcher to report the conclusions of the study?

Note

1. Psychological empirical aesthetics is attributed to the 19th-century German scientist and philosopher Gustav Theodor Fechner (Pickford, 1972). His initial project was to measure the length and intensity of sensory experience in response to aesthetic stimuli and analyze how the relationship of these qualities produced meaning. While Fechner's actual research remains controversial, it possibly contributed to John Dewey's argument for cognitive aesthetic thinking through qualitative relationships discussed in this chapter.

References

Alaimo, S., & Hekman, S. J. (Eds.). (2008). *Material feminisms*. Indiana University Press.

Arguëlles, J. (January, 2018). The heart of an image: Quantum superimposition and entanglement in visual perception. *arXiv*, 1–20. Cornell University. https://doi.org/10.48550/arXiv.1802.02216

Arguëlles, J., & Sozzo, S. (2020). How images combine meaning: Quantum entanglement in visual perception. *Soft Computing*, 1–10. Springer. https://doi.org/10.1007/s00500-020-04692-3

Arnheim, R. (1969). *Visual thinking*. University of California Press.

Arnheim, R. (1974). *Art and visual perception: A psychology of the creative eye*. University of California Press. (Original work published 1954)

Barad, K. (2007). *Meeting the universe halfway: Quantum physics and the entanglement of matter and meaning*. Duke University Press.

Barone, T. (2008). How arts-based research can change minds. In M. Cahnmann-Taylor & R. Siegesmund (Eds.), *Arts-based research in education: Foundations for practice* (pp. 28–49). Routledge.

Bauer, D., & Schwan, S. (2018). Expertise influences meaning-making with Renaissance portraits: Evidence from gaze and thinking-aloud. *Psychology of Aesthetics, Creativity, and the Arts*, *12*(2), 193–204. https://doi.org/10.1037/aca0000085

Baumgarten, A. G. (1954). *Reflections on poetry: Alexander Gottlieb Baumgarten's meditationes philosophicae de nonnullis ad poema pertinentibus* (K. Aschenbrenner & W. B. Holther, Trans.). University of California Press. (Original work published 1735)

Bennett, J. (2010). *Vibrant matter: A political ecology of things*. Duke University Press.

Berger, J. (1977). *Ways of seeing*. British Broadcasting Corporation; Penguin Books.

Bevir, M. (1999). Foucault and critique: Deploying agency against autonomy. *Political Theory*, *27*(1), 65–84. https://doi.org/10.1177/0090591799027001004

Braidotti, R. (2019). *Posthuman knowledge*. Polity Press.

Bullot, N. J., & Reber, R. (2013). The artful mind meets art history: Toward a psycho-historical framework for the science of art appreciation. *Behavioral and Brain Sciences*, *36*(2), 123–137, DOI:10.1017/S0140525X12000489

Clifford, J., & Marcus, G. E. (Eds.) (1986). *Writing culture: The poetics and politics of ethnography*. University of California Press.

Coole, D. H., & Frost, S. (Eds.) (2010). *New materialisms: Ontology, agency, and politics*. Duke University Press.

Deleuze, G. (1990). *The logic of sense* (M. Lester & C. Stivale, Trans.). Columbia University Press. (Original work published 1969)

Deleuze, G., & Guattari, F. (1987). *A thousand plateaus: Capitalism and schizophrenia* (B. Massumi, Trans.). University of Minnesota Press. (Original work published 1980)

Derrida, J. (1976). *Of grammatology* (G. C. Spivak, Trans.). Johns Hopkins University Press. (Original work published 1967)

Dewey, J. (1989). *Art as experience* [John Dewey: The later works, 1925-1953] (J. Boydston, Ed.), (Vol. 10: 1934). Southern Illinois University Press. (Original work published 1934)

Dretske, F. (1995). Meaningful perception. In S. M. Kosslyn & D. N. Osherson (Eds.), *Visual cognition* (Vol. 2, 2nd ed., pp. 331–352). The MIT Press.

Freedman, K. (1997). Artistic development and curriculum: Sociocultural considerations. In A. Kindler (Ed.), *Child Development in Art* (pp. 95–106). National Art Education Association.

Gayford, M. (2013). *Michelangelo: His epic life*. Fig Tree.

Geertz, C. (1973). *The interpretation of cultures: Selected essays*. Basic Books.

Gibson, J. J. (1950). *The perception of the visual world*. Houghton Mifflin.

Gibson, J. J. (1979). *The ecological approach to visual perception*. Houghton Mifflin.

Golomb, C. (1992). *The child's creation of a pictorial world* (2nd ed.). University of California Press.

Goodenough, F. (1926). *Measurement of intelligence in drawings*. Harcourt Brace and World.

Goodman, N. (1978). *Ways of worldmaking*. Hackett Publishing.

Harris, D. B. (1963). *Children's drawings as measures of intellectual maturity*. Hartcourt Brace and World.

Hespos, S. J., & Spelke, E. S. (2004). Conceptual precursors to language. *Nature, 430* (6998), 453–456. https://doi.org/10.1038/nature02634

Holton, G. (1996). On the art of scientific imagination. *Daedalus, 125*(2), 183–208.

Housen, A. (1983). *The eye of the beholder: Measuring aesthetic development*. Unpublished doctoral dissertation, Harvard University, Cambridge, MA.

Kellogg, R. (1959). *What children scribble and why*. N-P Publications.

Koffka, K. (1935). *Principles of Gestalt psychology*. Harcourt, Brace.

Kosslyn, S. M. (1995). Visual cognition: Introduction. In S. M. Kosslyn & D. N. Osherson (Eds.), *Visual cognition* (Vol. 2, 2nd ed., pp. xi–xiii). The MIT Press.

Lowenfeld, V. (1947). *Creative and mental growth*. Macmillan.

Norman, D. A. (1988). *The psychology of everyday things*. Basic Books.

O'Donoghue, D. (2019). *Learning to live in boys' schools: Art-led understandings of masculinities*. Routledge.

Packard, V. (1958). *The hidden persuaders*. Pocket Books.

Palmer, S. E. (1999). *Vision science: Photons to phenomenology*. The MIT Press.

Parsons, M. J. (1988). *How we understand art: A cognitive developmental account of aesthetic experience*. Cambridge University Press.

Pauwels, L., & Mannay, D. (Eds.) (2020). *The SAGE handbook of visual research methods*. SAGE.

Pickford, R. W. (1972). *Psychology and visual aesthetics*. Hutchinson Educational.

Polanyi, M. (1967). *The tacit dimension*. Anchor Books.

Popper, K. R. (1985). Scientific method. In D. Miller (Ed.), *Popper selections* (pp. 133–142). Princeton University Press.

Pratt, S. L. (2002). *Native pragmatism: Rethinking the roots of American philosophy*. Indiana University Press.

Rorty, R. (1980). *Philosophy and the mirror of nature*. Princeton University Press.

Schulte, C. M. (2015). Intergalactic encounters: Desire and the political immediacy of children's drawing. *Studies in Art Education*, *56*(3), 241–256. https://doi.org/10.1080/00393541.2015.11518966

Shelley, M. W. (2018). *Frankenstein: The 1818 text*. Penguin Books. (Original work published 1818)

Siegesmund, R. (2012). Dewey through a/r/tography. *Visual Arts Research Journal*, *38*(2), 99–109. https://doi.org/10.5406/visuartsrese.38.2.0099

Spelke, E. S., Gutheil, G., & Van de Walle, G. (1995). The development of object perception. In S. M. Kosslyn & D. N. Osherson (Eds.), *Visual cognition* (Vol. 2, 2nd ed., pp. 298–330). The MIT Press.

Spelke, E. S., & Kinzler, K. D. (2007). Core knowledge. *Developmental Science*, *10*(1), 89–96. https://doi.org/10.1111/j.1467-7687.2007.00569.x

St. Pierre, E. A. (2017). Deleuze and Guattari's language for new empirical inquiry. *Educational Philosophy & Theory*, *49*(11), 1080–1089. https://doi.org/10.1080/00131857.2016.1151761

St. Pierre, E. A., Jackson, A. Y., & Mazzei, L. A. (2016). New empiricisms and new materialisms. *Cultural Studies/Critical Methodologies*, *16*(2), 99–110. https://doi.org/10.1177/1532708616638694

Tufte, E. R. (1990). *Envisioning information*. Graphics Press.

Welsch, W. (1995). Aesthetics beyond aesthetics. In M. Honkanen (Ed.), *Practical aesthetics in practice and theory III: Proceedings XIIIth International Congress of Aesthetics* (pp. 18–37). International Association for Aesthetics.

Wilson, B. (2019). Art classrooms, comic markets, and the digital cosmos: Children's visual worlds as pedagogical spaces. In R. Hickman, J. Baldacchino, K. Freedman, E. Hall, & N. Meager (Eds.), *The international encyclopedia of art and design education* (pp. 1–16). John Wiley & Sons. https://doi.org/10.1002/9781118978061.ead011

CHAPTER 3

Visual Qualities and the Functions of Images in Research

Because some types of visual information are seen every day, viewers may assume that all visual information can be easily understood. However, this is not the case. Many layers of information exist, even in a single image. At one level, images contain visual symbols, and an image itself can act as a symbol. As a result, theorists often refer to the visual as a "language," and simple images, such emojis, can act as if they are part of a language. Emojis are easily understood because they reference the human face and mimic human expressions in an exaggerated and abstracted way, like a cartoon. Most comics and cartoons are relatively easy to understand because comics faces are simplified into basic facial components and expressions. In fact, it is easier to understand and relate to a simple drawing of a human face than a complex representation of a face (McCloud, 1993). However, as we discussed in the previous chapters, the visual is much more than a language. Most images are a blending of symbolic and tacit visual information, which, when perceived, will elicit a range of associative interpretations.

In the previous chapter, we provided a simple explanation of visual perception and how the use of visual research methods depends on it. The current chapter provides the visual basis on which images are made and valued by creators, researchers, and audiences, including research participants, as part of visual culture. In Figure 3.1, we present the second conceptual framework lens used in this book: components of visual culture. The areas in the lens are

Visual Methods of Inquiry

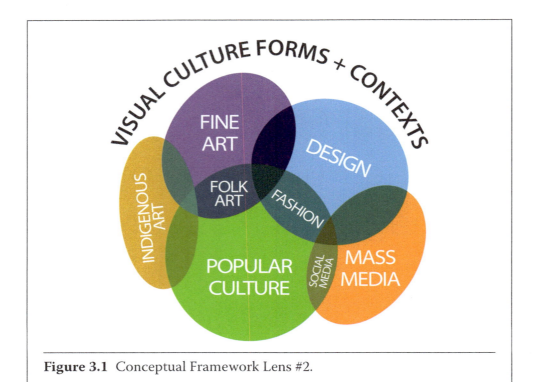

Figure 3.1 Conceptual Framework Lens #2.

examples of categorizations of images and objects. These categorizations are ways of classifying by materials and processes, social and cultural groups, uses and functions, and so on. The categories have meanings attached to them, which attach information to the images in the categories.

In the first of the following sections, we focus on the features of visual information applied to inquiry through three aspects of visual literacy needed by art and social science researchers: the use of reason in interpretation, the role of expressive content, and the context of a professional field. Second, we explain some of the formal visual qualities, known as the elements and principles of design, which are the foundations of images and used to express visual knowledge. Third, we discuss major concepts in social science research with regard to visual research methods, particularly as a form of evidence. Concepts foundational to scientific research, such as objectivity and subjectivity, are considered in relation to imagery and visual research methods. Validity and reliability are discussed in terms of communities of agreement, including the contexts and processes by which visual culture is judged and valued. Fourth, some of the ways that images function in research are surveyed. Fifth, we discuss in greater depth the ways that images can function in terms of visual criticism, particularly through the connection of recognition and feeling.

Visual Literacy and the Power of the Image

The cultural transformation discussed in Chapter 1 is based on the immense power of the visual, and the newer technologies that have enabled and enhanced that power by offering a hyper-reality and widespread distribution. The power of the visual comes from the ability of images to make us want to look at formal arrangements of aesthetic visual qualities. Images seduce us; they command our attention and compel us to linger with them. This is one of the reasons that an enduring prejudice against them has existed in social science research.

The visual arts work because they both attract and challenge expectations. Often, when audiences enter a contemporary art museum, they know that visual provocations await them because the artists who are selected to exhibit in these museums work to create images and artifacts that have not been seen before. If a work of art is new and disorienting, it can make people look longer to study it and discover its contents. Viewers who want to look longer and investigate the work are those who might have seen similar art and seek artistic differences in the new piece. If, however, the work is too new to viewers, some might reject it all together. When a work of art displayed in a museum is extremely outside a viewer's experience of valued art, it can cause stress, and some viewers might not want to look.

Visual Literacy and the Inferential Reasoning of Interpretation

Unlike reading and writing, most people can recognize images without art education. As discussed in Chapters 1 and 2, building inferential reasoning from visual gestalts precedes language. However, to use images and other visual cultures in research requires a greater knowledge of the visual than mere recognition. This requires the ability to look deeply into the structures of imagery and the ways they work to suggest and convey information. It means researchers need to do more than interpret the surface of an image, they need a deeper understanding of the ways the image works.

Geographer Gillian Rose called for "a grounding of interpretations of visual materials in careful empirical research of the social circumstances in which they are embedded" (2016, p. xxi). Her project is interpretivist, but interpretation does not mean anything goes and that one is expected to believe "alternative facts." As Rose notes, images have empirical evidence that supply the building blocks for inferential reasoning. Art educator Terry Barrett (1994) and other art theorists have argued that interpretation must be rooted in the work itself, and that some interpretations are better than others because not everyone is equally skilled at sustaining a chain of inferential logic. Rose also notes that careful empirical research should be based on interpretations of the image itself, both in how the image is situated in the social world and how the visual materiality of the image generates its own agency.

Engagement in tacit seeing has often been linked to aesthetic engagement with an object. When we feel a compulsion to aesthetically linger with an image, to surrender time to dwell with it, the tacit levels of meaning within an image are more likely to reveal themselves. As Rose advises, "Successful interpretation depends on a passionate engagement with what you see. Use your methodology to discipline your passion, not to deaden it" (2016, p. xxiii). Rose also notes that

> The "mood" or "atmosphere" of an image is both difficult to explain, often, and also crucial to compositional interpretation as a method. An important part of compositional interpretation is the evocation in writing of the "feel" of an image.
> (2016, p. 79)

Using visual research methods requires knowledgeable interpretation of the ways that the visual is mediated by material. As a researcher, you need to understand how to decode visual meaning from the symbolic content of images, but also have a literacy of the matter used to make images (Bennett, 2010). Material influences meaning in, for example, the ways that light imposes constraints and affordances on the physical apparatus of a camera, the intensity of color produced by a back-lit computer screen, the pliable yet resistant feel of clay spinning on a wheel. The meaning of a vibrantly intense neon sign takes is different if presented as a solitary beacon in a forlorn landscape than if that same sign appears as just one among a multitude of others in Times Square, New York. Knowledge of available materials, including digital media, how they act on each other, people, social contexts, and the environment, can help a researcher use visual methods.

Visual Literacy of Expressive Content

Rose and others have referred to this as *expressive* content. Rose turns to early 20th-century art historian Erwin Panofsky for guidance in the use of critical language to communicate expressive content. Panofsky is a good choice within the discipline of visual arts, but we prefer art historian Jakob Rosenberg's (1967) *On Quality in Art* as an incisive guide for articulating visual knowledge in language beyond simple meaning to felt significance. When Rose states, "Visual images have their own effects." (2016, p. 22), she is acknowledging that an image's own materialism is the catalyst that allows the image to assume its

Visual Qualities and the Functions of Images in Research

own agency. That is not Panofsky. This follows a heritage of art criticism that can be traced back to Dewey, and resonates forward in the work of critics, such as Clement Greenberg (2003), Harold Rosenberg (1972), and John Berger (2001). Qualitative material relationships generate tacit meaning—sometimes, but not always, intended by the image creator.

Rose cautions against the danger of allowing a methodology to constrain the dynamic nature of an image. Images have their own *nomadic materiality* (Siegesmund, 2023), which allows them to shift in unanticipated ways; the researcher follows, charting the movement. Following Rose, we maintain that the seeing and shaping these tacit levels of meaning is not just unconscious luck. It is a skill that can be developed through curriculum and pedagogy.

The use and analysis of imagery requires an understanding of both what the material can record and what can be interpreted from that recording. The foundation of these literacies is a working, practical knowledge of multiple, visual cultural forms and processes (Freedman, 2003).

Visual literacies demand an awareness of (a) *visual cultural forms*, (b) *making processes and materials*, (c) *delivery and viewing systems*, and (d) *viewer responses*. The first of these, *visual culture forms*, refers to humanly created or used artifacts or environments that have an impact on visual perception (Freedman, 2003). In the case of research, these could be, for example, images made by the researcher or by participants for analysis. Second, *making processes and materials* are the techniques, tools, and matter used to make, manipulate, or otherwise manifest artifacts and environments. The materiality through which an image comes into existence matters, and a researcher should be familiar with this whenever possible. Third, *delivery and viewing systems* refer to the ways in which artifacts and environments are then presented and used, such as how a research participant encounters an artifact in a research study. Fourth, *viewer responses* are the ways in which a researcher, participant, academic audience, or any other individual or group reacts to an artifact and the contexts that surround it.

The contemporary idea of needing multiple literacies revisits John Dewey's theory. Dewey stated, "if all meanings could be adequately expressed by words, the arts of painting and music would not exist" (Dewey, 1934/1989, p. 80). Richard Shusterman (1992) expanded Dewey's pragmatist aesthetics by reaching to the visual culture of everyday life, including images outside the traditional category of fine art, and theorizing experience as coming to know about the range of visual forms.

Dewey's life work was devoted to two questions: how do we come to forms of socially meaningful knowledge and how might these pathways be best taught (Dewey, 1916/1980)? Although Dewey always felt the best teacher was direct experience, it was only late in his life that he explored the idea that experience precedes language, and that art was the record of pre-symbolic thinking. In

1934, when he was 75 years old and published *Art as Experience*, he reached the conclusion of his journey, which began in *Experience and Nature* (Dewey, 1925/1981); the construction of meaning through relationships of subjective qualities is a separate form of intelligence, distinct from the construction of meaning through the manipulation of symbols. Words and numbers can bring us to a limited understanding of the visual arts, but attention to tacit somatic kinesthetic experiences, Dewey's "organization of energies" brings us to in-depth and dimensional understanding.

Dewey also appreciated the layers of information that contribute to the experience of art. Not only did experience stem from close attention to the object itself, but it also resonated from awareness of the practical, social context in which the object was situated. Knowing about art is not just a matter of learning about artists, art materials, or compositional qualities. It involves consciously immersing oneself in the experiential character of visual arts forms, contexts, and meanings. The art critic and social theorist John Berger (2001) further refined this approach to interpretation. One must deliberately look at and study images to analyze them and use them in research.

Building Visual Literacy in a Field: Connecting Visual Culture to Social Science

This sense of literacy can be seen in Pierre Bourdieu's (1984) argument concerning cultural capital, which directly connects knowledge to experience. Bourdieu's sociological research demonstrated that one of the reasons for learning about cultural forms is that the knowledge gives an individual cultural capital: the arts provide a core knowledge that allows individuals to navigate social situations. For knowledge to be considered cultural capital, it must be considered useful in gaining some sort of privilege, such as money or social influence. A possible outcome of cultural capital is expertise, which can be used in a livelihood.

From this perspective, the level of knowledge required for the cultural capital of visual, material, and digital media literacies can only be achieved through direct connections to cultural carriers and interactions within cultural fields, such as the fields of visual culture and social science. Literacy depends on an insider's view of a cultural form; that is, literacy is the ability to use cultural knowledge. For example, as Bourdieu suggested, greater knowledge of a visual cultural form means a greater ability to criticize the conditions under which the form delivers cultural capital. This enables the concept of literacy to be applied to a cultural field where literacy not only acts as an identifier for individual membership, but also enables members to determine which aspects or levels of literacy are needed for membership.

Visual Qualities and the Functions of Images in Research

Building visual literacy does not only involve individual members of a field, it also means increasing the visual literacy of a field, such as social science, at large. Literacies evolve and become more complex through attention to forms of social practice, which are closely tied to cultural conditions and responsibilities. In this case, visual literacy is connected to the wide range of visual culture forms and practices. The wider the range of visual culture applications, the greater the demand for visual, material, and digital media literacy. Knowledge in all social science disciplines can be advanced through the collection, interpretation, and assessment of visual information, but only if we build expertise in the critical analysis of the visual.

Interpretation and the use of visual culture in research are ways of coming to know the world, which require the acquisition of skills and concepts specific to the visual. Whether a researcher makes a picture, creates an image-based inquiry system, or collects visual creations made by other people, the interpretation of the image becomes paramount to the results of research. Interpreting images requires knowledge of visual qualities, such as the elements and principles of design, which are discussed in the following section.

Formal Visual Qualities: The Elements and Principles of Design

In a small, yet powerful book, *Picture This: How Pictures Work*, award winning children's illustrator Molly Bang (2000) demonstrated the basic parameters of visual knowledge by showing how to create a visual and wordless narrative of the Brothers Grimm fairy tale, *Little Red Riding Hood*. She applied what are referred to the elements and principles of design, which are the visual qualities of an image. The categories of elements and principles or design (Table 3.1) are

TABLE 3.1
Elements and Principles of Design Examples

Elements	Principles
Line	Movement
Shape	Balance
Form	Rhythm
Color	Contrast
Texture	Pattern
Space	Emphasis
Value	Unity

a loose set of Western imagery benchmarks articulated in the late 19th century by artist and art educator Arthur Wesley Dow (1899/1920), which were based on his structural analysis of European and Japanese fine art and design. Bang shows that the elements and principles of design open tacit, visual communication; pictures express meanings that we feel before we have language to articulate them.

The elements and principles of design are not only a foundation for what is seen, but also what is felt. The elements of design refer to visual qualities such as line, value, shape, form, space, color, and texture. The principles of design refer to the ways in which the elements form relationships in compositions, such as through balance, movement, pattern, rhythm, contrast, emphasis, and unity.

The elements and principles are not a static code. How we think about relationships of qualities in imagery continually evolves. Postmodern art and architecture in the late 20th and early 21st centuries changed the way people think about the elements and principles of design as fundamentally modernist concepts. Arthur Efland et al., (1996) argued that postmodern principles help to "raise the veil" on the limits of modernist principles and aid learning about contemporary cultural production and reproduction. Expanding the principles for organizing the visual, postmodern theorist Charles Jenks (1987) maintained that eclecticism, complexity, multivalence, double-coding, and inclusivity are principles that challenge modernist architectural design. Fredric Jameson's (1977) principles of postmodernism were pastiche, discontinuity, and double-coding. Robert Stern's (1977) principles, or at least attitudes (p. 275) of postmodern design were contextualism, allusionism, and ornamentalism. Kerry Freedman (2003) delineated a list of postmodern concepts, which act as principles of contemporary visual culture:

1. Art as Cultural Production
   reflections of cultural conditions
   cultural critique
   cultural symbols
   challenges to elitism of high modernism
2. Temporal and Spatial Flux
   environmentalism
   pastiche
   eclecticism
   recycling and transforming
3. A Concern for Otherness
   issues of power/knowledge
   pluralism
   popular culture
   questioning "good" aesthetics and "good" design

4. Acceptance of Conceptual Conflict
   fragmentation
   dissonant beauty
   collage
   deconstruction
5. Multiple "Readings"
   visual/textual interpretation
   issues of representation
   attached meanings
   double-coding

Olivia Gude (2004) proposed additional postmodern organizing principles including juxtapositioning and hybridity. The arts-based educational research methodology of a/r/tography includes contiguity and excess (Springgay et al., 2005). These elements and principles can be applied to the data analysis of images (Hannes & Siegesmund, 2022).

Materials, such as ink, pigment, canvas, paper, wood, steel, and light, all render different affects to visual qualities and each material will enable different expressive possibilities. The encounter with materials is catalytic, and often unexpected dynamics of visual qualities emerge during the process of production. However, images have remarkable similarities regardless of material. In the following two sections, we discuss some examples of visual qualities using visual culture applications.

Examples of Visual Elements: Line, Shape, Color, and Contrast

The quality of line, such as width, around and within a character can indicate whether an object or facial expression is strong, fragile, anxious, or some other characteristic. In the range of visual culture, from Michelangelo's Sistine Chapel paintings to comic books, line is used to define, contour, and express. For example, Shoujo manga artists use line quality to symbolize aspects of characters, such as highlighting youth and romance in the comics through the use of thin, light-weight lines in the characters' figural forms.

Color is also used selectively in visual culture. Color attracts attention; it creates richness, vibrancy, and depth. To stay with the comics example, not all comics depend on color; some comics forms, such as manga, have continued in their black and white tradition. However, colored covers are added to attract audiences. Color schemes are used in images to promote unity, emphasis, and rhythm, which visually holds the image together. Color schemes also work symbolically to convey tacit information, such as mood, because like the other elements and principles, they can elicit emotions. There are five color schemes considered standard and commonly used in Western imagery: monochromatic, analogous, complementary, split complementary, triadic, and rectangular. These refer to the color wheel hues, tints, and shades. For example, a monochromatic color scheme is made up of the same hue throughout, but includes a variety of tints and shades. An analogous color scheme is based on hues that are next to each other on the color wheel. A complementary color scheme depends on colors opposite from each other on the color wheel, and so on.

Human eyes and brains are hardwired to search for contrast, and contrast is used in imagery to attract. However, higher contrast does not always result in dwelling with an image longer. Higher contrast may make objects and figures (the term usually used to refer to human forms in an image) easily recognizable, but sometimes creators use low contrast to elicit complex feelings or convince people to try to find objects, figures, and meanings that are less clear.

Lines, colors, and contrast are used to distinguish shapes. Shape defines objects and spaces through size, scale, and solidity. In the visual arts, two-dimensional objects are referred to as having shape and three-dimensional objects are referred to as having form. However, when referring to images, either can be used. Shapes can be geometric or organic, continuous or broken, monomorphic or polymorphic. The phrase geometric shapes refer to standard polygons, whereas organic shapes are representations of natural or non-geometric forms.

Example of Visual Principles: Unity, Balance, Figure, and Ground

Visual compositions in imagery are created through the use of rules similar to other two-dimensional art forms. The repetition of line, shape, color, pattern, and other elements promote unity in a canvas, page, or screen. As we discussed earlier, viewers' eyes are led to look at places in an image as a result of visual qualities, such as bright colors or high contrast, and the objects or figures represented. Our eyes tend to search for intended meaning in an image—we try to find out what an image creator is trying to show us—although we will place our own interpretations on it. For example, the use of repetition with variation causes us to follow the repeated aspects of an image without getting bored. This is a centuries-old strategy used by artists to keep viewers' eyes looking within an image, but moving around the image to collect information.

Weight and distribution of visual elements cause a perceived symmetrical or asymmetrical balance, which can also be used to move the viewer's attention when looking at the form. Viewers will attend differently to a focal point, or center of interest, if it is in the center of an image than if it is to one side or partly outside of the frame. Directionality within a space suggested by elements of design can lead viewers to look into or out of the image.

This is the way compositional principles work, regardless of material or visual culture form. As in traditional painting, drawing, and other two-dimensional visual arts, comics artists use figure and ground to suggest space in each panel. Ground usually refers to a type of background and negative space is space not intended to be perceived as an object or figure. However, as we have discussed, backgrounds can work in a Gestalt manner and otherwise provide viewers with important information, which can influence viewers' experience and interpretation.

Empirical Evidence: Visual Qualities and New Materialism

In this section, we discuss new materialism in support of our focus on visual qualities, and the ways new materialist rethinking of empiricism reshapes traditional research conceptions of objectivity and subjectivity, validity and reliability, and evidence. Similar to ancient forms of indigenous knowledge and early fine art, new materialism offers a way to conceptualize the agency of objects as they reveal themselves through their posthuman entanglements with nature, culture, and technology (Barad, 2007; Braidotti, 2019; Haraway, 2004; DeLanda, 2021). From this perspective, images and their materials act on humans as we create with and interpret them. Creators can only do so much with the materials they use, and the human brain can only interpret images we see based on past our experiences in an ever-changing world.

New materialism theorists, like earlier postmodern artists, challenge the notion of dualisms, such as the opposition of the transcendental, the humanist, the anthropocentric, and logocentric foundations of modern philosophy. For this reason, an appropriate way to use language to describe our immersion in material is to say, for example, that we "think with" the material. Humans have only limited means for working with a material and interpreting what is made with it. The material and our psychobiology provide those limitations and making images can push boundaries as we think with the material. If our understanding, exploration, and analysis of new materialism remain within the limitations of language, we again run the risk of inscribing the dualisms that postmodernist and constructionist theorists have deconstructed (Coole & Frost, 2010; Dolphijn & van der Tuin, 2012). Visual research offers a fertile place of new materialist inquiry when the power of relationships of material and visual qualities are recognized.

Through the mechanisms and processes discussed in this book, new materialism can aid researchers in their work because it points to the integral relationships between and among aesthetic conditions, consciousness, ethics, and materiality in social science research. The recognition of meaning constructed through visual qualities is key. New materialism highlights the importance of our psychobiological visual systems as fundamental to the ways that images act upon us as we act upon them.

Objectivity and Subjectivity

Two foundational concepts of social science research are subjective and objectivity. Following our commitment to transversal theory, within visual culture the concepts of subjective and objective, rather than being opposites, are complex theoretical constructs that exist on a relational scale. For example, the visual is literally objective. We tend to accept empirical evidence as objective facts because the term "empirical" refers to that which is seen, and by extention, otherwise experienced through perception. Everything in an image is factual in the sense that visual qualities are facts—lines, shapes, and colors can be seen. They become manifest through material in different ways, which must be interpreted for meaning through the lenses of viewer experience. It is the experience of these qualities that has a subjective quality.

The use of elements and principles of design are one of the reasons that people associate images with language. The elements and principles of design are seen to function in the same way that letters, sentences, and paragraphs function. Letters make up words and words are organized to make up texts: the letters themselves are not challenged as facts on a page. Rather, it is the use of them in, for example, what has become a particular academic language that makes them valid as means of representation in research.

This is the case with professional agreements about the use of elements and principles of design—even as principles of design expand with postmodern considerations. In professional communities who work with visual images daily, such as art history, art education, media studies, digital design, communication, and advertising, the possibilities of visual qualities and their analyses are common knowledge. Agreements are made in these professional communities and changed when characteristics of images initiate or adapt to changes in visual technologies, social conditions or values, but the direct effects of visual qualities on the brain stay much the same. Yellow is "bright" because it is the hue that reflects the most light back into the eye, which stimulates ganglion cells, sending an impulse to the brain. Gray is "muted" as it dulls light reflection and stimulates fewer cells. Culturally, there may be a variety of interpretations of an experience that stimulates or dulls; however, the underlying psychobiology is consistent. Therefore, images are entangled so that no interpretation is either completely subjective or objective. In this sense, they are post-structural and post-qualitative. The researcher and participants cannot be erased. At the

Visual Qualities and the Functions of Images in Research

same time, judgments about images in social science research—where they come from and what they mean—are not just a matter of personal opinion; they are a matter of expert opinion. Analyses of images as data require professional expertise that both embeds and distinguishes the visual.

Validity and Reliability

As with other research methods, validity and reliability are important in the decision to use images in research. A valid judgment about the use of images in research depends on the quality of the image with regard to its ability to function in the intended manner. An image may not only function in the intended manner; it will likely function in other ways as well, perhaps even in contradiction. For example, an image chosen and used in a study may retrieve a response from a viewer that is related to the study, but it may also retrieve other memories and associations in viewers. We will discuss the ethics of this situation in Chapter 7, but for now, it is the accuracy with which the image has been chosen to function in a particular way that concerns us. Does the image elicit responses related to the study? Would another image be a better fit with the study? Does the image primarily or most immediately suggest the intended variable?

The reliability of an image in research depends on the extent to which the expert community will agree that the image works to function in a particular way in a particular situation. Often, this concerns the consistency with which the image would be interpreted in the same manner among viewers in the same general context. Several questions may be asked when selecting an image for consistency through the use of a pilot study, such as: Is the meaning of the image interpreted consistently? Is interpretation consistent with regard to related images? Is interpretation consistent across time?

Determinations of validity and reliability with regard to images in research depend on agreements within the professional communities who select, interpret, and judge images. For example, when an image is used as evidence in a court case, a professional community (usually lawyers) needs to come to an agreement about the types of evidence that can be attained from the image. The criteria for making determinations of validity and reliability in the use of images are still debated by social science research communities.

Four Sources of Evidence for Visual Interpretation

The process of finding visual evidence starts before the act of viewing through expectations based on one's iconic store. Expectations about the look of visual data can shape the way people "see" and interpret an image. If the new imagery is too far from expectations, a rejection of the image or data by the viewer can occur. When confronted by a new image that people find difficult to making meaning of, we either tend to maintain interest long enough to work out a meaning or reject the image and look away. This rejection can be the result of many causes. For example, when an avant-garde type or style of art is seen, viewers will search to see if a familiar meaning can be constructed. If not, a new meaning will be made, which could be a meaning like "too difficult to understand," resulting in the piece being rejected as without value. This often happens when naïve viewers see avant-garde artwork in a professional fine art community context, such as a museum. Such viewers may not want to look at the work or say that they do not think the work is art. Some years before the writing of this book, one of the authors brought classes of undergraduate, non-art major students to a contemporary art museum. On one occasion, three of the students in the class stood outside the museum in a group, not wanting to enter the museum. When I asked them what was wrong, they said that they felt unwell and described symptoms, such as sweaty palms, "butterflies" in their stomach, and a stress headache. I pointed out to them that these sounded like fear symptoms, which they admitted, but after some coaxing, they entered the museum. A knowledgeable museum docent directed them to works of interest and provided background information about the art on the tour. When it was time to leave the museum, the students who had reported fear symptoms reported that they felt quite well and had enjoyed the experience—they had even made a plan to return to the museum outside of class.

Images can be dismissed as a muddle, a mistake, or the work of a hack with poor artisanship. However, viewers can value the experience of seeing something new that makes meaning construction challenging. Viewers with this consciousness actually enjoy and invest in the process of constructing meaning from visual images, so may attend to and study a new image *because* it is challenging. So, before a researcher looks at visual evidence, it is important to have a clear idea what to look for, but also be open to evidence that may be unexpected. The following sections explain four sources of visual evidence: evidence within the object, evidence within the context, evidence of creator intent, and evidence of viewer association.

Evidence Within the Object

Humans must interpret visual qualities for meaning. It is not a question of whether the facts of the formal qualities exist; rather, it is a question of the acceptable range of interpretation of those qualities within the image. Once the acts of viewing begin, viewers tend to search for visual evidence in the image to build on and check interpretation. If the sensory evidence does not seem to coincide with an interpretation, then the evidence and the interpretation are usually reexamined, perhaps several times. This process of examining and reexamining an image is part of the normal, interpretive process.

Our saccadic (rapid, small) eye movements begin to facilitate this search process in a very short period of time. Cognitive scientists explain that the ability to engage our eye movements to follow an endogenous (intrinsic) impulse develops slowly and well into adolescence (Luna et al., 2008). Scanning saccades are intrinsically motivated by a decision to look at an image, but saccadic movements themselves cannot be consciously controlled. So, the saccadic eye movements of the viewer are, in a sense, controlled by artistic decisions in the creation of form. The image creator has the ability to seduce the eye. This is part of the power of imagery; images tell our eyes where to look. Humans are hardwired to look for certain configurations, such as facial features, because we know that these can provide helpful information. So, we search for faces as we look for information to construct meaning.

Image creators take advantage of endogenous (internal) viewer eye movement to maintain viewer attention. For example, artists will use color schemes and lines that do not go off the painted surface, to keep viewers' eyes moving within the image. Artistic training emphasizes ways the viewer's eye will track within an image. In contrast, scientists consider exogenous (extrinsic) eye movements to be the result of external distractions, such as a fast-moving car in our peripheral vision. These can override endogenous movements, which is why works of art placed in museums are spaced apart. To keep viewers interested, the marriage of endogenous and exogenous eye movements is ideal. Animation, television, movies, and video games all succeed in using both types of eye movement to keep viewers focused on a screen.

Evidence Within the Context

Another type of evidence that influences interpretation is in the viewing context. For example, people will approach an image differently in a museum than in an experimental study. Images are used differently in professional social science conferences than they are in political party conventions. Images may be viewed as a screen projection in a quiet, darkened room during a lecture or presentation in the first case and in the second case, the same image may be seen on multiple posters in bright, artificial light with crowds of people and other distractions. As a result, similar images will be interpreted differently in different viewing contexts. Suppose that someone sees an informational drawing of a spaceship on a wall at a NASA museum. If it is in the hallway and drawn in a generalizing style (like a cartoon) and has an arrow on it, it is likely to be showing people directions. However, if it is drawn as a plan and elevation for people on a flight, it is likely to be showing the interior layout of the ship. One could not reasonably be interpreted as the other; at least no more reasonably than the word "direction" could be mistaken for the word "interior" in a text. A long history of research on images as information exists. For example, research on museum information delivery began in the late 19th century to determine which types of visual qualities were most helpful to visitors (Kelly, 2004).

Human beings have a history of professional agreements about which types of visual presentation work for which types of information delivery. These agreements are influenced by cultural similarities and differences, which change over time and place. Staying with the example of museums, consider the following case: a type of beaded Northwest Coast Native American earrings is meant to be seen on a dancer at night in firelight, where the earrings disappear and only the sparkling, reflective light from the shiny beads is left, floating around the dancer's face. However, when those same earrings are shown in a museum, the cultural context is not the same. Viewers can appreciate the beauty of the earrings, but they cannot experience them in their original context, so will not have access to their intended formal qualities or original meaning (Freedman, 2003).

In research, these differences require attention because images are not viewed the same by difference audiences, in different places, and at different times. Whenever images are used in research, particularly images not created specifically for a research project, changes in context need to be considered. In these cases, researchers can address the issue in several ways, such as pointing to it as a limitation when reporting the research.

Evidence of Creator Intent

The influence of evidence from viewing contexts leads us to evidence of creator intent. Creator intentions are partly derived from their context; external motivations that surround a creator can influence their intentions. Factors that influence intention may include a creator's educational background, professional expertise, cultural background, identity, previous image-making, skill sets, and experience with the visual medium. So, knowing something about the motivations of a creator can be helpful in making meaning from an image. This is the reason, for example, that art education includes study of the lives of artists.

Sometimes, a research project will demand that images are created specifically for the project, which may be disclosed to participants or other viewers. Knowledge of creator intent is often considered a matter of disclosure in research when the researcher tells viewing participants the purpose of the image in the study. However, when participants are provided with creator

Visual Qualities and the Functions of Images in Research

intention, their interpretation of an image will likely be influenced. Since, this could make the image easier to interpret or direct interpretation so as to make the study invalid, careful consideration must be taken with such disclosures.

Often, viewers have no previous knowledge of a creator's intent, but will be able to gain knowledge of it by looking at the image. It is the task of a creator to make the image not necessarily represent, but to suggest meaning. A photographer may ensure that the intention of the image is understood by making the intention clear and direct. In contrast, the photographer may create an image that merely suggests through both the subject and the way it is portrayed. For example, when viewers look at a photograph of dead fish in a lake, they may discern that the photograph is intended as a commentary about water pollution.

Evidence of Viewer Association

The associations a viewer brings to an image also influence interpretation; this is how viewers create new meanings when seeing an image or remembering the image once it is in their iconic store. The evidence of viewer association is heavily influenced by other images in an individual's iconic store and by viewer's intentions, including the way they intend to use the image. When including images in research, several questions must be considered concerning viewer association: What are the viewer's aims when looking at the image? What previous knowledge and beliefs will be likely to influence viewer interpretation? What is the range of possible meanings that could be constructed by the viewer?

Images can affect people strongly and can even cause a rejection of all images thought to be of the same type. A strong reaction to a body of images based on a single image is an aspect of the power of imagery. Because images are highly associative, they can access deep meanings in viewers, including meanings that can have extreme emotional ties, such as love, hatred, justice, and fear. When experiencing an image, associative experience quickly comes into play. A viewer consciously or unconsciously attaches new meaning to the image as a result of associations made from previous knowledge and experience.

The associations people carry with them can even change their response to an image based on how it has been cropped. In a study of teaching difficult knowledge, Nurit Cohen-Evron (2005) first showed Israeli university undergraduates part of a photograph of a woman holding a child only showing the child and the woman's arm around it. Seeing that part of the image, the students in the study responded with compassionate sounds and terms. When the researcher showed the whole photograph, revealing that the woman was wearing Palestinian clothing, the students responded quite differently, using negative sounds and terms. The previous beliefs of the students influenced their interpretations based on the amount of the image they saw.

For these reasons, images need to be tested in pilot studies. Through a pilot study, you can discover whether the images selected to be used in a study will be interpreted by participants as intended. If pilot study participants do not interpret the images in the manner you intend, alternative images should be chosen, or the research question or study procedures may need to be adapted.

How Images Function in Research

In a research context, the creation and use of imagery can have many purposes, from eliciting information from research participants to presenting difficult data and tacit information through visual means. Here, we discuss four major functions of images important to research.

1. Images Attract Attention and Focus Thought

Philosophers have argued for centuries that art is about beauty, but perhaps a more accurate statement is that art is about attraction. Good art, or any compelling image, makes us want to look (or deliberately look away); it can hold a viewer's attention and cause an absorbing feeling, as if at once, the viewer takes in the image and the image takes in the viewer. Artists absorb other art from elite and popular visual culture and from other cultures, changing it and making it their own as they create.

Attraction to the visual occurs not only as a result of attraction to the topic suggested by an image or form, but also as a result of the way the topic is handled. In this sense, the formal qualities could be considered part of the content of an image. Visual form can produce desire, a desire to look, even a desire to possess, which has been taken advantage of historically by artists who, for example, seek to represent and elicit "the male gaze" at a sensuous female nude. The same seductive function works in advertisements that seek to make viewers want to look and to possess a product. However, imagery is more complicated than successfully seducing a viewer to look through the use of beauty. For example, the way an image is handled visually may be deliberately unattractive, but viewers may be attracted to it because we are curious. We are hardwired to want to look at human bodies, in order to recognize family and friends, for cues that indicate good health and suggest who might be a good partner for breeding, and to identify death. This attentiveness to the human form and interest in human narratives are why so much visual culture includes human figures. Throughout history, visual culture forms have often been about sex and death. Sex and death are used to sell products in advertising because these topics make us want to look.

Interest in images of the human form begins very early in life. Young children begin drawing human figures without direction using schemas for people just as they learn schemas for letter and numbers. They learn quickly that a schematic representation of a human can be changed slightly to mean "Mommy," "Daddy," a sibling, or a pet. Before children can write, they will draw, dance, and sing. Young children's drawings help them express ideas before they have the linguistic capacity to say or write those ideas. When collecting drawing data from participants, researchers must remember that children, youth, and pre-professional adults will have drawn figures more often than most other forms.

All images have the potential to attract, but choice of visual qualities in a stimulus image can produce a desire to want to look at an image longer or more deeply in order to better study and understand it. From a research perspective, the seductive capabilities of the visual offer opportunities to attract and maintain the attention of project participants who might otherwise lose focus or leave an image due to lack of interest. As well as helping to answer questions that otherwise might not be asked, visual research methods can be used as a participant motivation.

Asking participants to make their own images can motivate engagement in a project as well. Mihaly Csikszentmihalyi (1996) has done extensive research on the concept of *flow*. Flow is the pleasurable experience one feels while being creative; it involves complete absorption. Most creators, including children, can experience flow when making art.

2. Images Are Information

Images provide information and can be considered evidence as a result of their physical, or potentially physical, existence. They can be evidence of knowledge, thought, emotion, creativity, and critique. By documenting actions, environments, and ideas, they can reveal what would otherwise be hidden in the human mind and bring people, locations, and other experiences to viewers who would otherwise not encounter them.

The information of images is not only through the content; visual qualities also carry information. Two television series focusing on the Colombian war are good examples (Perez, 2019). Both were documentaries based on girls taken as children to fight in a war and contain visually powerful images. The guerilla forests are deep and dark greens of *La Mujer de los Siete Nombres* (Castro &

Ordóñez, 2018) leaving viewers with feelings of isolation. In *La Niña* (Martínez, 2016), the forests are a pale, sickly green, which changes to cooler, more intense colors as the action moves to a city. Both stories are about the efforts of female soldiers to recreate their lives away from war. However, the two characters focused on in these stories handle leaving the army in different ways. The main character in *La Mujer de los Siete Nombres* takes control over her life by becoming a doctor, but her anger and feelings of isolation stay close to the surface as the colors reflect their intensity. The lead in *La Niña* coolly takes on multiple identities of female physical and sexual power when she arrives in the city, as multiple, bright colors surround her. In each video, color is used both as a show of emotion and as a way of enabling viewers to have access to the emotion being shown. Color is, in a sense, a supporting character in these videos where the use of different colors produces different effects.

Because images are powerful carriers of information, when included in research, the information carried by any particular image should be considered in relation to the intentions of the researcher. As is the case with artists, researchers may intend for viewers to widely interpret the images they create or use. However, it is more common for researchers to intend a narrow range or a single interpretation when using images in research.

3. Images Are Didactic and Convince

The power of the visual is not only one that causes awareness. Once humans become aware of something that is visually interesting, we often desire more information about it. We study it, learn from it, and if we find it pleasing, we want to see it and things like it again and again. As a result, visual images have an immense didactic capacity, first drawing our eye and then teaching us how to look at them by guiding our eye movements, providing the information we seek through these movements, and convincing us to believe what we see.

Humans developed artistic skills prehistorically. Cave paintings appear to be the earliest visual form that art historians and archeologists can agree is imagery. Even before those paintings were created in an environment that enabled them to survive, it is likely that people were making art to aid instruction, perhaps to teach people how to hunt or serve other social functions. A leader of the hunt who had art skills may have used these to explain hunting strategies or stories on cave walls. This leader may not only have indicated the knowledge necessary for a viewer's own survival, but also used imagery to convince viewers to ensure the care and survival of the group. Therefore, that artist-leader would be particularly attractive for breeding and passing on their genes. In other words, it is likely that capabilities of art-making and the didactics connected to them have been culturally important and were increasingly expressed in our genes. As a result, humans have become a species who can create, value, and even search out increasingly sophisticated forms of images to learn from.

4. Images Recall the Past and Influence the Future

Ancient artworks suggest that art-making and appreciating capabilities evolved simultaneously with other higher order functions. It could even be possible that cave paintings of hunting are not just a visual record or an effort to teach skills and strategies, but were also a form of research. Perhaps the drawings were an investigation of what would happen on a hunt, through which the hunter could see which strategies and practices would be successful before endangering tribal member's lives. Perhaps the evidence of the image could have even convinced the hunters that the hunt would succeed.

The capacity of visual qualities to connect to previous experiences through association and the provocation of memories enables the use of visual research methods. This can be seen in the long history of empirical aesthetics. Daniel Berlyne (1971) contributed to research on the impact of the visual through studies suggesting that characteristics of visual aesthetics, such as complexity in images, have a greater impact on people's visual preferences than previously assumed. Visual preferences are constructed by and give coherence to social and cultural groups through the establishment of common meanings, narratives, and aesthetic experiences (Freedman, 2016). Access to global digital technologies and mass distributed popular culture have enabled humans to develop long-lasting allegiances to visual culture choices. These allegiances play a critical role in the formation of large and small communities that supersede geographic borders as visual culture mediates among people in and across sociocultural groups.

Thinking with Materials in and Through Qualities

Dewey's *Art as Experience* (1934/1989) attempted to unpack the ways that tacit relationships among qualities carried the significance of images. As stated earlier, his personal intellectual journey can be described as a search for thought. He was interested in where thought begins, the ways thought develops, and how thought is best nurtured. Dewey stated in his conclusion to *Art as Experience* that tacit knowledge constructed in the process of making exists in the place where original, autonomous thought begins to emerge: "Only imaginative vision elicits the possibilities that are interwoven within the texture of the actual" (1934/1989, p. 348). Visual analysis offers the step from the actual to the possible.

Quantitative Thought: The Amounts of Qualities

The visual qualities that make up images have amounts. An image may have more red than blue, or ten lines and three shapes. Humans are hardwired to find patterns and otherwise structured relationships of qualities that we tacitly hear, sense, smell, and feel. Most people can be educated to increase this perception by focusing attention on the amounts and placements of qualities that make up patterns and structures. Any quality that exists can be measured or assessed, at least approximately, in terms of the amount of that quality, which can be useful in research.

Qualitative Thought: Thinking in Relationships of Qualities

However, determining the amounts of visual qualities may not be the most important aspect of imagery used in social science research. Rather, the impact of the tacit aspects of those qualities may be the primary emphasis in the use of visual research methods. According to Dewey, finding meaning in the relationships of qualities is far more intellectually demanding than using semiotic rules, which involve thinking in terms of textual symbols. Dewey (1931) referred to this process of finding relationships of qualities as *qualitative thought*. At its core, qualitative thought is a recognition of tacit knowledge that allows one to sense, for example, organization, movement, and time. Dewey argued that the visual arts are an exemplary mode of this form of intellectual communication. His contemporary Martin Heidegger referred to it as a road to language (1959/1971). However, the visual can be an end in itself.

Conclusion

This chapter has focused on the empirical basis of visual qualities. Sensory information, which creates the look and feel of an image, hovers outside of articulated language and can inform without the attachment of language. However, through tools of visual analysis, such as art criticism, somatic data can be brought into language where criteria may be applied for judging the use of visual research methods. These tools can help researchers understand the importance of the visual in the construction of knowledge across disciplines, develop a high level of visual literacy in order to ask better research questions and apply visual methods, develop visual research methods skills, and assess visual methods applications.

As you decide which images might be relevant to your research, ask the following questions:

1. What elements and principles of design should the image(s) have?
2. How would you select, create, and analyze the image(s)?
3. Would the image(s) be made using digital or traditional material?
4. Who would have the skills to make or select the image(s)?
5. How has the image(s) of interest been used and judged by professional communities?

References

Bang, M. (2000). *Picture this: How pictures work*. Chronicle Books.

Barad, K. (2007). *Meeting the universe halfway: Quantum physics and the entanglement of matter and meaning*. Duke University Press.

Barrett, T. (1994). Principles for interpreting art. *Art Education, 47*(5), 8–13. https://doi.org/10.2307/3193496

Bennett, J. (2010). *Vibrant matter: A political ecology of things*. Duke University Press.

Berger, J. (2001). *John Berger: Selected essays* (G. Dyer, Ed.). Vintage Books.

Berlyne, D. E. (1971). *Aesthetics and psychobiology*. Appleton Century Crofts.

Bourdieu, P. (1984). *Distinction: A social critique of the judgement of taste*. Routledge & Kegan Paul.

Braidotti, R. (2019). *Posthuman knowledge*. Polity Press.

Castro, D., & Ordóñez, N. (2018). *La mujer de los siete nombres [The woman of the seven names] [Film]*. Cine Colombia, SA.

Cohen-Evron, N. (2005). Students living within violent conflict: Should art educators "play it safe" or face "difficult knowledge"? *Studies in Art Education, 46*(4), 309–322. https://doi.org/10.1080/00393541.2005.11651793

Coole, D. H., & Frost, S. (Eds.). (2010). *New materialisms: Ontology, agency, and politics*. Duke University Press.

Csikszentmihalyi, M. (1996). *Creativity: Flow and the psychology of discovery and invention*. HarperCollins.

DeLanda, M. (2021). *Materialist phenomenology: A philosophy of perception*. Bloomsbury Academic.

Dewey, J. (1931). *Philosophy and civilization*. Minton, Balch & Company.

Dewey, J. (1980). *Democracy and education*. In Boydston (Ed.), *The middle works, 1899–1899*, Vol. 9. Southern Illinois University Press. (Original work published 1916)

Dewey, J. (1981). *Experience and nature*. In Boydston (Ed.), *The later works, 1925–1953*, Vol. 1. Southern Illinois University Press. (Original work published 1925)

Dewey, J. (1989). *Art as experience*. In Boydston (Ed.), *The later works, 1925–1953*, Vol. 10. Southern Illinois University Press. (Original work published 1934)

Dolphijn, R., & van der Tuin, I. (2012). *New materialism: Interviews & cartographies*. Open Humanities Press.

Dow, A. W. (1899/1920). *Composition: A series of exercises in art structure for the use of students and teachers*. Doubleday.

Efland, A., Freedman, K., and Stuhr, P. (1996). *Postmodern art education: An approach to curriculum*. National Art Education Association.

Freedman, K. J. (2003). *Teaching visual culture: Curriculum, aesthetics, and the social life of art*. Teachers College Press & National Art Education Association.

Freedman, K. (2016). Interculturalism now: How visual culture has changed formal and informal learning. In P. Burnard, E. Mackinlay, & K. Powell (Eds.), *The international handbook of intercultural arts research* (pp. 444–453). Routledge.

Greenberg, C. (2003). *Late writings*. University of Minnesota Press.

Gude, O. (2004). Postmodern principles: In search of a 21st century art education. *Art Education, 57*(1), 6–14. https://doi.org/10.1080/00043125.2004.11653528

Hannes, K., & Siegesmund, R. (2022). An analytical apparatus for visual imagery applied in a social-behavioral research. *International Review of Qualitative Research, 15*(2), 278–302. https://doi.org/10.1177/19408447221097061

Haraway, D. (2004). *Donna Haraway reader*. Routledge.

Heidegger, M. (1959/1971). A dialogue on language: Between a Japanese and an inquirer. In *On the way to language* (P. D. Hertz, Trans., pp. 1–54). Harper & Row. (Original work published 1959)

Jameson, F. (1977). *Postmodernism, or the cultural logic of late capitalism*. Duke.

Jenks, C. (1987). *Post Modernism: The new Classicism in art and architecture*. Rizzoli.

Kelly, L. (2004). Evaluation, research and communities of practice: Program evaluation in museums. *Archival Science, 4*(1–2), 45–69. https://doi.org/10.1007/s10502-005-6990-x

Luna, B., Velanova, K., & Geier, C. F. (2008). Development of eye-movement control. *Brain and Cognition, 68*(3), 293–308. https://doi.org/10.1016/j.bandc.2008.08.019

Martínez, G. (2016). *La niña* [The girl] [Television series]. Caracol TV.

McCloud, S. (1993). *Understanding comics: The invisible art*. Kitchen Sink Press.

Perez, C. (2019). *A hall full of mirrors: A critical analysis of mass media post-conflict narratives in Colombia* [Paper presentation]. 15th International Congress of Qualitative Inquiry, University of Illinois at Urbana-Champaign.

Rosenberg, H. (1972). *The de-definition of art*. University of Chicago Press.

Rosenberg, J. (1967). *On quality in art*. Princeton University Press.

Shusterman, R. (1992). *Pragmatist aesthetics: Living beauty, rethinking art*. Rowman & Littlefield.

Siegesmund, R. (2023). The arts as research: Nomadic materiality and possible futures. In N. K. Denzin, Y. S. Lincoln, M. D. Giardina, & G. S. Cannella (Eds.), *The SAGE handbook of qualitative research* (6th ed., pp. 453–465). SAGE.

Springgay, S., Irwin, R. L., & Kind, S. W. (2005). A/r/tography as living inquiry through art and text. *Qualitative Inquiry, 11*(6), 897–912. https://doi.org/10.1177/1077800405280696

Stern, R. A. M. (1977). *New directions in American architecture*. Braziller.

CHAPTER 4

Visuality in Social Science Research

Visual research methods are cross-disciplinary. Scholars across the social sciences, such as sociology (Pauwels & Mannay, 2020), anthropology (Banks & Zeitlyn, 2015), and geography (Rose, 2016) have described methods of using visual images in research. In tandem, scholars in the visual arts fields have argued for the methodological foundations of image creation as fundamental to many types of inquiry (e.g., Rolling, 2013; Springgay et al., 2008; Sullivan, 2010). As a result, a wide variety of conceptual frameworks (e.g., content analysis, historical materialism analysis, structuralist analysis, post-structural analysis, psychoanalysis, or embodied analysis) have been used to drive inquiry through visual methods.

And yet, past approaches to the visual in social science research have generally relied on text-based metaphors. In a survey of more than 5,000 educational research articles published in 20 journals over a 10-year span, images were used overwhelmingly in an *illustrative* capacity (Roldán et al., 2017). The study found that the educational research analyzed tended to have an image analysis limited to textual "reading," merely identifying images and their contents as semiotic signs. The impact of the visual, aesthetic qualities—the formal properties and tacit power that give images their agency—were rarely considered. Yet, those tacit dimensions are a significant factor in the social science disciplines that use images (Berger, 2001).

In this chapter, we first discuss the relationship of science and aesthetics in Modernism and the impact of that relationship on contemporary images.

DOI: 10.4324/9780429285721-5

Second, we discuss visual criticism as a foundation of art and social science research and an example of the connection between knowledge and emotion. Third, we explore the phenomenological flexibility of images and their use in visual methodologies. Finally, we take a close-up look at visual research methods in the context of the professional disciplines, which developed and depend on them for inquiry. Figure 4.1 shows the third conceptual framework lens in the book, which focuses on the relationships among the research question or researcher's interests (partly determined by professional discipline), the research methods, the processes and techniques that method requires, and the research image(s). The lens shows the embedded nature of an image(s) in the practice of research across disciplines. These practices are interrelated and do not necessarily act in a stage-like manner, particularly when it comes to including images in research.

The Influence of Aesthetic Modernism on Contemporary Images

One of the hallmarks of the Modernist era, beginning at least by the 19th century (although its roots can be seen in art as early as the Renaissance), is that scientific theories emerged about art. Visual images are an empirical way to investigate the world. However, Modernism, as an aesthetic and artistic concept, holds that the purposeful disruption of prior expectations and the

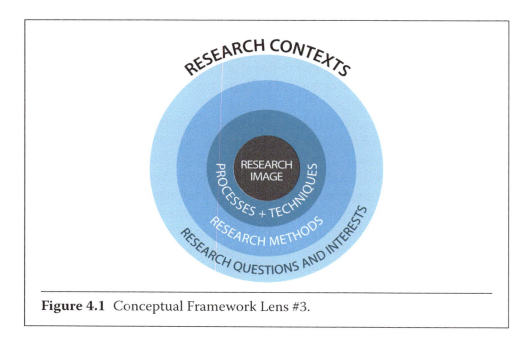

Figure 4.1 Conceptual Framework Lens #3.

Visuality in Social Science Research

Figure 4.2 *The Third of May*, Francisco de Goya, 1814.
Public domain, via Wikimedia Commons.

unsettling of beliefs about art and the world are necessary to broaden perception and open conditions for the creation of new knowledge. Visual images should add complexity to prior knowledge. The concept of avant-garde art—art that forces people to see in new and unsettling ways—was born of the Modernist project. Avant-garde art does not sooth the soul, but rather disrupts in order to build imaginative possibilities.

For example, one image that marks the beginning of Modernism is the 1814 painting *The Third of May 1808* by the Spanish painter Francisco de Goya (Figure 4.2). The image portrays war crimes committed against civilians during Napoleon's occupation of Madrid. It is not a pretty picture; but rather, it has an artistic beauty. It is a scream of anguish, and yet its beauty compels us to dwell with it. The artist has made clear to us whose side he is on. The humble people cowering to the left of the image are next to a standing individual in white. This standing figure is the lightest part of the picture and its focus; he is the center of interest.

87

A lantern in the image shines light on him. His outstretched arms suggest the martyrdom of Christ, as a faceless, repetitive line of solders aim their guns at him. We do not see the perpetrators of this crime – they are dehumanized, standing rather like a solid wall; we fixate on the anguish on the faces of the victims. It is an extremely emotional painting, a snapshot of a moment in time because the artist uses the power of imagery to generate empathy within viewers. The power of this painting, its seductive formal and symbolic qualities, makes us want to explore it and come to terms with the horror of war. Viewers can think through the implications of this painting as the image bears testimony and serves as a charge for ethical action.

Images have the ability to say something true about time and culture. At about the same time as Goya painted the *Third of May*, the Japanese artist Katsushika Hokusai created a series of landscape depictions of the sacred summit of Mount Fuji. However, Hokusai used these various views to create rich ethnographic studies of his culture (Figure 4.3).

Figure 4.3 *Fuji from the Katakura Tea Fields in Suruga,* from the series *Thirty-six Views of Mount Fuji* by Katsushika Hokusai, c. 1830.
CC0, via Wikimedia Common.

Visuality in Social Science Research

Images have not merely been a means to document an event, they became a tool for generating social indignation and political pressure for social change. The photographs by journalist Jacob Riis at the end of the 19th century of New York City tenement dwellers, now collected by art museums as early achievements of Modernist photography, inspired social scientists as a result of their evidential power to support civic reform. At the same time, the commitment of Modernist artists to apply visuality for social change is tied to a range of social science disciplines.

In the late 19th and early 20th centuries, new technologies enabled and advanced machine-made images and color reproduction to spread Modernist ideas developed in the visual arts to spread around the globe. Early social science theorists and researchers began to grasp the profound impact of visual imagery on knowledge. By the 1930s, several members of the neo-Marxist Frankfurt School of critical theory in Germany, such as Walter Benjamin, Theodor Adorno, and Herbert Marcuse, began exploring the "aesthetic dimension" (Marcuse, 1978) from a social science perspective. Benjamin and Adorno argued that the new machine technologies of the age, which enabled the increasingly realistic reproduction of a work of fine art, would damage the uniqueness of the original, but both saw the possibilities of visual reproduction as a tool for cultural and social change. They considered fine art as having the power to disrupt and even emancipate, not through explicit messaging with signs, but as an evocative space of aesthetic possibility. Marcuse realized that both the fine arts and popular arts can stimulate desire. He expressly pointed to forms of making and performance that mainstream culture sought to push to the margins (such as popular Black or Latinx arts, Asian somatic discipline, and international youth culture) as sites of imaginative social critique.

In contrast to Marcuse's Modernist argument that art can emancipate by gaining aesthetic access to the viewer's previously formed unconscious, Michel Foucault (1966/1970) reinforced a sentient interpretation of images through the conscious use of symbol systems, applying a constructivist and post-structuralist argument supporting the view that the audience works to compose the picture with the artist. He argued that the Renaissance confirmation of visual resemblance in images as corresponding to life was expanded in what he called the Classical period that followed (the art historical Baroque) by tying visual representation to systematic codes. This actually began well before the Renaissance, in the West for example in ancient Egyptian art, but Foucault claimed that the subject ("man") became entangled in a visual symbol system, in part, through art as exemplified in the trompe-l'oeil style of painting (Figure 4.4). From this perspective, the meaning of a painting is found in a precise identification of every object portrayed.

As culture enforced control through this web of signs, Foucault envisioned a post-representational, deconstructive, aesthetic resistance that would allow

Visual Methods of Inquiry

Figure 4.4 Trompe-l'oeil still-life by Samuel van Hoogstraten, 1664. Public domain, via Wikimedia Commons.

individuals to think beyond symbolic hegemony and discover a personal self-invention through a somatic art of living (Foucault, 1997; Ratiu, 2021). Foucault understood that the ties between deeply held emotion and knowledge made apparent by Modernist artists give art its power.

Research as Visual Criticism: The Connection of Knowledge to Emotion

In order to investigate the research uses of visual culture, we need to explore the relationship between knowledge and feeling with regard to images. This involves the connection between the formal and symbolic uses of visual qualities discussed in Chapter 3, which enable artists to create aesthetic form. Much of art is made up of symbolic content, such as a narrative, a portrait, or a landscape. However, the study of non-objective art (art not intended to represent) makes it easy to see that the elements and principles of design themselves can be interpreted independent of objects as well as being associated with multiple, cultural meanings. For example, colors can be used to suggest emotions, which are often culturally specific. In Western culture, traditional wedding dresses are white to suggest virtue and purity, whereas traditional Chinese wedding dresses are red to symbolize happiness and prosperity.

Because visual qualities act both formally and symbolically, creators use them to achieve both compositional and expressive goals. This connection between the formal and the expressive is how cultural knowledge is represented, which has an immense capacity to teach viewers ideas, values, and beliefs, even when viewers are unaware of this capacity. In a study of high school students responding to fine art and popular culture forms, the students demonstrated learning from both types of images, but did not appear to grasp

> the influential properties of imagery, even when asked directly about them. Purpose (whether conceived in terms of artist intent, cultural use, or personal appropriation) is a complex concept that we should not assume secondary students understand or are able to glean from an image. However, when actually forced to do so, students made a decision based on imagery and learned to analyze images critically when given the right conceptual tools. They began to understand that images convince.
> (Freedman & Wood, 1999, p. 139)

Some of what people obtain from visual experience can be described as a feeling of transformation. It is through the connection of knowledge and emotion that transformational, aesthetic responses to imagery may occur. In our view of aesthetic experience, emotions are not isolated from knowledge. Rather, the experience transports viewers to an emotional high at the same time as reaching into previous knowledge, some of which can be quite out of reach to the conscious mind. From a psychobiological perspective, knowledge and emotion work in unison to achieve this sense of elevation, in part, because viewing and making art result in increased levels of dopamine (e.g., Zeki, 1990), and drawing increases activity in the section of the brain that handles the feeling of being rewarded (Kaimal et al., 2017) Making and responding to art are cognitive processes dependent on multiple brain regions (Zaidel, 2010).

Observation as Visual Criticism: Coming to Know through Aesthetics

Elliot Eisner (1991) pointed out that observation in a social context, such as a classroom, is akin to the processes of art criticism through which the researcher makes sense of their variety of perceptual notations in a complex visual environment. For example, an experienced educational researcher conducting observation in a classroom is viewing a context that is at least somewhat familiar to them. It is likely that they have learned, taught, and observed in classrooms before. The classroom under observation has several component parts that are common to most classrooms, such as walls, floor and ceiling, people standing and/or sitting on chairs at tables, and someone in a position of leadership. However, this description could just as easily apply to a business meeting, a written traffic test, or a coffee shop, as it could refer to a classroom. What do the visual characteristics of a particular classroom convey to the researcher about its unique educational quality? What characteristics identify the people in the room? What behaviors can be ascertained through observation? The experienced researcher observes aesthetic aspects of the situation and compares it to their previous experiences in classrooms; observation and comparison are the foundations of visual criticism in the conduct of research.

Reporting as Visual Criticism: Connecting Knowing and Feeling

Contemporary cognitive scientists consider the connection between knowing and feeling as closer than conceptualized in the past (Lakoff & Johnson,1999). The aesthetic qualities of the visual provide more than a set of symbols to decipher, but can provide a felt experience that bridges the gap between knowledge and emotion. This enhances inquiry. If handled appropriately, visual qualities can be used to motivate coming to know, particularly with regard to learning about complex issues. Images draw the viewer in to dwell with their complexity.

Viewing can initiate a transformative feeling as a result of the visual qualities per se or in relation to the content or context the visual qualities represent. An example can be found in the aesthetic preferences that result from cross-cultural, psychobiological functions. However, within and across cultures, humans have also developed particular aesthetic preferences that have emerged as cultural groups chose, investigated, and created forms that became agreed upon as preferred over time.

The Visual as Both Made and Seen

The concept of image maker and image viewer as two separate and distinct activities has changed within contemporary Modernist practice. A major current of fine art in the early 21st century is called Social Art or Socially Engaged Art. Social Art rejects the idea of a single creative individual making an expressive statement, and instead sees the visual arts as generating a social dynamic that enables a sense of becoming to connect and increase knowledge and emotion. From this perspective, artists theorize change in complex, and often wide-ranging, social issues. As a strategy for dealing with the scale of these issues, the artists bring together social groups (often including local people who are not professional artists) as co-creators and researchers in order to address an issue or problem. Social artists may enfold quantitative data and qualitative knowledge and practices into their work. For example, they may collect data about a political event, local social problem, or environmental condition, then create a work of art using that data. The co-creators and audience visually or conceptually complete the work, in part, by considering the alternatives the work suggests. If successful, co-creators and audience may experience a type of transformation or change of mind. The work of art is a type of research through which co-creators theorize data.

The Phenomenological Flexibility of Visual Methodologies

As introduced earlier in this book, visual methodologies hold an inherent tension between suggestive possibility and fixed meaning. They reveal a generative process while enacting a disruptive process. This tension produces what philosopher Jacques Rancière (2010) calls *dissensus*, which is an unresolved element that sustains hermeneutic dialogue. Such a dialogue prohibits full closure even while the dialogue can forge robust communities of agreement. An image is never fully settled; it remains perpetually queered. Viewers return to discover more, to dig deeper, to reconsider. New interpretations are translucently layered upon older ones. As Dewey (1934/1989) enjoined, the flexibility of images is vital to social life and guards against intellectual stagnation. To arrive at a fixed conclusion diminishes our capacity to discover. These conditions make up one of the benefits of images in research.

In part, images are dynamic because they are situated in culture, which is vibrant and ever-changing. Therefore, addressing visual culture in research is a phenomenological issue. Phenomenology does not attempt to define how something is represented, but instead is concerned with becomings that an object and its human participant produce together (Vagle, 2018). These moments of mediated meaning—of what is seen, sensed, and thought—are *intentional* phenomena. Philosopher Mark Vagle argues that *post-intentional* phenomena play with Deleuze and Guattari's idea of starting in the middle (Deleuze & Guattari, 1980/1987). This is a particularly important concept in visual creation as the researcher brings an image out of invisibility into visibility through the conscious and unconscious use of images previously seen that are carried in the researcher's personal iconic store. Thus, the making of images in the context of research is seldom a mechanist system of recording. Rather, it is an iterative process of visualizing, sketching, erasing, re-envisioning, and re-drawing to bring forward an image that the creator feels can stand before critical analysis and carry the weight associated with labeling analysis as findings. Even with a camera, the image maker erases, re-envisions, and remakes their visual data as they seek for the right moment.

This flexibility is seen in the process of artistic production. Often, creators experience a thrashing in their discovery and development of an image. In this volatile, primordial state, multiple possibilities of becoming emerge, which Deleuze and Guattari (1980/1987) called *lines of flight*. A creator will juggle these possibilities until the image is released and eventually refined. These becomings are not limited to the making of images; they also apply to the ways an image is viewed within the dynamic of visual culture as it appears and reappears to the viewer in ever-changing contexts.

As an example of post-intentional phenomenal visual research, art educator Brooke Hofsess, who researches in the Appalachian Southern Highlands, conducted a project with local girls and their mothers called Ecologies of Girlhood. In this project, participants came to know the unique characteristics of their mountain heritage through material interactions and visual recordings (Hofsess et al., 2019). For example, the adolescent girls waded into a stream (a physical entry into a midpoint) to investigate aquatic life. Sensation and wonder guided them. They took samples as their interests unfolded, often inspired by a sense of beauty. They made records of discoveries using blue cyanotype printing (a process that seizes on available daylight to secure a permanent image), which allowed the girls to create immediate, visual field records. The prints served as both archival data of research subject to analysis and works of art that could be curated for public exhibition. In part, this research was a visual investigation of what it means to be in Appalachia. Although the researcher had a question in mind about what would happen under these conditions, this was a post-intentional phenomenological study, as participants are actively interacting with the world around them to make meaning. They do not simply encounter and experience a phenomenon; they contribute to generating the phenomenon with which they are engaged as they actively shape it.

Visual research continues to grow with specific methods like photovoice, photowalk, photo elicitation, and participant-created artwork. These methods emerge and develop within and across disciplines. A list of example methods with brief definitions and literature resources can be found in Table 4.1. Major visual research methods will be discussed in the context of a variety of visual arts and social science disciplines in the following sections.

Visuality in Social Science Research

TABLE 4.1
Examples of visual research methods

Visual Research Methods
A/r/tography
❏ A multimodal, emergent practice that incorporates artistic making with data generation, analysis, and presentation of research (Springgay et al., 2008).
Art Therapy Methods
❏ Methods used to promote and study therapeutic self-expression that aid the creator through engagement with artistic materials and processes to improve or resolve psychological concerns (McNiff, 1998a).
Artistic Iteration
❏ An image in development, or the process through which an image is developed, by selection, sketching, queering, and erasure, or other means of visual drafting (Sousanis, 2018).
Collage Methods
❏ The use of image juxtapositions and overlapping as a process of data collection and analysis (Butler-Kisber, 2019).
Close analyses
❏ Careful and slow looking at and analyzing of visual imagery or objects to interpret the impact of formal and symbolic qualities (Freedman et al., 2013).
Embodied Practice
❏ The physical manipulation of materials, images, and objects as a form of data analysis (Leigh & Brown, 2021)
Image Assembly
❏ The process through which an artist, researcher, or research participant collects and arranges a group of images, often seeking to create metaphorical meaning that generates new understanding (Marín-Viadel & Roldán, 2012).
Image Critique
❏ The practice of criticizing an image or images against an agreed upon set of criteria, either stated or presumed, which may be formative or summative (Soep, 2004).
Mapping, Mind
❏ Visual culture created to reflect thinking and decision-making processes (Ali et al., 2022).
Mapping, Geographical
❏ Illustration of visualized experience of land and space (Green et al., 2016).

(Continued)

Visual Methods of Inquiry

TABLE 4.1 (Continued)
Examples of visual research methods

Visual Research Methods
Participant-Made Images
❏ Participants make visual culture in response to a prompt (Mitchell & Sommer, 2016).
Performativity
❏ The visual enactment of identity in social situations (Butler, 2015), including the use of cosplay (Aljanahi & Alsheikh, 2021).
Phenomenology, Post-Intentional
❏ Researcher/participant image-making that creates a record of the ineffable (Vagle, 2018).
Photo Documentation
❏ A systematic record of objects or events taken with a camera as data for analysis (Karpati, et al., 2016).
Photo Elicitation
❏ Participants respond with a camera to visual prompts provided by the researcher (Harper, 2002).
Photojournalism
❏ Researcher use a camera to capture visual information as an image of record (Kobre, 2017).
Photowalk
❏ Photo documentation conducted while participants walk through a research site (Muszyński, 2022).
Photovoice
❏ Participants respond to a research prompt by creating photographs and discussing these with the researcher (Wang & Burris, 1997).
Post-structural approaches
❏ Visual research strategies that deliberately overwhelm or deconstruct thematic structures to provoke new appraisals (Manning, 2015).
Reflexive Making
❏ During the production of visual culture, systematic reflection where the maker looks back upon and analyzes the production process (Ritterbusch, 2016).
Scientific Visualization
❏ Visual representations of data that effectively communicate, for example, quantity, duration, weight, function, and/or metaphoric structure (Tufte, 1990).

(Continued)

TABLE 4.1 (Continued)
Examples of visual research methods

Visual Research Methods
Self-Portrait
❏ Image in which participant is aware of shaping their own appearance (see Chapter 3 this book).
Social Art
❏ Art that responds to felt or articulated social concerns (Cosier, 2019; de Azevedo & Peled, 2015).
Studio Inquiry
❏ Visual culture that emerges through a process of artistic inquiry (Sullivan, 2010), frequently following creative practices to discover a point of inquiry (LeBlanc, 2018).
Visible Border Exploration
❏ The method by which a social scientist or artist deliberately pushes previously established or assumed visual boundaries, particularly through the image creation (Wallin, 2012).
Visio-Textual Analysis
❏ Participants create images with critical-reflexive openness and the researcher systematically weaves visual analysis of the image with interview data from the participant (Brown & Collins, 2021; Hannes and Siegesmund, 2022).
Visual Advocacy
❏ The creation or use of critically insightful visual culture to promote a better and more inclusive future (Finley, 2018).
Visual Argument
❏ Creation or appropriation of an image to make a point and advance a claim (Frank, 1958/2008).
Visual Authenticity
❏ Determination of valid visual representation used as evidence in research (see Chapter 3 of this book).
Visual Choice
❏ The creation or arrangement of multiple visual culture objects for comparative purposes (Jensen, 2014).
Visual Co-Creation
❏ The researcher and/or participants make a visual culture object through a systematic, collaborative process (AmberBeckyCreative, 2022).

(Continued)

TABLE 4.1 (Continued)
Examples of visual research methods

Visual Research Methods
Visual De-Colonialization
❏ Visual imagery that purposively seeks to deconstruct colonial conceptual frameworks (Denzin, 2011; Staikidis, 2020).
Visual Ethnography
❏ The application of visual images within the framework of qualitative ethnographic research (Pink, 2013).
Visual Exhibition
❏ The curatorial selection and arrangement of visual objects to provoke audience interpretation (Hofsess et al., 2019).
Visual Journaling
❏ Visual images created or used as a form of qualitative notetaking (Gibson, 2018).
Visual Narrative
❏ Images in a sequential order that tell a story, such as through graphic novels (Kuttner et al., 2021).
Visual Sequence
❏ A series of images or digital video that show change over time (Trafí-Prats, 2012).
Visual Web
❏ Visualized entanglements of interacting data sets that invite comparison and discussion (Tufte, 1990).

Disciplinary Approaches to the Use of Visual Research Methods

Dewey (1934/1989) explained that perceiving art is an aesthetic experience, not just a process of recognition, in which the context of making, viewing, and judging interrelate. The contextual includes, for example, where, how, and by whom an image was created, how it is seen, its medium, and its viewers. As a result, determining the appropriateness of a visual research method should be based on several factors, including disciplinary context.

Studio Art

Studio art, or the personal expression of an individual artist (who may work in their own studio), has been a primary mode of visual communication

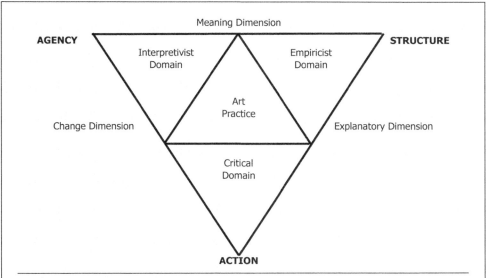

Figure 4.5 Sullivan's Framework for visual arts research with dimensions of practice.

about social information historically and a foundation of contemporary visual research methods. Now, art serves a wide range of functions, such as to represent the world through a personal style, for therapeutic expression, to maintain or change cultural traditions, and to promote social justice. The methods of the visual arts are widely variable, but have commonalities across functions, materials, and styles as discussed in Chapter 3. These methods have been part of the training of visual artists across cultures for millennia.

Artist and educator Graeme Sullivan (2010) proposed a framework for visual arts research focusing on the process of art making as inquiry (p. 102). His framework is useful for considering the purposes and goals of thinking through images. Originally conceived of as a method of understanding visual arts practice as a process of inquiry, his model applies to social science efforts directed at making visual images. Sullivan lays out an arena for practice established by the tension between three dimensions of visual research: empirical structure, personal agency, and social action (see Figure 4.5). These three horizon points establish domains of practice: the empirical, the interpretive, and the critical. Sullivan conceptualizes visuality as a terrain which the researcher journeys through while assuming different roles as the empiricist, the interpretivist, or the critical commentator.

Traversing Artistic Domains

Sullivan's three horizon points are different poles for research. *Empirical structure* focuses on investigating a world assumed to exist without human interference. *Personal agency* places personal growth and transformation at the center of research. *Social action* considers research as a form of civic engagement. These poles create dimensions of practice: *meaning, explanation,* and *change*. As one moves toward each pole, distinctive domains of practice emerge. This is not an index for pigeon-holing research. It is a cartographic chart serving to map entangling motions and tensions across the three domains. There is no checklist or recipes for successful completion; rather, research is evaluated by how one moves across this terrain.

James Rolling Jr. (2013) also sees the process of visual research as a journey over time. He frames the emergence, analysis, and interpretation of the visual as an unfolding dialogue among researcher, object, and audience where all have agency to shape a new emergent methodology. He claims that "research may now be viewed as a dynamic human engagement requiring a dialogical dance of inquiry that synthesizes multiple perspectives into an emergent, often transitory, theoretical point of view" (p. 88). Rollings makes Sullivan's map multi-dimensional by introducing audience reaction as an integral part of the research's unfolding path. This is a fluid process of inquiry "since not everything visible makes discursive sense, and not everything that makes sense is plainly visible" (p. 49). There is a complex interaction between the researcher's intent that drives the research, the resistance of the materials that redirects the trajectory of the research, and reverberations of audience feedback that alter constructions of meaning. The shaping and interpretation of visibility is where spontaneous discoveries of tacit qualitative meaning are made, which were not discursively articulated before the research commenced, but are discovered within the process of inquiry. These discoveries may serendipitously support the researcher's purpose or just as easily tacitly undermine it, thereby forcing a revaluation of the entire research project.

Approaches to Making

We conceptualize journeys in visual making as traversing four points: selection, sketching, queering, and erasure. As Deleuze and Guattari (1980/1987) suggest, research will always begin in the middle as the researcher wades into a stream in motion. The making or use of a visual image may not have a clear point of origin; nevertheless, a creator or researcher makes a *selection* of point of entry, which can be disorienting.

An emerging image can be an unsure, unsecured weight, like a cannonball on a ship's deck. In response to an initial move, the researcher begins *sketching* in order to capture the ball. The ball does not roll randomly; but each change in direction is fleeting, making the capture difficult. Sketching is a form of note taking. It can be done through drawing, of course, but also through, for example, the manipulation of clay, processes of sorting and rearranging images or bits of images, or taking snapshots. Sketching enables one to envision a global view or collect snippets of details. Sketching is not a transparent, representational transfer of external empirical data copied as a record to a data bank so that it becomes permanently available for future reference. Acts of transfer are acts of *queering* and every act of capture is an act of alteration. The researcher is responsible for a reflexive analysis of their intentional and unintentional interventions in the data recording process.

Neither is the visual process linear; it is hermeneutic, looping back and revisiting previous points of departure. Rather than being a sequential process of expansion with each new layer building upon previous layers, this process involves *erasure*, the removal of what was there before and the creation of absence. Erasure can be unconscious or unintentional—like rotating the brim of a cap for a photographed portrait (Jenoure, 2008).

Contemporary art practice provides numerous examples of the art of deliberately obliterating form in order for new thinking to emerge. An example is the drawing by Robert Rauschenberg (1953) entitled *Erased de Kooning Drawing*, which is little more than a framed blank piece of paper. Rauschenberg scrupulously removed all vestiges of semiotic markings from an original pencil drawing by Wilhelm de Kooning (with de Kooning's consent). Nothing remains, other than some faint indentations in the paper. Viewers must speculate as to what de Kooning's drawing might have been and dwell with implications of Rauschenberg's act of conceptual annihilation, which suggests that the importance of visuality is in what is thought and not just seen. Here Rauschenberg plays the provocateur by suggesting that while criticism is the enlargement of perception (Dewey, 1934/1989), a broader conceptual visuality might mean seeing less. Art educator John Baldacchino (2019) calls this *unlearning*—a deliberate effort to erase that has been constructed in order that new ways of thinking might appear in their place.

Through selection, sketching, queering, and erasure, image creators enable images to form. These images often become key to what we believe we know, but once images achieve form, they are still not permanent. Even if they seemingly endure, like da Vinci's Mona Lisa, they are changed and repurposed as they appear in new and ever-changing social contexts. Marcel Duchamp's (1964/1919) defacement of a print reproduction of the *Mona Lisa* does not destroy the original image, it layers on a new level of interpretation because when encountering a new image, you often compare it to one in your memory. Visuality consists of both the seen and unseen, or what was once seen and seen no more.

Critique as Visual Analysis

In the visual arts, images invite textual analysis through criticism. Textual analysis cannot fully explain or categorize a picture, it opens a dialogue to possibility based on visual, somatic evidence. In the visual arts, this process of criticism is called critique. Two manners of critique are common in studio art: a group feedback practice devoted to the formative process of making works of art communicate more effectively (Soep, 2004), and a summative process for assessing the success of a work. The purpose of critique is not to explain a work, rather it can identify sites of strengths and weaknesses, such as unintended ambiguity. Formative critique can serve as a reflexive dialogue throughout the image creation process between the creator and viewers, which sharpens the eye. The visual researcher needs to stay attuned to what an image becomes in the eye of interpreters, and critique can help to form communities of agreement among professional peers who assess the validity of visual research.

Anthropology

In the 19th century, equipped with the first portable cameras, anthropologists staged Indigenous peoples in compositions that conformed to what the white Western gaze wished to impose (Banks, 2001). Images, including drawings and sketches, were used as supportive evidence in ethnographic studies. These pictures speak as much, if not more, to the researcher controlling the camera than the individuals who were posed for this visual record. Nevertheless, these images were regarded as a representational truth and presented to the public as accurate descriptions of unfamiliar cultures.

The book *Writing Culture* (Clifford & Marcus, 1986) was a watershed moment that marked a cultural shift from representation to interpretation in anthropology. Clifford and Marcus flipped the script from social scientists as detached collectors and analyzers of data to synthesizers who shaped narratives, which often helped research participants better structure their lives, value their cultures, and guide future aspirations. This turn was driven in part by the realization that culture is not a constant, passively waiting to be documented and recorded, but a living, mutable, and ever-changing dynamic—one that the researcher cannot objectively observe—but rather a continuous transformational process in which the researcher participates and does their best to report. Besides introducing the idea that social science field work was fundamentally subjective and required a set of allegorical and metaphorical skills on the part of the researcher to report across diverse cultures, the book also opened the door to neo-colonial studies and hard fundamental questions about the ethics of recording, analyzing, and reporting on "the other." With the realization that images were more than simple pictures, there was a call for greater systematic methodological analysis of what images could do (Collier & Collier, 1986).

The move to subjective interpretation raised concerns that "aesthetic" outcomes might undermine the hard, critical work of anthropology and sociology that explore systems and patterns of culture and sustain ingrained injustice (Clifford, 1999). Aesthetics was seen as detracting from important social concerns. This point of view led to a lack of attention to aesthetic factors; in particular, how materials themselves shape meaning. Visual anthropologist Marcus Banks (e.g., Banks; 2001; Banks & Zeitlyn, 2015) has attempted to address this issue through his interest in the contextual materiality of the image, which extends to the way the image was made.

In all cases of mechanical image production and reproduction, such as video and still photography, as well as in many non-mechanical cases, the material characteristics of the form serve to shape or even constrain the possible content. Conversely, through paint and other traditional media, it is possible to represent both things that can be seen with the naked eye and those that cannot (Banks, 2001). As Banks suggests, the materiality of the visual media brings into visibility imagery that had not previously existed. It allows the researcher to see anew. Therefore, the analysis of an image requires an appreciation of its making. Images are formed and shaped by the apparatuses and the materiality through which these tools make cuts in the universe (Barad, 2007).

Researchers form representations just as the rich visual culture that surrounds us influences our concepts of identity (Pink, 2013). As suggested by feminist studies, we apply all our senses and awareness of our bodies as we move through space and travel in time (Pink, 2015). Visual research provides a record of the magnitude and duration of the embodiment of practices, perspectives, and beliefs that are fundamental to tacit experience.

Sociology

Sociology became recognized as an academic discipline in the 1890s, but visual sociology did not emerge as a field until the 1960s. Visual sociologists argued that images could shed a unique light on social conditions and behaviors. However, in Jon Prosser's (1998) groundbreaking work in visual sociology, the author pointed out that most social scientists limited their use of images to illustration.

In contrast, Donald Harper (1988) argued that images should be able to stand alone without interpretive text. For Harper (2002), visual images serve as effective means of studying challenging life circumstances of community members who may not be able to fully articulate their concerns through traditional research methods, such as surveys or interviews. For example, he championed fine arts photographer Robert Frank's photo-essay book, *The Americans* (1958/2006), as an evocative inquiry into the feeling of America (although images in the book were initially criticized as poorly composed and lacking professional technique). Furthermore, Harper argued that researchers should not fix the meaning of an image with their own interpretation, as in the case of illustration, but rather leave the task of meaning making to individual viewers to allow for multiple interpretations (Harper, 1998). The task of the visual sociologist is not to present a definitive meaning, but rather establish a context in which a sociological issue, problem, or state can be brought into conversation.

Luc Pauwels and his co-editor Dawn Mannay (2020) call on visual studies to continue cross-disciplinary dialogue and embrace approaches to visuality across a number of disciplines in the humanities, social science, and fine arts. Pauwels' Integrated Framework for Visual Research offers three critical dimensions of visuality: provenance, design, and dissemination (Pauwels, 2020, p. 16). The first dimension (provenance and nature of visuals) involves the ways images come into existence. Pauwels' second dimension deals with researchers' intentional desire to apply images to inquiry (research design and procedural issues). Here, Pauwels suggests systematic procedures for image identification, image creation, and image analysis. The third dimension involves audience interpretation (dissemination formats and research purposes). The researcher can offer an interpretation to the viewer, but the construction of meaning is dialogic and the viewer has agency to critically alter the researcher's meaning.

Through both anthropology and sociology, we see a growing awareness of the complexity of images as they are either found in society or brought into existence by participants and researchers. These images are frequently under analyzed by limiting possible interpretations to textual readings of what is overtly depicted. However, in both disciplines there is an increasing interest in an embodied approach to analysis, such as photo elicitation.

Communications/Journalism

Photojournalism (Kobre, 2017) has a distinguished history of producing memorial images that serve as lasting records of events small to large. Photojournalist John Filo's (1970) image of Mary Ann Vecchio kneeling in anguish over the body of student Jeffery Miller seconds after he had been gunned down by the Ohio National Guard on the campus of Kent State University is more than poignant. It captures the horror and angst of a generation. Adding to the remarkable nature of his photograph, it was the last image on Filo's roll of film. One shot, one instant, either caught by the photojournalist or lost forever. Even more amazing is how the picture seemingly references an entire canon of Christian religious iconography called the pietà.

The stunning quality of photojournalistic pictures often prompts accusations that the photos were either staged or manipulated. For years, in journalistic practice it was acceptable to manipulate photographs to remove ambiguity and improve aesthetic impact. Indeed, when Filo's picture of Vecchio and

Miller was first released, editors airbrushed away (in an era before Photoshop) the fence post behind Vecchio that appeared to be sprouting out of her head. As the image quickly became iconic—and charges of fabrication began to surface—the unadulterated picture was restored as the historical picture of record—although a question lingers if this official image may retain vestiges of editing as Miller's blood pooling around Vecchio's foot appears to be airbrushed away as well.

A signature of photojournalism is its professionalism. Photographers are highly trained technicians in the use of exquisitely calibrated equipment. Therefore, it was radical when photojournalist Jim Hubbard, who documented homelessness, put his equipment in the hands of children. In his work, he found that children were fascinated with his camera, wanting to hold it and take their own pictures. In 1989, he created the non-profit organization *Shooting Back* that sought to empower disadvantaged youth by teaching them photojournalistic skills in documenting their own lives (Hubbard, 1991). While photojournalism has long maintained a high demand of technical excellence and close textual readings of images, by shifting the camera into the hands of participants who lacked the high degree of technical training of photojournalists, Hubbard's work points to a move toward community-based image production through methodologies like photovoice (Wang & Burris, 1997).

Business, Advertising, and Performativity

Professors of Management and Organizational Studies Torkild Thanem and David Knights (2019) argue for an embodied approach to the engagement of text and images in understanding how groups of people extract meaning from an immersive process with their environment. While such meaning produces "incomplete findings" and "visceral experiences" (p. xii), nevertheless they inform the decisions people make in social association and personal consumption. Advertising images attract and can lead to increased attention and sales, and social scientists have long worked to discover the visual forms and mechanisms that are most successful in selling. Two of those are suggestions of sex and death because they make humans want to look.

Just as photojournalists pride themselves on exercising technical skill to realize the decisive moment (Cartier-Bresson & Tériade, 1952) creating the image of record, advertising focuses on the critical instance of desire. This is not a matter of capturing uniqueness, but rather of creating a fantasy of replication in which the consumer merges their identity with that which is being advertised (Wallace, 2008). Fashion photographer Steven Meisel has famously pushed the envelope of desire. His work for the fall 2000 Versace advertising campaign drew on what French philosopher Jean Baudrillard (1995) called a *simulacrum* where individuality is erased in pursuit of an idealized form (Meisel, 2000). Even more controversially, Meisel's 1995 photographs for Calvin Klein appropriated the visual vocabulary of child pornography. His 2006 contribution to *Vogue Italia* included misogynistic images that flirted with torture and rape—all as hooks for selling designer apparel (Meisel, 2006). However, the real story behind this work is that Meisel and the Calvin Klein company, which has had a history of using sex to sell, were wrong about this ad campaign. Viewers responded negatively, the FBI threatened an investigation, and the advertisements were pulled from public venues.

Feminist philosopher Judith Butler (2015) views the visual presentation of self as a form of performativity. The consumer is not a copy, but a distinctive variant on a theme. Humans shape our appearance to the world to fit a narrative that we wish to convey. It is possible for individuals to consciously perform different narratives by changing the visual form in which they present themselves. Visual images thus record a series of transitory moments. Each is a piece of the puzzle, but none is a whole representation. Images are clearly manipulations and thus need analysis with consideration of who is doing what to whom and the motivations behind the urge to manipulate.

Psychology

Images have long been associated with mapping the mind and are critical to understanding how the mind works. The discipline of psychology is the home to creativity studies, which directly explore how the intuitive blossoms into new knowledge. As a discipline that is concerned with the health of the mind, psychology also hosts therapeutic approaches which often engage visual imagery.

Creativity

Paul Torrance (1970) pioneered creativity studies exploring how some individuals can make critical, imaginative connections in ambiguous circumstances. He identified four key traits of creative people: fluency, flexibility, elaboration, and originality. Here is an example of the way these traits function: if a researcher showed a participant a picture of a duck floating on still water, fluency would be measured by how many similar cases the participant might name. The participant might respond with similar examples of the category, such as mallard, goose, or swan or even extend the train of thought to other kinds of avian and fowl. Flexibility is the ability to think in context. In this case, the duck is in a pond, but there might also be fish, algae, frogs, and other creatures of the environmental system that relate to the duck. Elaboration is the ability to drill down into detail, attending to the distinctive parts of the duck including the bill, crown, wings, and feathers. Originality is the ability to make abductive leaps to other examples of ducks: *Duck Soup* (McCarey, 1933) is the name of a Marx Brothers comedy film; a sitting duck is a person who can be victimized; Howard the Duck (Gerber, 1973) is a Marvel superhero.

Through these four traits, viewers see more than a portrayal of a duck. They extend and extrapolate the image, creating associative meanings. The degree to which someone is inclined to do this is a quantifiable measure of creativity. While some people are naturally gifted in fluency, flexibility, elaboration, and originality, these are teachable skills. Creativity is not only an endowed talent, but also an orientation to problem solving that can be learned (Harris, 2016; Kara et al., 2021).

Art Therapy

Tracing the development of an image is critical to the discipline of art therapy. Shaun McNiff (1998b) advocates for therapeutic research that embraces visuality as a process of open, sensuous, non-linear, studio practice in forming visuality. McNiff demonstrates that developing a visual image is a process of thinking that occurs before language. He stated, "images and processes of artistic creation are always at least one step ahead of the reflecting mind" (1998a, p. 27). McNiff pointed to the heightened tacit awareness of visuality, which develops through the creative process of image-making and precedes language, opening the mind of the researcher to possibilities for new conceptual frameworks in which language could later appear.

Contemporary art therapy practitioners use researcher-produced and researcher-instigated participatory methods for gaining access to tacit levels of knowing. Contemporary contemplative practices in education explore visual imagery as a catalytic agent, confirming the creator's ontological presence to promote learning and building relationships with human and non-human communities (Walsh et al., 2015). In such cases, visuality causes language to coalesce around meaning, providing the opportunity to form theory. Victor Lowenfeld's *Creative and Mental Growth* (1947) provided a template for art educators to apply these research approaches to building visual arts curriculum for primary and secondary schools.

Art Education

The discipline of art education focuses on how humans of all ages make meaning in and through the visual arts. The Picture Study Movement at the beginning of the 20th century focused on using fine art in classrooms didactically to teach moral messages (Efland, 1990). These were particularly aimed at immigrant students who did not possess English language skills. Pictures like George Henry Boughton's *Pilgrims Going to Church* (1867) or Jules Adolphe Breton, *The Song of the Lark* (1884) would teach culturally approved messages of faith, resilience, and ennoblement through hard work. Visual propaganda works in analogously coded ways to convey an approved, official message. However, even when images have fixed codes, they may contain tacit evidence that can be constructed to different ends.

The field of art education is informed by the early 20th-century research of Franz Cižek, among others, who saw in the art of young children forms of authentic expression that preceded formal education (Efland, 1990). Later psychological studies would suggest a natural innate pictorial system in small children that was pan-cultural (Kellogg & O'Dell, 1967). However, as children get older, human immersion in and the influence of visual culture become increasingly important to learning, teaching, and research about the visual arts (Freedman, 2003).

Art educators use a wide variety of visual research methods borrowed from the visual arts and social sciences, from collecting student-made art for content analysis to more contemporary arts-based methods. For example, the arts-based research methodology of *a/r/tography* was developed at the University of British Columbia and focuses on an overlapping and integrated form of art, research, and teaching (Springgay et al., 2008). A/r/tography emphasizes individual, Deweyian rebuilding with a keen eye on the perpetual verb of becoming through a process of reorganization and reinvention. The making of and exhibiting visual images in the reporting of research is an essential feature of a visual a/r/tographic methodology.

An inquiry of becoming can be disruptive and throw the researcher out of balance (Siegesmund, 2012). Recovering from disruptions that come in the form of chance, unexpected tacit knowing, and the reinvention of ourselves in the process of being in our research is key to inquiry. As discussed earlier in studio art practice, the queering of form prevents an image from settling comfortably within a category. It promotes weak theory (Saint-Amour, 2018), which recognizes that the forms and methods of visual culture will slip classifications and assume different interpretations, which can be overwhelming for learners with both positive and negative effects.

Spectacle is a form of visual disruption that intentionally overwhelms through excess. It is a purposeful extravagance that silences discordant thinking (Garoian & Gaudelius, 2008). It mesmerizes; spectacle sweeps the viewer up in a dazzling array of visuality that suspends personal reflection and critical assessment. Spectacle, by design, is anti-analytic and can defer inquiry. A historical example of the masterful use of spectacle is filmmaker Leni Riefenstahl's 1935 Nazi propaganda film *Triumph of the Will*. The film suspends the viewer's judgment and uncritically accepts the producer's narrative with enthusiasm

Visuality in Social Science Research

Figure 4.6 A Carnival costume in Trinidad and Tobago, 2006.
Courtesy Jean-Marc/Jo BeLo/Jhon-John from Caracas, Venezuela, CC BY 2.0, via Wikimedia Commons.

(Taylor, 1998). The tradition of Carnival in Trinidad and Tobago creates riotous, visually wondrous, juxtapositions meant to overwhelm constraint to provoke uninhibited celebration (Figure 4.6).

Contemporary popular visual culture can have the same effect on young people and many other effects, such as influencing body image. Art educators use visual research methods to better understand the relationship among visual culture, learning, and social issues and to teach students how to inquire through artistic production and viewing.

Geography

The discipline of geography focuses on the ways that things relate to each other in space and time. In this context, images are important for their capacity to show relationships and transitions. Professor of Geography Gillian Rose's

(2016) *Visual Methodologies: An Introduction to Researching with Visual Materials* is based on a conceptual framework for visuality that has a radial design of three concentric circles of modalities: the technical, the compositional, and the social. A research project would spiral up through these three modalities, touching on each level, through four forms of interpretation: the image itself, the image's production, circulation, and audiencing.

Geographers depends on drawn and photographed images of rock and other land formations, as well as methods of cartography. They also attend to plants, animals, and human cultural relationships with land and environment, which are studied through the use of qualitative methods, such as ethnography. Geographers use visual methods to collect information, study human performances related to space, use newer technologies to visualize space, and present their research (e.g., Oldrup & Carstensen, 2012). As a result, visual literacy has become essential knowledge for geographers.

Conclusion

We began this chapter in the methodology of visual making as it has been traditionally taught in schools of art and design. However, we are not just addressing art school talk. Images have their own agency independent of the creator. Meaning becomes manifest through the tools we employ to engage with the materiality of the world. Our tacit sense precedes what we can articulate or read through language. These are now principles that belong to all qualitative inquiry. Returning to Pauwels and Mannay's (2020) call, the application of visual imagery in social science research is a multi-disciplinary endeavor. Across disciplines, visual analysis is a nomadic journey. It is a process of discovery, reconsideration, and revision. As Rolling (2013) observes, the construction and interpretation of images is a hermeneutic process. Yet it is important to remember that this is not merely an additive process; it demands attention to erasure and unlearning (Baldacchino, 2019). The construction of an image ebbs and flows as it is situated in an ever-changing context.

Our recommendation for qualitative researchers is greater than acquiring a course in studio methods or art history in their graduate program of study. Like artists, if qualitative researchers seek to embrace the visual, they need to dwell in the visual. Course work helps, but becoming critically reflexive consumers of art and popular visual culture is essential. Researchers need to engage in critical conversations oriented toward enlarging perception. How do we reside in this place of being? This is a challenge that Elliot Eisner (2005) says pushes us to the edge of incompetency (p. 160), but it is here that we fashion new understandings, which propel us into the future and help us avoid merely replicating the past.

To make decisions about which types of methods are appropriate for your inquiry, ask the following questions:

1. What discipline(s) was foundational to the research question(s)?
2. How phenomenologically flexible is the research?
3. How much does the research connect knowledge to emotion?
4. How would visual methods contribute to this research?
5. What type of image(s) would the study require (historical or contemporary images, participant or researcher made or selected)?

References

Ali, S. H., Merdjanoff, A. A., Parekh, N., & DiClemente, R. J. (2022). Development of an integrated approach to virtual mind-mapping: Methodology and applied experiences to enhance qualitative health research. *Qualitative Health Research*, *32*(2), 571–580. https://doi.org/10.1177/10497323211058161

Aljanahi, M. H., & Alsheikh, N. (2021). "There is no such thing as copying in cosplay": Cosplay as a remixed literacy practice. *Journal of Adolescent & Adult Literacy*, *65*(3), 209–218. https://doi.org/10.1002/jaal.1193

AmberBeckyCreative (2022). (k)not mattering: Ethical (re) considerations of material, methodological, and pedagogical responsibilities. *International Review of Qualitative Research*, *15*(2), 248–277. https://doi.org/10.1177/19408447221090658

Baldacchino, J. (2019). *Art as unlearning: Towards a mannerist pedagogy*. Routledge.

Banks, M. (2001). *Visual methods in social research*. SAGE.

Banks, M., & Zeitlyn, D. (2015). *Visual methods in social research*. SAGE.

Barad, K. (2007). *Meeting the universe halfway: Quantum physics and the entanglement of matter and meaning*. Duke University Press.

Baudrillard, J. (1995). Absolute merchandise (D. Britt, Trans). In *Andy Warhol: Paintings 1960–1986* (pp. 18–21). Kunstmuseum Luzern & Hatje.

Berger, J. (2001). *John Berger: Selected essays* (G. Dyer, Ed.). Vintage Books.

Boughton, G. H. (1867). Pilgrims going to church [Painting]. New York Historical Society. https://emuseum.nyhistory.org/objects/22545/pilgrims-going-to-church.

Breton, J. A. (1884). *The song of the lark* [Painting]. Art Institute of Chicago. https://www.artic.edu/artworks/94841/the-song-of-the-lark.

Brown, N., & Collins, J. (2021). Systematic visuo-textual analysis: A framework for analysing visual and textual data. *The Qualitative Report*, *26*(4), 1275–1290. https://doi.org/10.46743/2160-3715/2021.4838

Butler, J. (2015). *Notes toward a performative theory of assembly.* Harvard University Press.

Butler-Kisber, L. (2019). Collage-making. In P. Atkinson, S. Delamont, A. Cernat, J. W. Sakshaug, & R. A. Williams (Eds.), *SAGE research methods foundations* (pp. 2–9). SAGE.

Cartier-Bresson, H., & Tériade, E. (1952). *The decisive moment.* Simon and Schuster.

Clifford, J. (1999). After writing cultures. *American Anthropologist, 101*(3), 643–645. https://www.jstor.org/stable/683864

Clifford, J., & Marcus, G. E. (Eds.) (1986). *Writing culture: The poetics and politics of ethnography.* University of California Press.

Collier, J., & Collier, M. (1986). *Visual anthropology photography as a research method.* University of New Mexico Press.

Cosier, K. (2019). What can art and art education do in the perilous present? *Studies in Art Education, 60*(3), 260–268. https://doi.org/10.1080/00393541.2019.1632635

de Azevedo, E., & Peled, Y. (2015). Socially engaged art as a methodological strategy in social science. *International Journal of Contemporary Sociology, 52*(2), 167–188.

Deleuze, G., & Guattari, F. (1987). *A thousand plateaus: Capitalism and schizophrenia* (B. Massumi, Trans.). University of Minnesota Press. (Original work published 1980)

Denzin, N. K. (2011). *Custer on canvas: Representing Indians, memory, and violence in the new west.* Left Coast Press.

Dewey, J. (1989). *Art as experience* [The later works, 1925-1953] (J. Boydston, Ed., Vol. 10). Southern Illinois University Press. (Original work published 1934)

Duchamp, M. (1964) L.H.O.O.Q. *[Altered image].* Norton Simon Museum. (Original work created 1919) https://www.nortonsimon.org/art/detail/P.1969.094.

Efland, A. (1990). *A history of art education: Intellectual and social currents in teaching the visual arts.* Teachers College Press.

Eisner, E. (1991). *The enlightened eye: Qualitative inquiry and the enhancement of educational practice.* Macmillan.

Eisner, E. W. (2005). *Reimagining schools: The selected works of Elliot W. Eisner.* Routledge.

Filo, J. (1970). *Mary Ann Vecchio grieving over the body of college student Jeffery Glenn Miller shot by National Guardsmen during an antiwar demonstration at Kent State University, Ohio* [Photograph]. The Museum of Fine Arts, Houston. https://emuseum.mfah.org/objects/59183/mary-ann-vecchio-grieving-over-the-body-of-college-student?ctx=dadb2e76a13173489627fe0298e602afe49dd007&idx=0

Finley, S. (2018). Critical arts-based inquiry: Performances of resistance politics. In N. K. Denzin & Y. S. Lincoln (Eds.), *The SAGE handbook of qualitative research* (5th ed., pp. 561–575). SAGE.

Foucault, M. (1970). *The order of things: An archaeology of the human sciences.* Pantheon Books. (Original work published 1966)

Foucault, M. (1997). *Ethics: Subjectivity and truth* [The essential works of Foucault, 1954–1984] (P. Rabinow, Ed; R. Hurley, Trans.). New Press.

Frank, R. (2008). *The Americans.* Steidl. (Original work published 1958)

Freedman, K. (2003). *Teaching visual culture: Curriculum, aesthetics, and the social life of art.* Teachers College Press.

Freedman, K., Heijnen, E., Kallio-Tavin, M., Karpati, A., & Papp, L. (2013). Visual culture learning communities: How and what students come to know in informal art groups. *Studies in Art Education, 53*(2), 103–115. https://doi.org/10.1080/00393541.2013.11518886

Freedman, K. & Wood, J. (1999). Reconsidering critical response: Student judgements of purposes, interpretation, and relationships in visual culture. *Studies in Art Education, 40*(2), 128–142. https://doi.org/10.2307/1320337

Garoian, C. R., & Gaudelius, Y. (2008). *Spectacle pedagogy: Art, politics, and visual culture.* State University of New York Press.

Gerber, S. (1973, December). *Adventure into fear* [Comic book]. Marvel Comics.

Gibson, D. (2018). A visual conversation with trauma: Visual journaling in art therapy to combat vicarious trauma. *Art Therapy: Journal of the American Art Therapy Association, 35*(2), 99–103. https://doi.org/10.1080/07421656.2018.1483166

Green, E. P., Warren, V. R., Broverman, S., Ogwang, B., & Puffer, E. S. (2016). Participatory mapping in low-resource settings: Three novel methods used to engage Kenyan youth and other community members in community-based HIV prevention research. *Global Public Health, 11*(5-6), 583–599. https://doi.org/10.1080/17441692.2016.1170178.

Hannes, K., & Siegesmund, R. (2022). An analytical apparatus for visual imagery applied in social-behavioral research. *International Review of Qualitative Research, 15*(2), 278–302. https://doi.org/10.1177/19408447221097061

Harper, D. (1988). Visual sociology: Expanding sociological vision. *The American Sociologist 19*(1), 54–70. https://doi.org/10.1007/BF02692374

Harper, D. (1998). An argument for visual sociology. In J. Prosser (Ed.), *Image-based research: A sourcebook for qualitative researchers* (pp. 24–41). Falmer Press.

Harper, D. (2002). Talking about pictures: A case for photo elicitation. *Visual Studies, 17*(1), 13–26. https://doi.org/10.1080/14725860220137345

Harris, A. (2016). *Creativity and education.* Palgrave Macmillan.

Hofsess, B. A., Ulmer, J., Carlisle, J., & Caldwell, S. (2019). Curating with ecologies of girlhood. *International Journal of Education Through Art, 15*(3), 357–368. https://doi.org/10.1386/eta_00008_3

Hubbard, J. (1991). *Shooting back: A photographic view of life by homeless children.* Chronicle Books.

Jenoure, T. (2008). Hearing Jesusa's laugh. In M. Cahnmann-Taylor & R. Siegesmund (Ed.), *Arts-based research in education: Foundations for practice*. Routledge.

Jensen, S. (2014). *A long walk*. Open Society Foundations–New York. Retrieved from https://www.movingwalls.org/moving-walls/21/long-walk.html.

Kaimal, G., Ayaz, H., Herres, J., Dieterich-Hartwell, R. Makwana, B. Kaiser, D. H., & Nassar, J. A. (2017). Functional near-infrared spectrospop assessment of reward perception based on visual self-expression: Coloring, doodling, and free drawing. *The Arts in Psychotherapy, 55*, 85–92. https://doi.org/10.1016/j.aip.2017.05.004

Kara, H., Lemon, N., Mannay, D., & McPherson, M. (2021). *Creative research methods in education*. Policy Press.

Karpati, A., Freedman, K., Kallio-Tavin, M. Heijnen, E., & Castro, J. C. (2016). Collaboration in visual culture learning communities: Towards a synergy of individual and collective creative practice. *International Journal of Art and Design Education, 36*(2), 164–175. https://doi.org/10.1111/jade.12099

Kellogg, R., & O'Dell, S. (1967). *The psychology of children's art*. Random House.

Kobre, K. (2017). *Photojournalism: The professionals' approach* (7th. ed.). Routledge.

Kuttner, P. J., Weaver-Hightower, M. B., & Sousanis, N. (2021). Comics-based research: The affordances of comics for research across disciplines. *Qualitative Research, 21*(2), 195–214. https://doi.org/10.1177/1468794120918845

Lakoff, G., & Johnson, M. (1999). *Philosophy in the flesh*. Basic Books.

LeBlanc, N. (2018). The abandoned school as an anomalous place of learning: A practice-led approach to doctoral research. In M. Cahnmann-Taylor & R. Siegesmund (Eds.), *Arts-based research in education: Foundations for practice* (2nd ed., pp. 174–189). Routledge.

Leigh, J., & Brown, N. (2021). *Embodied inquiry*. Bloomsbury.

Lowenfeld, V. (1947). *Creative and mental growth*. Macmillan.

Manning, E. (2015). Against method. In P. Vannini (Ed.), *Non-representational methodologies: Re-envisioning research* (pp. 52–72). Routledge.

Marcuse, H. (1978). *The aesthetic dimension: Toward a critique of Marxist aesthetics*. Beacon Press.

Marín-Viadel, R., & Roldán, J. (2012). Quality criteria in visual a/r/tography photo essays: European perspectives after Daumier's graphic ideas. *Visual Arts Research, 38*(2), 13–25. https://doi.org/10.5406/visuartsrese.38.2.0013

McCarey, L. (1933). *Duck soup* [Film]. Paramount Pictures.

McNiff, S. (1998a). *Art-based research*. Jessica Kingsley.

McNiff, S. (1998b). *Trust the process: An artist's guide to letting go*. Shambhala.

Meisel, S. (1995). Calvin Klein advertisement campaign [Advertisement].

Meisel, S. (2000). Versace fall 2000 campaign [Advertisement].

Meisel, S. (2006, September). State of emergency [Editorial]. *Vogue Italia*.

Mitchell, C. M., & Sommer, M. (2016). Participatory visual methodologies in global public health. *Global Public Health*, *11*(5/6), 521–527. https://doi.org/10.1080/17441692.2016.1170184

Muszyński, M. (2022). The image of old age emerging from place personalization in older adults' dwellings. *Journal of Aging Studies*, *63*, 1–10. https://doi.org/10.1016/j.jaging.2022.101075

Oldrup, H. H., & Carstensen, T. A. (2012). Producing geographical knowledge through visual methods. *Geografiska Annaler, Series B, Human Geography*, *94*(3), 223–237. https://doi.org/10.1111/j.1468-0467.2012.00411.x

Pauwels, L. (2020). An integrated conceptual and methodological framework for the visual study of culture and society. In L. Pauwels & D. Mannay (Eds.), *The SAGE handbook of visual research methods* (pp. 15–36). SAGE.

Pauwels, L. & Mannay, D. (Eds.) (2020), *The SAGE handbook of visual research methods*. SAGE.

Pink, S. (2013). *Doing visual ethnography* (3rd ed.). SAGE.

Pink, S. (2015). *Doing sensory ethnography* (2nd ed.). SAGE.

Prosser, J. (Ed.). (1998). *Image-based research: A sourcebook for qualitative researchers*. Falmer Press.

Rancière, J. (2010). *Dissensus: On politics and aesthetics* (S. Corcoran, Trans.). Continuum.

Ratiu, D. E. (2021). The "aesthetics of existence" in the last Foucault: Art as a model of self-invention. *Journal of Aesthetic Education*, *55*(2), 51–77. https://doi.org/10.5406/jaesteduc.55.2.0051

Rauschenberg, R. (1953). *Erased de Kooning drawing* [Drawing]. San Francisco Museum of Modern Art. https://www.sfmoma.org/artwork/98.298/

Riefebstahl, L. (1935). The triumph of will [Film]. Reichsparteitag-Film.

Ritterbusch, A. E. (2016). Exploring social inclusion strategies for public health research and practice: The use of participatory visual methods to counter stigmas surrounding street-based substance abuse in Colombia. *Global Public Health*, *11*(5–6), 600–617. http://dx.doi.org/10.1080/17441692.2016.1141971

Marin-Viadel, & Roldán, J. (2012). Quality criteria in visual a/r/tography photo essays: European perspectives after Daumier's graphic ideas. *Visual Arts Research*, *38*(2), 13–25. https://doi.org/10.5406/visuartsrese.38.2.0013

Roldán, J. Pinola-Guadielo, S., & Rubio-Fernández, A. (2017). Images in educational reports: A literature review of the journal *Educational Researcher. Ideas Visuales*, 216–229. https://dialnet.unirioja.es/servlet/libro?codigo=685106

Rolling, J. H., Jr. (2013). *Arts-based research primer*. Peter Lang.

Rose, G. (2016). *Visual methodologies: An introduction to the interpretation of visual materials* (4th ed.). SAGE.

Saint-Amour, P. K. (2018). Weak theory, weak modernism. *Modernism/Modernity, 25*(3), 437–459. https://doi.org/10.1353/mod.2018.0035

Siegesmund, R. (2012). Dewey through a/r/tography. *Visual Arts Research Journal, 38*(2), 99–109. https://doi.org/10.5406/visuartsrese.38.2.0099

Soep, E. (2004). Visualizing judgment: Self-assessment and peer assessment in arts education. In E. W. Eisner & M. D. Day (Eds.), *Handbook of research and policy in art education* (pp. 667–687). Lawrence Erlbaum.

Sousanis, N. (2018). Thinking in comics: An emerging process. In M. Cahnmann-Taylor & R. Siegesmund (Eds.), *Arts-based research in education: Foundations for practice* (2nd ed., pp. 190–199). Routledge.

Springgay, S., Irwin, R. L., Leggo, C., & Gouzouasis, P. (Eds.) (2008). *Being with a/r/tography*. Sense.

Staikidis, K. (2020). *Artistic mentoring as a decolonizing methodology: An evolving collaborative painting ethnography with Maya artists Pedro Rafael González Chavajay and Paula Nicho Cúmez*. Brill | Sense.

Sullivan, G. (2010). *Art practice as research: Inquiry in visual arts* (2nd ed.). SAGE.

Taylor, R. (1998). *Film propaganda: Soviet Russia and Nazi Germany* (2nd ed.). I. B. Tauris.

Thanem, T., & Knights, D. (2019). *Embodied research methods*. SAGE.

Torrance, E. P. (1970). *Encouraging creativity in the classroom*. W. C. Brown Co.

Trafí-Prats, L. (2012). Urban children and intellectual emancipation: Video narratives of self and place in the City of Milwaukee. *Studies in Art Education, 53*(2), 125–138. https://doi.org/10.1080/00393541.2012.11518857

Tufte, E. R. (1990). *Envisioning information*. Graphics Press.

Vagle, M. D. (2018). *Crafting phenomenological research* (2nd ed.). Routledge.

Wallace, I. L. (2008). Sex, sameness and desire: Thoughts on Versace and the clone. In E. Shinkle (Ed.), *Fashion as photograph: Viewing and reviewing images of fashion* (pp. 154–167). I.B. Tauris.

Wallin, J. (2012). Graphic affects. *Visual Arts Research, 38*(1), 34–44. https://doi.org/10.5406/visuartsrese.38.1.0034

Walsh, S., Bickel, B., & Leggo, C. (Eds.) (2015). *Arts-based and contemplative practices in research and teaching: Honoring presence*. Routledge.

Wang, C., & Burris, M. A. (1997). Photovoice: Concept, methodology, and use for participatory needs assessment. *Health Education & Behavior, 24*(3), 369–387. https://doi.org/10.1177/109019819702400309

Zaidel, D. (2010). Art and brain: Insights from neuropsychology, biology and evolution. *Journal of Anatomy, 216*(2), 177–183. https://doi.org/10.1111/j.1469-7580.2009.01099.x

Zeki, S. (1990). A century of cerebral achromatopsia. *Brain, 113*(6), 1721–1777. https://doi.org/10.1093/brain/113.6.1721

CHAPTER 5

Description of Visual Methods

The Research Image Framework

Throughout the first four chapters of this book, we have explored conditions, examples, and applications of prominent visual research methods. This chapter further delineates those methods and provides a framework for image use in research. The chapter has three purposes. The first purpose is to help researchers build their iconic stores, essential to understanding and using the range of visual research methods. Humans understand the visual by looking and we each must see many images to improve our judgments about any single image. Images can illustrate and clarify social science research strategies and practices, as well as help to answer research questions. As Dewey (1934/1989) (Watson & Rayner, 1920/2013) observed, describing the visual in words can improve perception, but it cannot replace perception. This is one reason that a researcher's iconic store is so important to their work.

Second, we describe and explain specific visual research methods. Some of these methods have been labeled, defined, and redefined in the literature of anthropologists, sociologists, educational researchers, and other social scientists for decades. Others have emerged more recently, such as those of arts-based research, and we seek to further refine aspects of their description in this chapter. Still other methods have been used by artists for centuries, but are translated here to enable researchers to investigate social science issues and questions.

The third purpose of the chapter is to present the Research Image Framework (RIF), which is a taxonomical framework of imagery to aid

Visual Methods of Inquiry

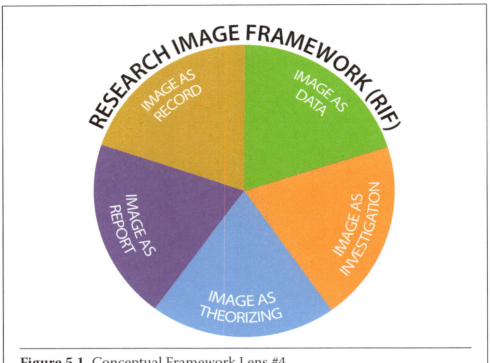

Figure 5.1 Conceptual Framework Lens #4.

researchers in their use and reporting of visual research methods. The fourth conceptual framework lens in the book is shown in Figure 5.1. It illustrates the general ways images are used in research as laid out in the RIF discussed below.

Figure 5.2 shows the interactions among all four conceptual framework lenses. We look through the lenses to see and address issues of visual research methods.

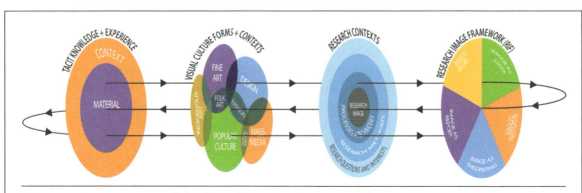

Figure 5.2 Interaction of the four Conceptual Framework Lens.

Description of Visual Methods

Building an Iconic Store to Support Visual Evidence

Adults in the United States have a wide range of common ground images in their iconic store. The national flag, Grant Wood's *American Gothic*, the *Statue of Liberty*, Martin Luther King giving his "I have a dream" speech, the *Vietnam Veterans Memorial* in Washington D.C., and the "Buffalo Nickel" (which actually has a bison on one side and a Native American man's profile on the other) are all iconic representations in American culture. They each connote a sense or a feeling of some aspect of national culture, as well as representing or symbolizing their role as national icons through their form. These examples of visual culture are recognized and carry strong associations with them, which have both commonality and difference for different individuals and groups. As a result, the memory of these examples of visual culture is carried in the iconic store of many people's memory.

Internationally, the common ground images in people's iconic stores overlap with those in the United States. Many people in the world have seen the Mona Lisa painting, or reproductions of it, and the Wonder Woman comics character. Not only are these referenced widely as familiar images, but they are also commonly used in advertising, products, and memes. Seeing such visual culture supports a common iconic store, image recognition, and image association. This is one reason why logos, such as the Nike logo, promote sales effectively.

Professionals in the visual arts, and people in general, interpret and reinterpret such common images to refresh their meanings. However, most people have a fairly narrow range of interpretation for them. As a result, they can be used to communicate intended ideas beyond those of the creators through attached meanings. For example, the Mona Lisa is often used as an icon of excellence, a meaning that has become attached to the image over the centuries. Wonder Woman's first appearance in 1941 in *All Star Comics* represented feminist ideals (e.g., Serna-Gutiérrez, 2018) and she has been used as a feminist icon for decades. Researchers cannot assume that all other researchers or participants will be familiar with such images enough to recall them, and even if those people can recollect them, the images may have a different interpretative meaning for any individual or cultural group. However, images that are common to a population's iconic store can be used as a starting point in a research environment to pilot test for their use across researchers and participants. Also, new images can be created to meet the specific needs of a particular study.

As we discussed in Chapter 3, humans are hardwired to remember high volumes of images, and for eons, our capacity for these memories have kept images alive. However, as technology developed, from the drawing and painting techniques on cave walls to digital visual imaging, the iconic store no longer rested only in our brains. Anyone who can use the Internet can now access a multitude of online images, which aids the development of our individual iconic stores and connects those stores to other individuals and populations.

In Chapter 3, we also introduced the idea of visual evidence and discussed ways of finding visual evidence in an image by "close looking" at its elements and principles of design. In the current chapter, we discuss uses of visual evidence in research, and specifically the ways that visual methods can aid knowledge construction and memory. When used as evidence, photographs in particular can reduce the cognitive effort required to understand new information by making information easy to interpret (Carney & Levin, 2002; Marcus et al., 1996; Mayer, 2008; Sargent, 2007). Visual evidence is used in courts of law to prove claims by scaffolding information and supporting prior knowledge, as might be reported by a witness. Many disciplines depend on visual evidence. In court, photographs are considered the best evidence of an occurrence because people remember events differently. Because of the human capacity to remember a large number of images with relative clarity, photographs are also used as prompts to help people in a courtroom remember an event, to "jog their memory". Art historians, media professionals, and other visual culture professionals use the visual evidence found in works of art and design as data on which to base inferences and draw conclusions. Photographs and videos are used on television news to make stories more believable than with words alone. Art educators use the visual evidence in student art to make determinations of quality when assessing and grading student work.

However, viewers can confuse information in a photograph and replace memories of an event with an inaccurate photographic image (Lindsay et al., 2004). Falsified images can cause people to believe that a fictitious event really happened (Newman & Feigenson, 2013). In one study, seeing a manipulated photo of Obama shaking hands with the former Iranian President, Mahmoud Ahmadinejad—a fabricated event—led people to remember having witnessed that false event on the news (Frenda et al., 2013). In another study, a doctored childhood photograph caused people to remember taking a hot air balloon ride they had never taken (Wade et al., 2002). People tend to evaluate new information by starting with the assumption that it is true (Gilbert, 1991). This can lead to a confirmation bias, which is the interpretation of new evidence as confirming a viewer's previously held beliefs. The new information then filters and influences a viewer's meaning construction and trust in related, subsequent information (Nickerson, 1998). As a result, images used in research should be selected and analyzed in other contexts for meanings that are both valid and reliable.

Choosing the Right Visual Research Method

Historically, the use of visual research methods has been challenging. Images can be expensive to create and publish and permissions can be costly and difficult to secure. However, this has begun to change as a result of newer technologies. Personal computer digital imaging capabilities and mobile phone cameras have lowered costs, making the creation and use of imagery in research and reporting more attractive to researchers, funders, and publishers now than in the past. Some countries are now connecting inquiry in the visual arts to social science research in their national funding. At the time of writing of this book, Europe was beginning to require a Ph.D. in order to teach art and design in universities, which has opened up new opportunities for collaboration in the use of visual methods for scientific study. Across Europe, independent schools of art have become part of departments of social research, and some national social science research proposals must include artists who receive mandatory minimums of approved research funding. In Canada, the national Social Sciences and Humanities Research Council granting agency uses the term "research creation" to refer to "an approach to research that combines creative and academic research practices and supports the development of knowledge and innovation through artistic expression, scholarly investigation, and experimentation" (SSHRC, Oct. 14, 2020).

Posing Research Questions

In order to determine which visual research method to use, a researcher needs to have formulated a research question or purpose, which will direct the researcher to the method. If a researcher begins with a research question, the question should be *clear* (Freedman, 2004). When research questions are not stated clearly, they lack a focused pathway for study, making it difficult to determine which methods are appropriate. A clear pathway is needed for determining appropriate research methods, analyses, and peer assessments, even when the intention is to allow the creative process to take the researcher or participants on a journey. In some arts-based research and insights are allowed to emerge. In such cases, when the question and purpose is left open-ended or not actually stated as a question, a question like "What will happen if I(we, they, it…) do(see, respond to, create…) under these conditions…?" is often being asked.

The question should be *answerable* (Freedman, 2004). Although good questions can lead to other questions, they must also lead to some end point in inquiry, even if momentary. They should be able to provide some conclusive results, given the resources available, even when the conclusion is that more work is needed. A difficult part of creating a research question is finding the right scope to balance breadth and depth in order to make the research manageable. Unmanageable research questions may be too big to be completed in a single project or series of projects.

Research questions should have *relevance* to other related research, theory development, and practice (Freedman, 2004). Questions must be pertinent in contexts; for example, they must be relevant to their time. Although some research questions are intended to replicate previous research results, new research questions should intend to fill gaps in the body of research of a field, expand the field, or in some other way add to the field.

A research question should also be *important* enough to study (Freedman, 2004). Conducting research is a type of service to a professional community, so research questions should help researchers contribute new knowledge to a field. Questions that are worthy of investigation result in reports that are important contributions to the literature in a field. It may be easy to decide what you want to study; it is harder to determine what the field needs to learn. So, when choosing a visual method, consider how images will be used (for example, as evidence), and how they will serve the purposes of the research.

Enabling Insights to Emerge

Post-qualitative researchers argue that social scientists need to be open to new opportunities that can bestow insight, which requires that some research questions may be structured in terms of process, such as: What will emerge…? The process that allows a visual metaphor to surface into consciousness from work in the unconscious or sub-conscious brain involves insightful connections or combinations that the mind constructs as a mental image. Artists learn to take advantage of such insights, and many examples exist of physical science researchers gaining from visualization, sometimes through abduction. Pierce's theory of abduction refers to the "ah-ha" moment, or the eureka effect. Here leaps in clarity are made (Douven, 2021). For example, August Kekulé famously claimed to have discovered the structure of benzene in the late 18th century after an abductive association from viewing an image of a snake biting its own tail. Einstein said that he visualized the theory of relativity in a dream involving cows: he had a sudden insight and seized the opportunity of an abductive moment.

Although many attempts have been made to discover the brain locations and processes that enable this effect, little is known about the ways that visual metaphors come into consciousness. Abduction is only one of many forms of abstract thinking that are difficult to capture and leave no apparent, identifying trail. The emergence of visual metaphors seems to involve a jump to visual consciousness of an insightful problem resolution. So, although researchers can gain from the abstract thinking and tacit knowledge of visual metaphors, logical systems can help set up situations to enable the visual work of the brain to occur.

The Research Image Framework

In this section, we discuss the RIF, which can aid researchers thinking about and classifying images used in research. These classifications can help with the selection of images for research, the benchmarking of images created or chosen as data, the use of imagery in illustrating or exhibiting research, and the building language to use in research reports. Each of these classifications overlaps and inter-relates, and each can depend on multiple methods. We lay out the five main categories of image use first, then explain a more fine-grained analysis of image use in the following sections.

Image as Record

Image as Record refers to the documentation of what can be seen and represents its subject in as direct and straightforward manner as possible. Although the visual can carry and suggest a wide range of interpretive meanings, this way of using images deliberately seeks to narrow interpretation so as to make a one-to-one correspondence between the image and that which it is intended to represent. It is an attempt to reveal the symbolic real through photographs, scientific visualizations, graphs, charts, and so on.

Image as Data

Image as Data refers to the use of visual culture, including art created by participants, as a source of information. For example, public images such as product and political advertisements have been used to study viewer response. This category refers to selection and sorting exercises where participants use previously made images as information or make their own images during the research project. Researchers often use such exercises to determine individual and group preferences, decisions, and beliefs. These exercises are powerful tools to gain insights into people's choices and decision-making in ways that text cannot because images can convey or suggest complex attached meanings. The vast amount of visual culture prevalent today makes it easy to find already-made images to use as data in research.

Image as Investigation

The creation and use of visual culture by participants in a study as a process of coming to know is *Image as Investigation*. As part of a research project, participant-made photographs, drawings, or other images can provide more information than participant-written text, interviews, or other behavioral observations. The images themselves may be analyzed for form and content, and the process of creation can reveal information that otherwise would be difficult to see, such as attitudes, mindsets, and points of view. Also, the creation of images can aid participants in talking about difficult knowledge. For example, one of the authors of this book used an adapted version of the International Baccalaureate interview process to interview hundreds of high school students about their autobiographical artwork in order to answer questions about adolescent and young adult social development. The students used the creation of artwork to investigate aspects of themselves they found difficult to describe or explain in words alone but were able to discuss when explaining their work to the researcher.

Image as Theorizing

Image as Theorizing highlights the use of imagery for the clarification of researchers' theoretical ideas through visual representation. For example, this manner of using visual culture can help a researcher to understand and see the implications of information, particularly information leading to and from tacit knowledge, in a manner that circumvents the limitations of textual interpretation. A classic example of this process is the discovery of the structure of DNA. Researchers James Watson and Francis Crick were unable to visualize the structure of DNA until they saw the spiral helix configuration in Rosalind Franklin's X-ray crystallography images. The images helped them make sense of their other data and based on the combination of these, they were able to conceptualize the DNA model.

Image as Reporting

Image as Reporting refers to the use of imagery in the public representation of research results. The image itself (or other visual forms) may be presented as part of, or a complete, publication or as an exhibition or installation to convey the results of research for an audience. Typically, the visual information used in social science publications are charts and graphs, which are intended to show a one-to-one correspondence between data and image. However, because images and other visual forms carry more information than words, they can be used to translate data and results to readers in aesthetic ways. For example, a popular culture representing human development from apes shows successive figures standing increasingly upright. Such a shorthand image is based on decades of research. In a more complex example, DaVinci's *The Last Supper*, the artist created a mathematically constructed composition to communicate the idea of an eternal order in the moment he sought to represent. The structure illustrates relationships and hierarchies, and our brains find the mathematical structure satisfying to see and explore. Dynamic engagement can be used in conjunction with *Image as Investigation*, so that investigation and reporting are simultaneous. For example, an arts-based research project in a gallery might include an installation, which has visual qualities and asks audience members to become participants in research. The participants then make or add to visual information, which then becomes part of the installation and reporting.

Expanding the Research Image Framework

A few organizing frameworks have been developed for visual research methods. For example, Luc Pauwels (2010) conceptualized the use of visual methods as a single methodology and produced a framework for "issues and aspects" (p. 547) of the visual in social research. Our RIF is a conceptual framework of the ways that imagery is created, selected, and used for research across methodologies based on the major categories just discussed: (1) Image as Record, (2) Image as Data, (3) Image as Investigation, (4) Image as Theory, and (5) Image as Report. Each of these categories has two subsections, and each subsection has two subsubsections, resulting in 20 different approaches included here that a researcher may take when creating, interpreting, and presenting the visual (see Table 5.1). Of course, more categories, subsections, and subsubsections could be developed, but we have chosen to focus on these examples.

The RIF does not suggest a hierarchical scale in value (Image as Record is just as significant to research as Image as Theory). Rather, it recognizes that images are chameleonic. They function differently at different times in both intended and unintended ways, which have as much to do with the research questions, interests, and plans of researchers as with the characteristics of the images. However, the RIF offers the grounding of a benchmarking system. It can help investigators both articulate their research intentions through the visual and analyze what the image itself—in its non-human agency—does independent of the investigator's research plan.

TABLE 5.1
Overview of the Visual Benchmarking Framework

I. Image as Record
Visual Documentation
❑ Visual Facts
❑ Visual Sequence
Visual Authenticity
❑ Visual Argument
❑ Visual Recording
II. Image as Data
Artifact Collection
❑ Participant-Made Art
❑ Visual Choice
Visual Ethnography
❑ Textual Response to Images
❑ Visual Field Notes
III. Image as Investigation
Image Assembly
❑ Collage Methods
❑ Scientific Visualization
Studio Inquiry
❑ Artistic Iteration
❑ Visible Border Exploration
IV. Image as Theorizing
Reflexive Making
❑ Therapeutic Expression
❑ Embodied Practice
Envisioned Futures
❑ Visual Advocacy
❑ Social Art
V. Image as Report
Research Illustration
❑ Correspondent Figures
❑ Visual Webs
Research Presentation
❑ Visual Narrative
❑ Visual Exhibition

Description of Visual Methods

In the following, we fully explicate the ten subsections and their 20 subsubsections of the RIF. Because images can be nomadic, and the RIF categories refer to ways images are used, the categories are non-binding, their boundaries are fuzzy, and images move across them. This does not make images unreliable; rather, it renders them dynamic. It is the task of the researcher to understand the dynamic nature of any particular image—the diverse ways it functions and can be interpreted—and to apply this nature to an analytic end. Some of the images connected to the examples in the subsections and subsubsections described here are in the Image Analysis Matrix in Chapter 6. We hope that you will look online for these and other related examples to build your iconic store.

I. Image as Record

The first category of visual image use is based on the idea of rendering the world as it is. This category has two subsections: **Visual Documentation** and **Visual Authenticity**.

Visual Documentation

Realistic images may serve as evidence of reality. The effort to make such proofs is accomplished by documenting what is seen in reality or suggested as comparisons to reality. Within this subsection are two subsubsections: **Visual Facts** and **Visual Sequence.**

Visual facts The visual may be conceptualized as a mirror of nature. Cameras and lens-based apparatuses use natural and artificial light to capture apparently mimetic images of the world. These are *photodocuments*. Before cameras, when artists sought to reproduce the visual world, they worked to create meticulous hand-drawn recordings of what they saw. These visual artifacts report facts of the world as it appears. Stock commercial images, such as photographs of nature, are meant to stand for basic types of objects and are photodocuments. A photodocument, such as Joshua Wilking's image of a coyote in Death Valley, can show a two-dimensional representation of the animal as it is at that moment, but it can also provide more information about the animal by showing an environmental context, which suggests additional attributes of the animal. Other types of visual documentation can render non-ambiguous information (or at least limit ambiguity) as well, such as a typographical map of the lay of land. Edward Tufte (1990) points to the Swiss typographic map as a classic example.

Visual sequence Efforts to carefully document the living world around us is a human urge, ranging from the prehistoric cave paintings of Lascaux, France, to the detailed Renaissance notebooks of Leonardo Da Vinci, Chinese handscroll paintings, and sequential art (e.g., comics and graphic novels). Visual sequences are series of still images. For viewers to see growth, development, and other forms of change over time, images may need to be sequenced.

Visual Authenticity

This use of visual records can illustrate authentic experiences by showing real-life human and non-human interactions. Efforts to produce realism in visual methods, such as the use of *photojournalism*, focus on the critical moment and often seek to expose conditions that not only inform but also authentically evoke emotion. This can be done through either **Visual Argument** or **Visual Recording**.

Visual argument Images may serve to record a critical moment, which visually presents a case. Photographs, such as Lewis Hine's, can document a **Visual Argument**. We mentioned Jacob Riis in Chapter 4. He was a photojournalist at the close of the 19th century, who photographed tenement slums in New York City, which spurred political reformers like Theodore Roosevelt to effect social change. Photojournalism seeks to inform and evoke human concern for the non-human world as well as the human, as in the case of global warming (Kobre, 2017). In such cases, images can present information with an authenticity that illustrates not only the facts that can be seen but also information about the point of view of the creator.

Other forms of representational art can document events and circumstances, as in the Social Realism paintings of Jacob Lawrence, Diego Rivera, and Ben Shahn. Artists, like Carmen Lopez Garza or Willie Birch, bring the viewer into cultural worlds they may not have known existed.

Visual recording Images can serve as authentic records of communication over time using film, video, and digital recording. Researchers often record their real-life observations and research participants may make their own real-time recordings. By presenting the context of research over time, video recording can provide documentary evidence difficult to achieve with still images.

However, visual recordings create conditions where individuals perform their own appearance in subtly intentional ways (Butler, 2015). In such cases, participants in a recording act as co-creators in an effort to produce an authentic fabrication of the visual artifact. That is, participants who know that they are being recorded cannot help but act as they try to reveal the authentic, but in that acting, their performance may make their intentions even more clear than a hidden camera would reveal.

Description of Visual Methods

II. Image as Data

Visual images can function as data when they have been created outside the research study taking place, as a result of their internal qualities (formal, symbolic, and material), and the people who make them. Images can act as data through simple *Artifact Collection* and through the more complex processes of *Visual Ethnography*.

Artifact Collection

Artifact Collection can aid researchers in efforts to uncover research participants' preferences, tacit knowledge, emotions, and practices. There are two traditional approaches to visual data collection. Researchers may choose to gather **Participant-Made Art** as data or the researcher can analyze the ways that participants select, sort, and use visual culture through **Visual Choice**.

Participant-made art An approach to visual research is to ask participants to provide works of art they have made in the past with traditional materials or newer technologies, such as student art made in a classroom based on an assignment or during the research project, which the researcher collects and interprets as data. **Participant-Made Art** may be analyzed in terms of formal qualities, symbolic content, and technical skills. However, art may also be analyzed in terms of qualities of self-expression, such as the intended message of the creator, their ability to convey their intention, and the power with which they convey it. The emotional impact of such works of art may be critical to the analysis.

Such participant-made arts may be created using any traditional or newer visual arts media and may be two-, three-, or four-dimensional. Another form of making is performance (such as theater, role play, or cosplay) when the body becomes the material, which may be recorded over time or collected as a single image. For example, as part of their research on the phenomenon of Lolita fashion and behavior, Yoshinaga and Ishikawa (2007) photographed young women who posed and performed their interpretation of a culturally prescribed Lolita appearance.

Visual choice In the process of visual research, an investigator can gather or describe visual culture that participants have selected and used in some way, such as to decorate their home, wear as a fashion statement, show in their social media pages, or use in their own artwork. This may be an intentional or unintentional reworking of visual culture made by others but selected by participants and invested with new layers of significance.

For example, the image on the cover of the September 1994 issue of *Mirabella* fashion magazine purported to be the female "face of America." The issue started a search by modeling agencies and advertisers to locate the model who posed for this picture. Only later did the editors of *Mirabella* admit that the woman pictured on the cover did not exist; she was a digital fabrication. Surrealist fashion photographer Hiro (Yasuhiro Wakabayashi) blended the facial features of multiple professional supermodels to create this fictional character. Blending new realities from visual culture existed long before digital technologies. The 16th-century Italian artist Giuseppe Arcimboldo made a career of it, often painting pictures of fruits and vegetables formed into a portrait.

Visual choice may also present the reviewer with repeated forms of evidence to compare for similarity and contrast. Photojournalist Shannon Jensen Wedgwood documented the suffering of the Sudanese civil war by photographing the pairs of shoes war refugees wore as they walked out of their war-torn country to the relative safety at the northern border of South Sudan. Photographing the footwear of adults, children, and infants, these artifacts transformed by the participants' harrowing journeys became eloquent evidence of the human catastrophe (Jensen, 2014). The choices of visual culture in these examples reveal preferences, values, techniques, and skills of not only the original producers of the photographs of the models and the makers of the shoes but also the creators who chose to use those makers' work to convey a message. This can be seen in the artist Laurie Ourlicht's print *I Come Warm, I Come Gentle, I Come Strong* as she explores the tacit significance of African-Caribbean female clothing.

Visual Ethnography

Ethnography is the deep, scientific study of cultures and people, which involves methods often used by anthropologists, sociologists, educational researchers, and other social scientists. Anthropological research methods have long focused on ethnographic ways of studying, analyzing, and otherwise using visual culture to promote engagement with informants, such as to encourage responses during interviews. We call this **Textual Response to Images**. Ethnographic methods also include visual images as a form of on-site notation and method for the collection of raw data, which we refer to as **Visual Field Notes.**

Textual response to images The research method of *photo elicitation* uses images as interview prompts. The photographs open research participants to verbal reflection (Harper, 2002). In photo elicitation, participants may select the images to be discussed, but the emphasis of this method is on participant responses to them. The researcher's focus is on the "thousand words" that an image may generate while following the steps of interviewing (Kvale, 1996).

Description of Visual Methods

When a researcher provides the visual culture that participants discuss (Gold, 2015), an image can be an effective catalyst in allowing a participant to interpret the tacit into linguistic expression. An image may be a prompt for forgotten information or a window into personal values, ideas, and opinions. Images used in this way can reveal an aspect of experience that the researcher may otherwise not have access to through language alone because the tacit aspects of an image can stimulate pre-conscious or pre-linguistic responses.

Use of the method *photovoice* leads participants to take pictures of what they wish to talk about (Bowling et al., 2018; Rayment et al., 2019). Photographer Wendy Ewald's work was an inspiration for the *photovoice* method (Wang & Burris, 1997) and provides an example of an open participatory response. She worked with the community media arts organization, Appalshop, in the Eastern Kentucky mountains. Her participants were local impoverished children. Ewald led art classes where she prompted children to photograph their dreams. This prompt inspired the children to go beyond simply photographing the visual artifacts of their world, and instead focus on their imaginary lives and aspirations to begin to critically deconstruct their culture (Ewald, 1985). Focusing on a participant's intentions is key to the *photovoice* method (Wang & Burris, 1997), which enables participants to take their own photographs as data and talk about them. Researchers (Kelly et al., 2018) have used this method to critically study the manipulative practices of commercial marketing and contemporary visual culture.

When participants are too young to write, children may be especially interested in talking about images (Schulte, 2015). When working with adults, images can be useful prompts, for example, when the image is remembered from the past. In this case, the image itself is not the primary artifact (Aghasafari, 2022); rather it is the written or spoken text generated by the image. Even when an image is not significant to the study itself, it can be a powerful agent in promoting participant reflection.

Visual field notes Since prehistoric times, humans have used visual notation to reflect on daily human activity and social interactions. As well as artists, anthropologists, archeologists, and sociologists have used sketches as a form of note-taking when conducting research in the field. While everyone may not have the dexterity of the 17th-century artist Rembrandt van Rijn to elevate a quick gesture drawing of a telling moment to the level of fine art, digital drawing and other imaging tools make the creation of rapid and accessible field notes easy for qualitative researchers. These notes can have additions or subtractions later as a researcher theorizes about what they saw. These notes—drawn or photographed snap shots taken in the field—provide strategies for personal visual reflection on field experience and are a valuable part of the qualitative researcher's tool kit.

Maintaining a visual journal is a means of capturing impressions (Gibson, 2018). Art educator Sara Scott Shields uses different forms of media as she physically alters the pages of her journal as her ideas come into view. Also, collaborative visual notation can be used as a form of call and response in team-based research (Hofsess & Rhoades, 2022).

III. Image as Investigation

Methods of finding and creating visual objects, information, and entanglements may be pre-defined, or they may develop as part of an exploratory process. In the case of **Image as Investigation**, images and other visual culture forms (including, for example, landscape and architectural design in walking research or maps and sketches made during the walk) are used by a researcher to set up their own iterative and reflexive process of gathering, questioning, and ultimately distilling information to define or refine research questions and answers. In such cases, a researcher is not responding to a hypothesis; rather, they seek to understand what questions might be asked, how an investigation might take place, or how the resulting information might be visualized. Images help researchers think about hypotheses or uncover points of inquiry using *Image Assembly* and *Studio Inquiry*.

Image Assembly

Image Assembly is a way of arranging or creating original visual compositions by recycling and transforming sources of information, such as other images and numerical data. It helps researchers investigate by enabling them to visualize nonlinear relationships and non-visual information. *Image Assembly* can be further understood as the use of **Collage Methods** (a process of organizing previously collected images or objects) or **Scientific Visualization** (a process of visualizing previously collected information).

Collage methods Collage is the process of building up imagery from previously made objects and images. Often, it involves layering images and materials to investigate an idea, perception, concept, or space. For example, researchers use visual mapping, such as concept mapping, as a form of cartography: both seeing the lay of the land and charting a course. As part of a team of scholars working on a government-sponsored urban planning report in Panama, anthropologist Kimberly Powell (2016) asked researchers to collage by employing a variety of materials and methods to make visible "residents' sense of place and place-making" (p. 402). The goal was to understand the multiple levels of human interaction that sustain communities as illustrated by the visual records and designs that these interactions leave as traces. Perception normally functions as a process of selecting, distilling, and clarifying; researchers may challenge how they see by seeking to be overwhelmed and collage methods can be used to distill that experience. Professor of Education Lynn Butler-Kisber (2019) argues that collaging allows for a layering of senses so that new forms can emerge.

Scientific visualization Form conveys numeric information; as a result, people can understand numeric data through graphical inscription. Strings of numerical data prompt the mathematical imagination to find visual form because geometry requires the visualization of three-dimensional objects. Three-dimensional surface plots lead to the visualization of data landscapes that can be mentally traversed. Mathematics educator Elizabeth de Freitas (2016) claims that these exercises in making mathematics visible, and creating imaginative spaces to inhabit with our bodies, are acts of literally making sense of data. From this perspective, the mathematical image is not just a record or a map, but an active event, a kind of virtual spectacle, that serves to invite the viewer into its potentiality.

As mentioned earlier in this chapter, an example of visual inferential reasoning that enabled the clarification of patterns is the development of the diagrammatic figure for DNA. Artist Odile Crick created the figure after her husband, Francis Crick, described to her the pattern of relationships imagined by his research partner, James Watson. That image was an amazing breakthrough; it enabled the expression of tacit knowledge about the foundation of life on Earth.

Artistry can represent and provide a source of feedback in response to large data systems. Like the assignment of 18th-century artist-illustrators to European voyages of discovery, the inclusion of data visualization specialists in research teams is becoming an increasingly common to enable scientists to "see" their data. The nanoscience visualizations of Michael Oliveri, who works in conjunction with the University of Georgia's nanotechnology laboratory, demonstrate how an artist's interpretation of data can add to formal applications of science. Oliveri's artistic speculations about the look of the nano-world can serve as metaphoric prompts for scientific speculation.

Studio Inquiry

Researchers often investigate by playing with images to allow ideas to emerge. The creation of a visual image may or may not be a process of progressive refinements; frequently, it is the product of expression and abductive metaphoric leaps. Because metaphoric juxtapositions expand human brain capacity to conceptualize a problem when pursued reflectively (Lakoff & Johnson, 1999), a question may be refined and answered through the process of making.

This process of investigation may include strategies where the visual is designed to disrupt and disorient. The reflexive process for coming to understand tacit knowledge that has developed through metaphors—an essential part of investigative methods that count on emergent structures—includes multiple types of formative feedback loops. ***Studio Inquiry*** can be explicated as either **Artistic Iteration**, which involves the development of an image through a cyclical process of drafting and revision, or **Visible Border Crossing** that exploits disruptive metaphorical thinking.

Artistic iteration Visual ideas can develop through iterative drawing processes, such as thumbnail sketching, which parallel journalist Donald Murray's (1984) five-stage writing pathway: collect, focus, order, draft, and clarify. Although sustained and deliberate, this is an approach (rather than a methodological rule) used to achieve visualization of an imaginative idea. Such visual ideas are often more felt or sensed than verbally articulated. The artist struggles to bring an intuition into view, with the final visual image being the record of the visual investigation. Art educator Nick Sousanis (2018) documents the development of research analysis through sequential art in the form of a graphic novel. While Sousanis can document the process of his visual investigation through sophisticated hand/eye skills of iteration in representational drawing, digital technologies can help researchers who lack hand rendering abilities to engage in a similar process of visual idea development.

Images evolve not only by parts added (an additive process) but also by parts taken away or erased (a subtractive process). Through additive and subtractive processes, the reading of an image continually shifts. By altering juxtapositions through the manipulations of symbols and visual elements, new metaphoric combinations emerge that expand thinking (Boulton et al., 2017).

Photographer and art educator Natalie LeBlanc (2018) documented abandoned Canadian schools as places of educational memory through an iterative method of locating phenomenological compositions as she moved through deserted spaces. She was not seeking out evidence to photograph, she trusted that her artistic training—the development of visual attention, selection, and judgment—would enable the pictures to come to her. Through this open process of visual discovery for gathering images, the schools revealed themselves. The individual pictures were not only individual records of representational significance; through their juxtapositions they generated metaphoric understanding.

Visual border exploration As well as thinking of research as an analysis of fixed properties that effect change with validity, reliability, and generalizability, research may also be seen as a process of potentialities that points to future possibilities (St. Pierre, 2020). As we discussed in Chapter 4, art is nomadic. Images exist before language, and they resist the language that we attempt to place on them to harness them to a specific purpose. Before a coalescing gestalt suggests the form of an image, raw visuality invites a free-fall of the imagination in which new possibilities may emerge. At this moment, the visual can break codes and remain formless for the purpose of allowing previously unconceived stories to emerge. Likewise, for the purposes of post-qualitative research, the visual image may not only seek to tell a story or represent a past event, but it is also a projection into the future "of what art can do" (Wallin, 2012, p. 35).

Thinking of inquiry as an exploration of what an image might be, rather than asking the image to answer a question, relates to Deleuze and Guattari's (1987) idea of starting in the middle. Visual investigation shifts researchers "from thinking about methods as processes of gathering data towards methods as a becoming entangled in relations" (Springgay & Truman, 2018, p. 83). In so doing, one can find a previously unconceived point of inquiry into the world. Such a search for becoming is present in the paintings of Shei-Chau Wang, who reconstructs Asian and Western artistic canons.

The virtual worlds of Sandrine Han create an existence that relies on a sentient and moving body to investigate it. This prosthetic digital world depends on new forms of looking, being, and communicating. Visual borders are explored as the creator crosses over traditional means of image-making, material, and techniques.

IV. Image as Theorizing

Theory can drive the creation of visual images. Glaser and Strauss (1967), who coined the phrase "grounded theory," argued that the researcher can begin as a blank slate and trust the process of making, allowing the research to manifest. While we do not agree that Glaser and Strauss's starting point (a blank slate researcher) can exist, the process of grounded theory is helpful in explaining **Image as Theorizing** because theorizing identifies points of origin rather than a destination. When researchers are involved in theorizing, planning, comparing, and changing images as they change or substantiate their points of view, they are using ***Reflexive Making*** and ***Envisioned Futures***.

Reflexive Making

Theory is developed through an iterative, comparative process of data collection, coding, analysis, and planning next steps in the research. Throughout the making process, parts of images are created and relationships among them emerge, which may change as theory develops. This type of making involves many processes; we highlight **Therapeutic Expression** and **Embodied Practice** here for use in theorizing.

Therapeutic expression The creation of art can be a therapeutic process. Even when not addressing a specific psychological issue or concern, the creation of art engages, releases, and transports creators, resolving a felt need to work with a material, realize a mental image, or struggle with difficult knowledge. Creating art can be so immersive that a creator can lose a sense of time.

Visual imagery is a tool to make manifest reflexive processes. Once visualized, it may not be a statement as much as a site of theorizing, of opening oneself up to possibilities. In the fine arts, the artist Matt Mullican presents himself as the vessel through which his alter ego, whom he calls That Person, creates work. Although the works on display are theoretically by That Person, officially Mullican is credited as the author. Mullican's transmissions of the work of That Person have been collected by major museums around the world like the Museum of Modern Art in New York.

Making art can be similar to the use of walking methodologies in the social sciences, which open a researcher up to unexpected encounters (Springgay & Truman, 2018). Walking a labyrinth, a form of visual culture, makes apparent the connection between the walker's internal experience and their physical experience of the world, which can be as simple as attending to the way one foot is placed in front of the other. From a therapeutic perspective, seeing the world in a new way allows one to think from fresh perspectives. Moments of openness encourage new emergent forms of relationality to the world to emerge (Walsh et al., 2015).

Embodied practice Visual methods can be a coming to know through doing involving trained gestures that articulate thought (Manning, 2016). In these cases, the process of inquiry employs prosthetic devices—such as a pencil, paint brush, or camera—which support and extend the body's movement through space (Garoian, 2013). The visual records produced through these inquiries can initiate beginning points of theorizing. Often, the researcher and/or artist works within parameters that establish how the body will move in order to produce theory. The gesture of the sentient body is a form of tacit thinking that eludes linguistic mental processes (Manning & Massumi, 2014). As an example of this approach, Professor of Social Work, Paula Gerstenblatt (2013) fashioned portraits (Lawrence-Lightfoot & Davis, 1997) of her research participants by writing next to images.

Artist and art educator Jorge Lucero follows a method for working with a single magazine page to generate a new idea through a subtractive collage process. Lucero works within these rules: the page may only be folded one to three times and the page cannot be cut, torn, or glued in any way. The result is a reimagining of the initial content of the visual culture object that presses a new theory of meaning on the maker and viewer by extending or disrupting its original meaning.

Artists often realize a theoretical vision or position in their work. The paintings of Sam Gilliam exemplify another aspect of theorizing through making. Gilliam was an African-American artist of the Washington School of Abstract Expressionism, specifically the Color Field painters. He was criticized in the 1970s and 1960s because he worked non-objectively at a time when many activists argued that Black artists should make clear anti-racist visual commentaries. However, Gilliam's work is being re-considered as a radicalism of form that continually renewed itself over many decades until his death in 2022. He theorized that his work could change viewers' minds by causing them to think about acceptance and what it means to be different (Chambers, 2021). Gilliam's idea was that viewers see his work in comparison to other (more typical fine art) work and this comparison, which leads viewers to think differently. We have discussed the limit of influence of a creator over the interpretation of their work, but *Embodied Practice* focuses on intention by considering an image as the embodiment of theory.

Envisioned Futures

Qualitative research has a history of engagement for social justice (Denzin & Lincoln, 2018). A researcher may approach the relationship between images and social theory motivated by a sense of inequity, oppression, or unfairness. Visual advocacy does not simply establish a record of events; it is a means of speaking truth to power, of theorizing a better world through the concerted use of **Visual Advocacy** and **Social Art**.

Visual advocacy The search for social justice not only compels researchers to conduct inquiry but also ensures that the results of that research reach broad audiences to promote civic dialogue. **Visual Advocacy** is a form of cultural critique. Social science inquiry may lead both researchers and participants to arts-informed practice (Nelson, 2013), such as critical theorizing, where images help a researcher to discover and respond to structural systems of oppression. Creating images as theory allows the researcher to address social change by assisting in the self-actualization of participants (Finley, 2018), where images not only illustrate a problem but also effect a heighten social awareness and civic engagement on the part of the makers. In such cases, the researcher's focus is not just to document or even criticize a situation, but to come to know and represent a theory of possibility that compels a public response to effect change.

The imagery of **Visual Advocacy** can have high stakes, as in the case of the *Hope* poster portrait of presidential candidate Barack Obama by Shepard Fairey. In her work *Sun Raid*, artist Ester Hernandez protests the working conditions of farmer workers in California's San Joaquin Valley. **Visual Advocacy** enables a researcher to theorize a response mediated by an image and discover whether viewers have that response, which is sometimes the act of dialogue. Contemporary artist Kehinde Wiley problematizes the tradition of the soldier on horseback as a public war memorial by replacing the white general with an African-American cavalryman. His provocative reimagining of this form of public remembrance opens a critical dialogue about why these public sculptures were made and the messages they convey. Similarly, the work of Robert Pruitt places an African-American figure in an unconventional heroic narrative.

Social art **Social Art** is a process of collaborative art-making that takes the form of social action to promote future outcomes, such as change in a community. The critical education theory of Paulo Freire (1970) contributed to specific forms of artistic and research participatory practice. Freire's student, artist Tim Rollins, worked with high school youth in New York City's South Bronx neighborhood. Rollins titled his efforts the "Art and Knowledge Workshop." *Tim Rollins and Kids of Survival* was the official attribution of the artwork produced by the participants in the workshop, which was purchased by leading art museums all over the world. (Rollins took credit in the attribution as he played a guiding role in forming and selecting the final work exhibited.) From Freire's perspective, once individuals are able to conceptualize and accurately articulate their situation, they will mobilize politically to improve it. Freire's philosophy also animates the ethnographic art-making of Kryssi Staikidis (2020) who works collaboratively with Maya artists in Guatemala to explore decolonializing methodology.

Visual images can be forms in which oppressed populations can reveal these conditions to others outside of their local communities. As demonstrated by the socially engaged work of art educator Kim Cosier, the creation of visual imagery can be an effective means of community mobilization. Cosier's participatory visual methods of **Social Art** can create resistance to dominant, hierarchal, and heteronormative assumptions, which work to impose colonial control over non-conformist thinking and behavior (Mitchell, 2011; Mitchell & Sommer, 2016). **Social Art** is also used for other social, political, and economic purposes, such as to promote environmental and climate justice and sustainability.

V. Image as Report

Image as Report is the use of images to show research to peers or other audiences who may find value in the results. As visual researcher Gillian Rose (2016) points out, researchers present visual images with an eye to the ways that audiences will interpret them. Often a visual researcher will specifically work to narrow report results within specific parameters so that viewers will see the results of research clearly or they will seek to broaden interpretation in a more open presentation. We refer to these two types of visual reporting as ***Research Illustration*** and ***Research Presentation.***

Research Illustration

Research Illustration is a visual culture form that represents or closely adheres to data in **Correspondent Figures** or **Visual Webs**. In the first circumstance, the figures illustrate the raw data. In the second, the report represents information associated with the project visually, in a way that opens up a broad interpretation from viewers.

Correspondent figures Visual images can have a direct relationship to numerical data. Commonly associated with bar graphs, histograms, and pie charts, **Correspondent Figures** can have a great visual range. For example, artist Stephen Cartwright's mesh works map the daily amount of time he engages in human-powered activity plotted against month and day. This act of mapping is a form of self-portraiture: a log of personal endeavors. Art educator Daniel Barney's study of the statistical range of human hat sizes points to the differences that correspond to the ends of a normal curve. (The equipment that Barney used to produce the hats failed when producing the normal curve tails, speaking to ways that our systems of statistical measurement falter when dealing with exceptional cases.)

Visual webs Statistician Edward Tufte (1990) argues that data is best understood in terms of dynamic interactions. Creating a **Visual Web** enables researchers to illustrate complex systems, such as French civil engineer Charles Joseph Minard's 1869 webbed map of Napoleon's Russia campaign of 1812. By displaying the interaction of five different data sets, Minard graphically displays the human cost of Napoleon's adventurism. His map was a political statement, challenging the rise of a romantic interpretation of Napoleon's reign. Similarly, the sculptures of Natalie Miebach are based on the meticulous collection of data around meteorological events like Hurricane Sandy, which inflicted extensive damage along the New Jersey shoreline in 2012.

Research Presentation

Arts-based researchers often present a research project, or the creation or cumulation of visual culture from the project, in a way that enables participants and other viewers to construct their own story about the research, or more broadly, interpret what is present outside a narrative. These methods are forms of *Research Presentation*, which enables viewers to be invited into a **Visual Narrative** or **Research Exhibition** through their own experiences and meanings.

Visual narrative When researchers report by combining or developing images to tell a story about research, the report can be thought of as a **Visual Narrative**. A narrative of this type is useful when complex and tacit interactions of a project are difficult to write about and can only be conveyed through visual experience. Fact-based graphic novels, such as biographies or memoirs, are good examples of this method. Creator-researchers create visual narratives to inform about many topics based on research. For example, Scott McCloud's (1993) celebrated *Understanding Comics: The Invisible Art* is a graphic novel about the history and making of sequential art. Education professor Marcus Weaver-Hightower works in the format of the graphic novel to tell an easily accessible story about the health sciences.

Time arts are also used as a means of telling stories. In a research study, Laura Trafí-Prats (2012) gave digital video recorders to urban children to allow them to film and discuss their environments through activities such as a tour of the local Walmart or a walk-through of a relative's home. The images, unfolding and recorded in real time, impel a sustained narrative.

Visual exhibition Visual images and three-dimensional objects that are exhibited adjacently appear to speak to each other because we perceive their selection and arrangement in terms of their relationship. This is brilliantly demonstrated by museum curators. For example, working with the permanent collection of the Maryland Historical Society in Baltimore, Fred Wilson curated the 1992 exhibition *Mining the Museum*. Wilson presented the museum's objects in ways never before displayed, such as a grouping of ornate colonial lounge chairs clustered around a slave whipping post or cigar store Indian statues turned to confront authentic images of Native Americans. Wilson forced a new conversation about the ways a colonial society of refined tastes and privilege was sustained.

Social science researchers can curate their own exhibitions in real life or the virtual life through accessible on-line gallery environments such as www.artsteps.com. Here, researchers and participants build open access exhibits that invite audience participation and feedback (Gerber et al., 2022). Such a democratic environment can serve to promote public dialogue through visual inquiry.

With this introduction to the Research Image Framework—the five major themes supported by the two-by-two underlying structure—we have introduced 20 distinct methods of using visual images in research. Chapter 6 will explore applying the RIF to the specific analysis appropriate to these distinctions.

Conclusion

The intricacies of attaching language to the visual have been a challenge for centuries. The authors of this text found that we had difficulty writing this chapter until we set the outline up as a series of PowerPoint slides so we could easily scroll through images in order to attach language to the uses of visual qualities we were trying to describe. However, with care, researchers can use visual research methods with the clarity of other, more commonly used methods in the social sciences.

Consider the commonly used method called front-end, semi-structured interview. The process of conducting a front-end, semi-structured interview is generally understood by most qualitative researchers in the social sciences as an interview during which an individual or group of participants are asked a series of questions by a researcher, who then may go on to facilitate conversational discussion based on answers to the questions. An understanding among professionals to agree to use a common professional language enables research funding, practice, and refereed publication. This text attempts to add a common language to image use and analysis in social science research.

> When choosing which method to use with research, or which category your research fits in the matrix, ask the following questions:
>
> 1. Are images, visuality, or visual culture embedded in the research question(s) or interest?
> 2. Which method(s) have been used in the past to study similar question(s)?
> 3. Which method should be used based on the research question(s) or interest?
> 4. How does the image(s) relate to the researcher's, participants', and viewers' iconic stores?
> 5. What knowledge, skills, and additions to your iconic store do you need to use the research method?

References

Aghasafari, S. (2022, February 3). *Examining how bi/multilingual high schoolers construct meaning through the integration of visual art and biology* [on-line paper presentation]. European Congress of Qualitative Inquiry, European Network Qualitative Inquiry.

Boulton, A., Grauer, K., & Irwin, R. L. (2017). Becoming teacher: A/r/tographical inquiry and visualising metaphor. *International Journal of Art & Design Education*, *36*(2), 200–214. https://doi.org/10.1111/jade.12080

Bowling, J., Dodge, B., Banik, S., Bartelt, E., & Mengl, S. (2018). Social support relationships for sexual minority women in Mumbai, India: A photo elicitation interview study. *Culture, Health & Sexuality*, *20*(2), 183–200. https://doi.org/10.1080/13691058.2017.1337928

Butler, J. (2015). *Notes toward a performative theory of assembly*. Harvard University Press.

Butler-Kisber, L. (2019). Collage-making. In P. Atkinson, S. Delamont, A. Cernat, J. W. Sakshaug, & R. A. Williams (Eds.), *SAGE research methods foundations* (pp. 2–9). SAGE.

Carney, R.N., & Levin, J.R. (2002) Pictorial illustrations still improve students' learning from text. *Educational Psychology Review*, *14*(1), 5–26. https://doi.org/10.1023/A:1013176309260

Chambers, T. (June 20, 2021) Sam Gilliam: Disrupting American abstraction. *The Collector*. https://www.thecollector.com/sam-gilliam-american-abstraction-color-field/

de Freitas, E. (2016). Material encounters and media events: What kind of mathematics can a body do? *Educational Studies in Mathematics*, *91*(2), 185–202. https://doi.org/10.1007/s10649-015-9657-4

Deleuze, G., & Guattari, F. (1987). *A thousand plateaus: Capitalism and schizophrenia* (B. Massumi, Trans.). University of Minnesota Press. (Original work published 1980)

Denzin, N. K., & Lincoln, Y. S. (Eds.) (2018). *The SAGE handbook of qualitative research* (5th edition. ed.). SAGE.

Dewey, J. (1989). *Art as experience* [The later works, 1925-1953] (J. Boydston, Ed.), (Vol. 10). Southern Illinois University Press. (Original work published 1934)

Douven, I. (2021). Abduction. In E. N. Zalta (Ed.), *The Stanford Encyclopedia of Philosophy* (Summer Edition). Center for the Study of Language and Information https://plato.stanford.edu/archives/sum2021/entries/abduction/

Ewald, W. (1985). *Portraits and dreams: Photographs and stories by children of the Appalachians*. Writers and Readers.

Finley, S. (2018). Critical arts-based inquiry: Performances of resistance politics. In N. K. Denzin & Y. S. Lincoln (Eds.), *The SAGE handbook of qualitative research* (5th ed., pp. 561–575). SAGE.

Freedman, K. (2004). Editorial: Becoming a researcher in art education: Forming research questions. *Studies in Art Education*, *45*(2), 99–100. https://doi.org/10.1080/00393541.2004.11651759

Description of Visual Methods

Freire, P. (1970). *Pedagogy of the oppressed* (M. B. Ramos, Trans.). Continuum.

Frenda, S. J., Knowles, E. D., Saletan, W., & Loftus, E. F. (2013). False memories of fabricated political events. *Journal of Experimental Social Psychology, 49*(2), 280–286. https://doi.org/10.1016/j.jesp.2012.10.013

Garoian, C. R. (2013). *The prosthetic pedagogy of art: Embodied research and practice*. State University of New York Press.

Gerber, N., Biffi, E., Biondo, J., Carriera, L., Centracchio, M., Gemignani, M., Hannes, K., & Siegesmund, R. (2022). Sustaining life on earth: Arts-based responses to the lived experience of covid-19. In K. Hannes, F. Truyen, H. Vrebos, A. Benozzo, M. Gemignani, P. Issari, C. A. Taylor, & J. Wyatt (Eds.), *European congress of qualitative inquiry: Fifth edition – qualitative inquiry in the online technological realm* (pp. 63–68). European Network Qualitative Inquiry.

Gerstenblatt, P. (2013). Collage portraits as a method of analysis in qualitative research. *International Journal of Qualitative Methods, 12*(1), 294–308. https://doi.org/10.1177/160940691301200114

Gibson, D. (2018). A visual conversation with trauma: Visual journaling in art therapy to combat vicarious trauma. *Art Therapy: Journal of the American Art Therapy Association, 35*(2), 99–103. https://doi.org/10.1080/07421656.2018.1483166

Gilbert, D.T. (1991). How mental systems believe. *The American Psychologist, 46*(2), 107–119. https://doi.org/10.1037/0003-066X.46.2.107

Glaser, B. G., & Strauss, A. L. (1967). *The discovery of grounded theory: Strategies for qualitative research*. Aldine.

Gold, S. J. (2015). Panethnic mobilisation among Arab Americans in Detroit during the post-9/11 era: A photo-elicitation study. *Visual Studies, 30*(3), 228–243. https://doi.org/10.1080/1472586X.2015.1017348

Harper, D. (2002). Talking about pictures: A case for photo elicitation. *Visual Studies, 17*(1), 13–26. https://doi.org/10.1080/14725860220137345

Hofsess, B. A., & Rhoades, M. (2022). P(l)aying attention: Wilding correspondence as methodological possibility. *International Review of Qualitative Research, 15*(2), 216–247. https://doi.org/10.1177/19408447221090650.

Jensen, S. (2014). *A long walk*. Open Society Foundations–New York Retrieved from https://www.movingwalls.org/moving-walls/21/long-walk.html.

Kelly, K., Lee, S. H., Ray, H. B., & Kandaurova, M. (2018). Using the photovoice methodology to increase engagement and sharpen students' analytical skills regarding cultures, lifestyles, and markets internationally. *Marketing Education Review, 28*(2), 69–74. https://doi.org/10.1080/10528008.2018.1450093

Kobre, K. (2017). *Photojournalism: The professionals' approach* (7th ed.). Routledge.

Kvale, S. (1996). *Interviews: An introduction to qualitative research interviewing*. SAGE.

Lakoff, G., & Johnson, M. (1999). *Philosophy in the flesh*. Basic Books.

Lawrence-Lightfoot, S., & Davis, J. H. (1997). *The art and science of portraiture*. Jossey-Bass.

LeBlanc, N. (2018). The abandoned school as an anomalous place of learning: A practice-led approach to doctoral research. In M. Cahnmann-Taylor & R. Siegesmund (Eds.), *Arts-based research in education: Foundations for practice* (2nd ed., pp. 174–189). Routledge.

Lindsay, D. S., Hagen, L., Read, J. D. Wade, K. A., Garry, M. (2004). True photographs and false memories, *Psychological Science, 15*(3), 149–154. https://doi.org/10.1111/j.0956-7976.2004.01503002.x

Manning, E. (2016). *The minor gesture*. Duke University Press.

Manning, E., & Massumi, B. (2014). *Thought in the act: Passages in the ecology of experience*. University of Minnesota Press.

Marcus, N., Cooper, M., & Sweller, J. (1996). Understanding Instructions. *Journal of Educational Psychology, 88*(1), 49–63. https://doi.org/10.1037/022-0663.88.1.49

Mayer, A. (2008). Aesthetics of catastrophe. *Public Culture, 20*(2), 177–191. https://doi.org/10.1215/08992363-2007-022

McCloud, S. (1993). *Understanding Comics: The Invisible Art*. Tundra.

Mitchell, C. M. (2011). *Doing visual research*. SAGE.

Mitchell, C. M., & Sommer, M. (2016). Participatory visual methodologies in global public health. *Global Public Health, 11*(5/6), 521–527. https://doi.org/10.1080/17441692.2016.1170184

Murray, D. (1984). *Write to learn*. Holt, Rinehart, & Winston.

Nelson, R. (2013). *Practice as research in the arts: Principles, protocols, pedagogies, resistances*. Palgrave Macmillan.

Newman, E., & Feigenson, N. (2013). The truthiness of visual evidence. *Jury Expert, 25*(5), 1–4. https://www.thejuryexpert.com/wp-content/uploads/1311/JuryExpert_1311_TruthinessVisuals.pdf

Nickerson, R. S. (1998). Confirmation bias: A ubiquitous phenomenon in many guises. *Review of General Psychology, 2*(2), 175–220. https://doi.org/10.1037/1089-2680.2.2.175

Pauwels, L. (2010). Visual sociology reframed: An analytical synthesis and discussion of visual methods in social and cultural research. *Sociological Methods & Research 38*(4), 545–581. https://doi.org/10.1177/0049124110366233

Powell, K. (2016). Multimodal mapmaking: Working toward an entangled methodology of place. *Anthropology & Education Quarterly, 47*(4), 402–420. https://doi.org/10.1111/aeq.12168

Description of Visual Methods

Rayment, G., Swainston, K., & Wilson, G. (2019). Using photo-elicitation to explore the lived experience of informal caregivers of individuals living with dementia. *British Journal of Health Psychology, 24*(1), 102–122.

Rose, G. (2016). *Visual methodologies: An introduction to the interpretation of visual materials* (4th ed.). SAGE.

Sargent, S. L. (2007). Image effects on selective exposure to computer-mediated news stories. *Computers in Human Behavior, 23*(1), 705–726. https://doi.org/10.1016/j.chb.2004.11.005

Schulte, C. M. (2015). Intergalactic encounters: Desire and the political immediacy of children's drawing. *Studies in Art Education, 56*(3), 241–256. https://doi.org/10.1080/00393541.2015.11518966

Serna-Gutiérrez, J. I. O. (2018). Critical discourse analysis of Wonder Woman's appearance in "All Star Comics No. 8": Uncovering feminist ideologies. *Open Journal for Anthropological Studies, 2*(1), 13–26. https://doi.org/10.32591/coas.ojas.0201.02013s

Social Science and Humanities Research Council. (Oct. 4, 2020) *Definitions of Terms.* https://www.sshrc-crsh.gc.ca/funding-financement/programs-programmes/definitions-eng.aspx

Sousanis, N. (2018). Thinking in comics: An emerging process. In M. Cahnmann-Taylor & R. Siegesmund (Eds.), *Arts-based research in education: Foundations for practice* (2nd ed., pp. 190–199). Routledge.

Springgay, S., & Truman, S. E. (2018). *Walking methodologies in a more-than-human world: Walkinglab.* Routledge.

St. Pierre, E. A. (2020). Why post qualitative inquiry? *Qualitative Inquiry,* 1–3. https://doi.org/10.1177/1077800420931142

Staikidis, K. (2020). *Artistic mentoring as a decolonizing methodology: An evolving collaborative painting ethnography with Maya artists Pedro Rafael González Chavajay and Paula Nicho Cúmez.* Brill | Sense.

Trafí-Prats, L. (2012). Urban children and intellectual emancipation: Video narratives of self and place in the City of Milwaukee. *Studies in Art Education, 53*(2), 125–138. https://doi.org/10.1080/00393541.2012.11518857

Tufte, E. R. (1990). *Envisioning information.* Graphics Press.

Wade, K.A., Garry, M., Read, J. D. & Linsday, D. S. (2002) A picture is worth a thousand lies: Using false photographs to create false childhood memories. *Psychonomic Bulletin & Review, 9,* 597–603 (2002). https://doi.org/10.3758/BF03196318

Wallin, J. (2012). Graphic affects. *Visual Arts Research, 38*(1), 34–44. https://doi.org/10.5406/visuartsrese.38.1.0034

Walsh, S., Bickel, B., & Leggo, C. (Eds.) (2015). *Arts-based and contemplative practices in research and teaching: Honoring presence.* Routledge.

Wang, C., & Burris, M. A. (1997). Photovoice: Concept, methodology, and use for participatory needs assessment. *Health Education & Behavior, 24*(3), 369–387. https://doi.org/10.1177/109019819702400309

Watson, J. B., & Rayner, R. (2013). Conditioned emotional reactions: The case of Little Albert (D. Webb, Ed.). CreateSpace Independent Publishing Platform. http://a.co/06Se6Na (Original work published 1920)

Yoshinaga, M., & Ishikawa, K. (2007). *Gothic and Lolita*. Phaidon.

CHAPTER 6

Making Judgments

Analyzing the Visual as Evidence

In this chapter, we discuss types of qualitative and quantitative analyses that can be conducted when using visual research methods. Each visual research method is appropriate to a particular research context, and likewise, to an analysis of information resulting from use of the method. The choices researchers make about analytical processes and techniques with regard to imagery can be vital to research outcomes and conclusions, and so must be carefully considered.

First, we present ways to determine the quality of images in research through the engagement of an expert community. We discuss visual analysis as critique, judgment versus taste, making reliable judgments about images and establishing criteria for judgment. Second, we discuss the selection of analytical criteria and the loci of analysis. Third, we compare qualitative and quantitative analyses connected to images, including analyses of participants' comments about images. Finally, we present the Image Analysis Matrix (IAM), which visually illustrates the Research Image Framework (RIF) discussed in Chapter 5 and how it can be used for image analysis.

The key idea throughout this chapter is judgment of quality. Even in quantitative studies, judgments of quality are essential; it is of little value to know how much of something you have if you do not know the relative quality of that thing. Determining quality is a matter of judgment, and judgments are always formed within contexts.

The word *quality* has multiple meanings. As used in the preceding paragraph, quality means high in value or the best of its class. When it comes to research, judgments of quality in this use can refer to a variety of determinations of value, such as the contribution or fit of a particular image to a research project or the significance of an image created by a participant. However, quality has a second meaning that is core to the argument of this book. *A quality* represents a marker of non-semiotic experience of a specific intensity and duration. The color crimson has qualities. The swoop of a line has qualities. Multiple qualities, when placed in relationship to each other, evoke meanings that are felt before they are known (Dewey, 1934/1989). Thus, a meaning that is relayed somatically through the relationship of qualities can be appraised for its own quality of expression.

Quantitative and Qualitative Analyses from Visual Sources

As well as being the artist who painted the *Mona Lisa*, Leonardo DaVinci is well known for his *Vitruvian Man* drawing, which demonstrates that the proportions of a human body with arms and legs outstretched in a horizontal plane equal the geometric proportions of a circle. This was not a new idea when DaVinci drew his version of it. Rather, his version is an example of the search for visual clarity; it showed the proportions of human anatomy more clearly than previous textual or visual descriptions. Such drawings, referencing the RIF introduced in Chapter 5, were a method of Image as Investigation for DaVinci. He left notebooks that explain and illustrate his visual research methods, which appear to be highly creative for his time. Yet DaVinci, in describing his own abilities, did not claim to be creative. Rather, he said that his work was excellent. He asserted that he could complete multiple practical projects—building war machines, designing bridges and buildings, executing public sculpture (maybe even a painting or drawing)—as well if not better than anyone else (Isaacson, 2017). History says he was right. Qualities have identifiable strengths and weaknesses. DaVinci's images were better than those done by most other people. How does one judge what is "better" when it comes to imagery? How does one judge quality in visual research methods?

The quality of images is continually judged in everyday life. People judge the quality of visual images whenever they see them, even when they see themselves in a mirror or a selfie. These analyses are often a matter of personal preference: things we determine we like, things we reject as unpleasing. However, they are often based on the influencers in social groups, including family, friends, and creators of media acting as persuaders who consciously and unconsciously influence us through a range of processes, from manipulating us through seduction to convincing us through expertise (Berger, 1977).

Professional communities, like visual arts communities who have been analyzing visual qualities for centuries, have come to know the range of possible interpretations made by human viewers when seeing certain characteristics of line, shape, or color in the support of intended meaning and representation. If line width, shape definition, color saturation, and the character of other visual qualities support the overall meaning of the image, the image will more likely be considered effective than if the visual qualities chosen by the creator challenge or conflict with the intended meaning.

Visual images may be analyzed in ways that are similar to analyses of other types of information, such as textual or numerical data. Evidence can be measured: visual occurrences within a picture can be counted; the length of time that a viewer maintains engagement with an image can be clocked (Kopatich et al., 2021). Evidence can be assigned in terms of, for example, visual weights, saturations, lengths, occurrences, and time. Statistician Edward Tufte (1990) demonstrates how visual qualities help us evaluate and successfully navigate complex everyday problems. Through one's active participation in making and viewing, visual literacy increases because the processes of creating and analyzing imagery includes the enactment of learning (Freedman, 2015).

When it comes to making judgments about images, communities may not all agree, but will often have a clear majority of judgment because those judgments are often based on psychobiological responses to the visual. As in any endeavor that requires the exercise of judgment (scoring an Olympic gymnastics performance, an art portfolio for International Baccalaureate academic credit, or ranking international whisky) by a professional community, finding a level of consensus matters. One idiosyncratic interpretation is not considered reliable. Interpretations must be sustained through an agreed upon set of qualitative evidence and transparent processes that others can evaluate. We have discussed examples of information distortion that can be realized through images and their analyses. Statistical analysis is open to similar judgments by professional communities, for numeric data can easily be distorted into fantastic claims (with potentially devastating real-world consequences). Quantitative analyses also demand communities of agreement informed by professionals who understand and agree on best practices.

Communities of agreement are all around us. Imagine that a pre-school administrator has commissioned a creator to make an image of a bunny to use as the school logo. The creator is asked to provide a couple of options based on a photograph the administrator provides of a baby bunny. Two options are provided: a bunny made with pastel colors and soft, organic lines, and another bunny made in red with thick, jagged lines and pointy teeth. It is safe to predict that most pre-school children's parents would choose the soft-edged bunny. Thick, jagged lines and the color of blood are interpreted in most cultures as more aggressive than organic lines and pastel colors. We have discussed the powerful and long-term impact on imagery. Pre-school professionals have an unwritten, but shared agreement to avoid the use of aggressive or frightening imagery around young children. The jagged, aggressive bunny might be appropriate for the specialized audiences of an art museum or a horror movie, but such an image would probably come with advisories that it would be disturbing to young children.

Visual Analysis as Critique

From a social science perspective, critique is an examination and a phenomenological analysis (What is this object? Where did it come from? How do we experience it?). Historically, critique is particularly associated with the 18th-century Enlightenment, a scientific movement that sought to answer questions about the world through active, rational investigation, rather than passively accepting metaphysical explanations. However, methods of textual critique began much earlier, for example, in the early analysis of Talmudic scriptures. By the 19th century, through the work of Karl Marx, critique became an analytical method that probed how the material objects that surround us in our daily lives unconsciously influence human actions and can manipulate us in systems of cultural power and control.

However, well before Marx, the fine arts adapted critique as a process of baring the object to scrutiny so as to gain a fuller understanding of not just how the object appears, but how it is seen. In the visual arts, critique is used by creators, instructors, art critics, and art historians to analyze, judge, and improve works of art. As we mentioned in Chapter 2, 2,200 years before the surrealist René Magritte's witty caption "Ceci n'est pas une pipe" (This is not a pipe) to his 1929 painting *The Treachery of Images*, Plato considered mimesis—visual records of how the world apparently appears—an illusionist's trick. In Plato's day, it may have been as easy for viewers to believe what they saw painted as real as it is now to believe a computer-manipulated photograph. Critique is a means of taking Plato's accusations seriously. It as a process of deconstruction, which reveals the inner workings of an image. It provides a means to press through the illusions that Plato found so troubling.

Critique probes past the initial gestalt reading of an image. It seeks to look carefully at the component parts, which successfully came together to construct a first, indelible impression. It unpacks form to reveal internal, emergent dynamics that maintain a roiling fluidity. By trying to understand the dynamic, qualitative relationships at the core of visual experience, critique perpetually challenges fixed interpretations and demands the reapplication of judgment in the formation of interpretation.

When critique is practiced at its best, it is a dialogic process that recognizes the agency of the object. The creator of the work does not "say" what a work means. Rather, the work suggests meaning. It has a phenomenological presence. In art school, critique is frequently a formative process that allows the artistic creator to better understand the agency of their own work. The tools that schools of art have devised for critique as assessment (Buster & Crawford, 2009) also function as tools of analysis when visual images are included in research.

Judgment Versus Taste

Because so much visual information is currently available, its quality may seem difficult to determine. As is often the case when difficult choices are present, there can be tendency to evoke personal preference or taste. Any individual preference is claimed to be appropriate: whatever you like is okay. In contrast, judgment suggests that some choices are better than others. Adaptive Comparative Judgment (ACJ) assessment systems (Buckley et al., 2022), which work much like an eye exam, have been applied to scoring academic design portfolios in order to establish a rank order. ACJ models have demonstrated remarkable validity and reliability in rendering high-stakes judgments when assessors come from a community of agreement.

Like any subject, accurate judgments of quality require training. Long before digital visual culture existed, people knowledgeable about the visual arts used the concept of connoisseurship to characterize the requisite expertise for making reliable and generalizable judgments about artworks. People who were concerned about the question of quality in professional art, and its price, realized early on that connoisseurship was difficult to master without training and guidance. Early in the 20th century, first Harvard and then other universities across the country began offering courses in connoisseurship for wealthy, young men (specifically) who would become the collectors of great art. These university students were the first group formally trained in the United States to make judgments about fine art for collection, meaning that they were intended to learn about judgments of visual quality that would stand the test of time beyond fashion or taste.

At the time, an alternative to formal course work was personal experience with original art that usually included travel to visit the great art museums of Europe. A famous example from the period, which illustrates both the value and complexities of judgments based solely on direct experience with artwork, is the chemical engineer and art collector Albert C. Barnes. Barnes first went to France in 1911 to purchase paintings, with little more knowledge than tips from an artist friend, William Glackens, on painting qualities and names of some new, young Parisian artists. Applying Glackens' insights to his own direct experience with artists, Barnes built one of the world's greatest collections of modern art.

When Barnes brought paintings by Paul Gauguin home from Europe, few people even in the art world had heard of the artist. Barnes was not only able to see value in Gauguin's work overall, but see value in particular pieces by the artist, which have since become hallmarks of the artists' work and archetypes of French Post-Impressionism. Barnes taught himself to appreciate the possibilities of images and not simply buy any works created by Renoir, Cezanne, Matisse, and Picasso—he acquired outstanding exemplar works (Argott, 2009). As John Dewey (1934/1989) explained in *Art as Experience*, Barnes' efforts to then teach Dewey what he saw in art became the foundation for Dewey's own theory of thinking in qualitative relationships outside of language or number systems to make analytic judgments.

Barnes chose only certain examples of Gauguin's work to purchase, which had unique depths and flatness of color, decorative compositions, and sensuality of line—although these qualities were not the aesthetic preferences of the time, which were based on representational color mixing and modeling of brushwork to create an illusion of three-dimensional form. Gauguin was not making painting to conform to the visual expectations of his age; he was proposing a new way of seeing. For many, this was unsettling, and the works appeared crude and ill-formed, but Barnes grasped that Gauguin was changing how people could see.

One measure of Gauguin's success was in the reaction of viewers who have appreciated and been influenced by his work, such as historical fine artists Henri Matisse and Pablo Picasso (whose work Barnes also collected). That other artists adapted and advanced this new way of seeing—that innovation became convention—was a benchmark for judgment. Barnes put all of this work on public display to emphasize this new approach to perception, which was another benchmark. By creating a common iconic store among certain audiences, Barnes allowed a community of agreement to emerge, a third benchmark.

The example of Barnes is particularly interesting because audiences often go to exhibitions to learn about what is considered good; they assume, rightly so, that judgments about the work they see in those cultural institutions are based on expertise used to guide viewers. In fact, most art museums in the United States specifically state education as an aim of the institution in their charters. However, peoples' responses to expert judgments about the value of an image are not universal; those responses depend on context, and contexts change. In the case of Gauguin, debates have been raging for decades about the Polynesian fiction he created in his Tahitian paintings. As a result, his work, while long been shown in museums, has been criticized as racist and sexist. In addition to those concerns, the influence of Gauguin can be seen in the use of his idiom in contemporary, native Polynesian-made tourist trade art and by contemporary fine artists, such as Namsa Leuba and Kehinde Wiley, who suggest it in pastiche to inscribe their own and their subjects' identities on it. Gauguin's paintings survive in the lively complex world of visual culture judgments and are some of the most expensive paintings in the world.

The story of Gauguin's work illustrates that the problem of judging images often has to do with a lack of consensus about *how to judge them*. Should they be valued based on formal qualities alone, on suggested meaning, influence, use, or function? We discuss the ethics of imagery more in Chapter 7, but for now it is important to remember that while the ethics of images may not be a primary consideration when a work of art is displayed in a museum, they are critical to visual methods in social science research. This is a frequent point of confusion as the processes for creating an image for the fine arts world are muddled with the creation of images to advance social knowledge. This condition is further entangled as the outcomes of social science increasingly acknowledge the role of individual insight and personal, transformational experience to build broad generalizable knowledge of the human condition (Bochner & Ellis, 2016). Nevertheless, from the quality of images in stimuli photographs to the quality of selfies in photo elicitation, the ethical positions of images must be considered.

It is our view that the difficulty of making judgments about images has led, in part, to the lack of images in social science research journals and other publications. However, making judgments about the quality of any research tool, strategy, or process is a researcher's responsibility and making such judgments in a reliable manner is key to good research.

Making Reliable Judgments: The Concept and Practices of Provenance

The processes of making reliable judgments about the use of images in research require decisions about how the images will be used and analyzed. Each decision rests on the establishment of criteria for judgment and each can be used in relation to the purposes of the RIF categories.

Judgments while Collecting, Sorting, Reviewing, and Comparing

Some research requires that the researcher studies images, shows participants images, or asks participants to collect or sort images by reviewing and making comparisons. These processes can be used for any of the RIF functions. *Image and Record* and *Image as Data* can involve collecting, sorting, reviewing, and comparing information about particular images or a group of images as a whole. *Image as Investigation* and *Image as Theorizing* can involve collections used by a researcher to develop complex ideas, bring forth memories, and organize thoughts. Collecting images for public display or publication can be used to show the results of a research project (*Image as Report*). Images are often repurposed as part of a research project to enable the study of many topics and problems. For example, collection, sorting, review, and comparison can aid researchers' and participants' thinking about a problem and reveal choices and decision-making.

The most effective way of knowing whether an image is legitimate is through the use of *provenance*. The term provenance is used in art history to indicate the verified history of an image or object. Provenance helps determine the legitimacy of claims made about and within images. Basically, determining the provenance of an image involves processes of searching for documentation and other evidence to demonstrate who the creator was, how the image was made, when it was made, and if and when it was changed after it left the creator's hands. It can be used to prove that an image is an original creation and in its original form. This is the best way to determine whether an image should be believed in terms of original intention. If a researcher knows and reveals the background of an image, and its creation, then the researcher, funders, readers of the research report, and other stakeholders can feel confident that the image is reliable. Knowing the provenance of images used in research, particularly those found online, has become critical now that images can be digitally manipulated.

Sketching and Creating

In Chapter 3, we discussed four dimensions of *making* an image: (a) selection, (b) sketching, (c) queering, and (d) erasure. Sketching can be used to help a researcher plan a project; it does not require talent or a high level of drawing skill. A first sketch does not tend to be reworked to completion; sketches tend to be developed in series (iteration). If a new idea needs to be represented visually, we recommend that you make a new sketch, rather than reworking the old one. Researchers can use this type of *Image as Investigation* to work out a plan or study some aspect of a project close-up using snapshot photographs (a type of metaphorical sketching). Sketching and creating can help researchers use *Image as Theorizing* to help them see what they may have difficulty saying or writing. Theorizing is helpful for probing the possibilities of an image, both queering it into new possibilities and erasing previous assumptions so that new information can emerge. Once an idea is made visual, it often becomes easier to explore and explain because one can then describe what one sees.

For final, high-quality images that must meet certain criteria for appropriate use in a project, such as *Image as Record* photographs to be used for participant response, the researcher might want to hire a professional creator. Participants can also be asked to create images as evidence of their own thinking or experience. However, image creation is not always a process of building up, it is also a process of altering and taking away (queering and erasure). Depending on the project, this use of *Image as Data* may be more successful a way of gaining information than writing. For example, in a situation where a researcher needs participants to document their activities, participant-made sketches or photographs can be very effective. Sketched or created, final images can be used as *Image as Report* by including them in an exhibition or publication that illustrates the research process, data, and results.

Establishing Criteria and the Zone of Image Interpretation

In order to determine the appropriateness of a chosen image for use in research, the appropriateness of its formal qualities should be considered. For example, let's say that a researcher hires a creator to make the images that participants will respond to in a study of attitudes toward pollution from plastic bottles. How should the researcher judge the validity of the images? The images could show pollution as a major or minor part of the composition. They could choose to show an area and type of pollution that has sickly colors or highlights the bright, cheerful colors of the labels. The pollution could be hidden by grasses or floating on the ocean. Each of these choices could influence the level of response. In other words, the formal qualities of the images a researcher chooses can have a profound impact on respondents.

> When choosing images for participant responses, five main questions need to be asked about each image:
>
> 1. What is the intention of the image use in the research?
> 2. Does the content of the image support that meaning?
> 3. Do the formal qualities (line, shape, color, etc.) support that meaning?
> 4. Is the intended meaning of the image clear? Is it easy to interpret the image in terms of a single meaning? If the intention of the meaning is ambiguous or intended to be interpreted widely in the research, is that clear?
> 5. Does any formal or conceptual aspect of the image distract from its intended purpose in the research?

Researchers need to exercise caution when working with professional creators/designers for the presentation of research findings. Creators will make pictures that look good; however, a picture that looks good may be at odds with the researcher narrative, so the researcher's narrative and the visual images may work at cross purposes. In such a case, the image can skew the research findings.

The Zone of Image Interpretation

Some visual methods of research are used to narrow in on a single aspect of a problem, while other visual methods reveal the scope of a problem. An image can consolidate or crystalize a problem, but it can also broaden and generalize it. Since visual methods often involve a reorganization of references in viewers' iconic stores, an image can intentionally converge meaning by limiting *the zone of image interpretation*.

Any particular image can potentially have a wide range of possible, individual interpretations, including those based on unique, personal experiences and feelings. In contrast, the zone of image interpretation is the range of potential interpretations that can be made as part of the consensus of a group using reason and evidence (which may include evidence connected to group feelings). A zone of image interpretation can emerge through discussion and debate as part of the creation of a community of expert, visual researchers, or it may have been determined by, for example, art historians previous to a contemporary research project. This zone emerges, in part, as a result of the construction and enrichment of commonalities in researchers' iconic stores through experience, education, and debate. As is the case with other research, visual research should occur in a community of shared knowledge and, at least to some extent, shared agreement. Shared agreement permits consensus about what counts as visual evidence. The boundaries of interpretation that enable visual research can be conducted by researchers using visual references available in their iconic store, which can lead to a communal agreement.

Approaches to an Analysis of Research Images

A rhetorical analysis for images is essentially a textual model. Aspects of imagery are equated with aspects of text. This approach to analysis may have limited use, but as we have discussed, textual models raise problems when used with images. For example, a common model for rhetorical analysis included in the Texas A & M university writing center website includes taking stock of the "rhetorical situation," which is knowing the intended audience, medium, creator's background, purpose, and genre (Texas A & M University, n.d.b.).

Making Judgments

Although the "rhetorical situation" is generally the context, which we have discussed as being important to analysis, the context is not always rhetorical. Part of the context of an image is other images, which have their own tacit information that cannot be limited to rhetoric. Also, rhetorical models like this attempt to fit images into a language of writing. For example, the term "genre" in the visual arts differs in meaning to the term used in literature. In the visual arts, genre refers to a particular type of painting that deals with scenes of everyday life, such as ordinary people working, and these scenes are intended to be highly representational, so a genre painter uses a style that is conventionally realistic. Genre painting is different from landscape, portraiture, still life, non-objective and most other imagery. The same writing center website states that "the image's style, placement, format, and message will be influenced by the rhetorical situation" (Texas A & M University, n.d.b., para. 2). Actually, an image's style, "format" (which we assume means visual composition), and "message" (suggested meaning) are all found in the formal visual qualities, so it is more appropriate to ask questions regarding form, such as: How are the formal qualities used to convey style? Why is the figure placed in that location? How is color scheme used to create the composition? How are viewers' eyes directed so as to influence interpretation?

Image analysis requires visual literacy, not just the ability to describe what one sees. Visual description is only a first-level response to an image. Good visual literacy usually enables a viewer to discern the qualities of the medium used and how the artist is intending to affect an audience; it enables visual criticism. For example, a researcher may decide to use fine art still lifes in a project to study eye movements. In this case, the images may be chosen for their composition, so knowing the background of the artists who painted them may not be necessary. However, in this case, formal analysis of visual qualities is necessary because the formal qualities and the ways they are used directly influence eye movements.

Applying Criteria for Analyses: Research Questions and Purposes

If the research is intended to discover what a coyote looks like in life, a photograph would be more effective than a child's drawing. If, however, the research question asked about the ways that people interpret coyotes, participants' drawings of coyotes could be appropriate data. In either case, judgments of the formal qualities will help in the analysis. For instance, a researcher might ask of an image whether it has realistic color or whether the color is used symbolically. Such queries have to do with the formal qualities of the images and should be answered when coming to conclusions about whether an image will help to answer the research question. The conditions, such as medium, are also important to analyze in judgments of quality. What range of drawing implements were the participants allowed to use in their drawings? Was the participants' drawing paper well suited for the drawing implement? Were the participants given enough time to do their drawing?

The analyses of visual research should take into account the materiality of images, which have lives of their own and will influence different viewers in different ways. So, visual analysis needs to relate to the impact the image has on viewers and be judged based on that impact.

Loci of Analysis: Attending to Relevant Qualities and Contexts

While we were writing this chapter, one of the author's young granddaughters came home from school with a lovely small watercolor painting she had created of water lilies in a beautifully blended pool of color representing water. Of course, both parents and grandparents were delighted, but at the same time knew the source of the image to be the work of French Impressionist painter Claude Monet's water lily series of 1897–99. That knowledge did not diminish the child's or the family's delight in the copy—but when copies are made as part of a research project, a lack of knowledge about a source could influence a researcher's analysis.

In research, the locus of analysis is where one focuses their attention when analyzing an image. Based on our discussions about the conceptual location of evidence, four loci of analysis can be stipulated: (a) formal evidence, (b) symbolic evidence, (c) creation context, and (d) viewer context. Researchers who have a broad and deep knowledge of the relevant imagery can analyze these loci interactively. For example, in analyzing Monet's water lily paintings, a person familiar with the history of late 19th- and early 20th-Century European art, or one who had seen or visited Monet's home in Giverny, France, could interactively analyze the artist's intention and use of color and technique, which Monet developed over the course of over 250 water lily paintings while living with the plants in his garden. The analyst would know that Monet planted the water lilies at Giverny and saw his garden almost every day, studying the way light reflected on the water, the relative sizes and shapes of the plants, and their visual and emotional effects. Monet focused his work on the surface of the water and his water lilies became increasingly abstract over time—the area around the water and the trees, sky, clouds were only suggested by reflection—possibly because of cataracts developing in his eyes. By focusing on the light and color reflected by the surface of the water, Monet's work ushered in new aspects of abstraction in Western fine art. However, it was not only a technical exercise that motivated the painter. In the Museum of Modern Art in New York, three water lilies panels (1916–1926) are displayed as a triptych, each 6-1/2 ft. high x 14 ft. wide, but he wanted the paintings in his series to be displayed in a continuous fashion around a room so that no walls showed between. Monet created his garden as a work of art and intended to generate a similar, immersive impact on the viewer with these panels through the use of color, light, and scale. Much has been written about Monet's water lilies and a researcher certainly could read the analyses of experts before writing one oneself based on reproductions, but physically being in the environment of the lilies' exhibition changes the loci of analysis to the feel of Monet's garden.

In summary, it is important to remember that images far exceed rhetorical analysis and that claims of visual interpretation must be backed by evidence. An image may or may not represent the creator's intent, but if the image is a copy, a researcher who views it may not know whose intent is represented, the creator or the person who reproduced it, without further investigation. We now look at data information derived from visual sources.

Analyzing through Deep Study

A qualitative analysis of an image in research requires deep study. Pushing beyond the textual, a symbolic analysis requires study of the influence of formal qualities, which reveal the visual character of an image that support the content. Several stepwise models exist for analyzing images, most coming from the visual arts and grounded in art criticism—which Elliot Eisner (1991) drew on in his arguments for arts-based research. Several authors writing on methods of art analysis have created models based on a simple to complex process of description, formal analysis, interpretation, and evaluation (Barrett, 1988; Chapman, 1978; Feldman, 1970, 1994). Freedman (2003) challenged assumptions about the use of these practices as stepwise, pointing out that they do not occur independently when people view art; rather, they are interrelated and influence each other as the brain processes visual information. Other researchers have used similar models. In her review of visual analytic techniques, Susan Culshaw (2019) delineated three stages, which can be seen in the earlier models: descriptive, analytic, and interpretive.

1. Descriptive—focusing on how the image is produced, what it contains (factual and expressional representations, content and color) and how it conveys meaning—its visual impact,
2. Analytic—focusing on aspects such as compositional context, spatial relationships, significance of content/color/placement of items, and "visual syntax," and

3. Interpretive—beginning with the most obvious reading of the image, then generating alternative readings (Culshaw, 2019, p. 275).

In addition, Culshaw intermingles collage and interview data to stimulate visual thinking and reveal what cannot be expressed in words alone in holistic, non-linear ways.

As researchers across disciplines in the social sciences recognize, the use of imagery as data often necessitates a visual form of analysis. In their book, *Embodied Research Methods*, professors of business Torkild Thanem and David Knights (2019) insist on an analogue approach to visual analysis, which involves making juxtapositions. Professor of education, social research and practice, Nicole Brown, presents her research through a variety of arts-based forms, including visual installation where the analysis is the process of selecting, positioning, and interpreting how, what, and where to install (e.g., Brown & Collins, 2021). Art therapist Mandy Archibald (2022) provides an example of visual research analyzed by having another researcher respond with visual imagery.

Professor of social work Paula Gerstenblatt (2013) argues that collage portraits made by a researcher in a variety of media, including photography, provide opportunities for analysis of qualitative interview data. Such portraits can help a researcher establish a foundation for analysis that emphasizes inclusion, interdisciplinary and group connections, and authentic experience. Gerstenblatt generates her collage portraits by assembling photographs, field notes, newspaper articles about the project, and other data on paper, creating a visual presentation of a participant's story. She states,

> In reviewing the initial analysis I stated the following in my field notes: "I was able to feel words not just comprehend them. I could visualize the participants sitting on the lot with family members in the wee hours of the morning after a full day of work under the hot summer sun, telling stories, and sipping beer."
>
> (p. 299)

Gerstenblatt highlighted the dancing quality of the analytic process as she moved between and within the methodological steps and the artistic arrangement. She shifted back and forth from the interviews to the portrait, using drawing implements to connect parts on its background, drawing over them, and writing quotations from the participants to develop their stories. Gerstenblatt had been a practicing artist for decades before pursuing this strategy of analysis. However, it can be adapted depending on the experience of any researcher.

Making Judgments

Analyzing Participants' Textual Comments About Imagery

Because the tacit is difficult to put into words, participants often find responding to images verbally or in writing a challenge. However, such responses can aid researchers in seeing what participants see, and so can be valuable when trying to reveal aspects of their interactions with visual culture. Participant comments about images collected through interviews, surveys, or observations can be used to compare and contrast with a researcher's visual analysis.

As a researcher analyzes an image, questions to ask of the image may focus on formal qualities and meanings, but they can also include inquiry about participants' interactions with and decisions about creating or selecting the image: How did the participants respond during the creation or selection process? How did the material of the image influence participants' creation or selection? How and why did participants make decisions about formal qualities, such as scale or distance of the creator's eye or camera from the subject? Partial information about choices and interpretations can be seen in the images participants create and select, but their comments about images can also aid analysis.

Social science researcher Karin Hannes asked questions of participants about the formal qualities of the images they made or selected as part of a research project stating the following:

> We argue that visual data can do more than just illustrate ideas or concepts, particularly in the process of research where participants contribute to the data collection phase. Visual images record the tacit meanings of the person who makes them, and they can—with the help of a researcher skilled in qualitative reasoning—form another stream of textual analysis.
> (Hannes and Siegesmund, 2022, p. 278)

Hannes and Siegesmund (2022) developed a series of questions as part of their analytical protocol that enabled participants to aid in the analysis of imagery. They asked participants the following to dig deeply into the visual qualities of the images to understand how those qualities supported meaning:

1. What title would you give to the visual image you created?
2. What is the meaning or point of the image? (What does it represent? What do you want to tell?) Which visual details

or symbols are helping to tell the story? Which visual detail or symbol is referring to which meaning?
3. What is the character of the visual image? (Staged or spontaneous? Manipulated? Why?)
4. What is the perspective of the visual image? (Close-up/long distance? Central focus?)
5. What are the contrasts and contexts? (Background/foreground? Conflict/harmony?)
6. What are the attitudes, body language, and emotional expressions of the human figures displayed in the image?
7. What is the (bigger) context? (Representation of what is happening)
8. What if the qualities of the picture were different? Would it have changed its actual meaning?
9. Do the materials you used, such as paint, wood, metal, and paper, have a particular meaning at all? (If so, explain) (p. 286)

To illustrate this point, consider educational environments where the intention of research is to document experiences of students who are learning to articulate tacit knowledge. In a study by Jessica Vivirito (2012), students were asked to respond to images depicting difficult knowledge, such as photographs of torture taken at Abu Ghraib. The student respondents had difficulty expressing themselves in language at all when looking at the images. As the researcher pointed out, "one important finding from this inquiry is that difficult visual culture requires a deeper understanding of why transformative 'dialogue,'—as a key component of critical pedagogy—is especially difficult when confronting tragic visual images" (p. 170).

In such situations, side-by-side comparisons of respondent comments can be extremely effective in revealing how language is used when talking about images. For example, categorizing comments in terms of types, levels, or stages can reveal participants' attitudes, beliefs, and practices when it comes to imagery. In Table 6.1, Deborah Filbin (2020) compared and categorized comments made by high school art teachers about the assessment requirements for student art placed on them by school district administrators. The teachers offered alternative methods to the requirement that quantitative measures must be used to assess student art. The researcher organized the comments by art teachers' levels of resistance to meeting the assessment requirements.

Analyzing participants' comments connected to imagery they encounter in everyday life can be an effective way to engage verbal or written information

TABLE 6.1

Abridged Table of High School Art Teachers' Statements about Student Art Assessment Requirements (Filbin, 2020)

Covert Resistance	Overt Resistance	Pragmatic Compliance
I'll get a pie chart from Google that tells me where my students were ... during the beginning of the class, and then I'll do it again the last week and they can't not grow.	Art is in a weird spot with data... We have to fake it. And it's so fake I don't know how else to say it.	I'll do surveys throughout the school year that show data. I'll just give surveys randomly just to get numbers.
When are you ever going to do a one-day project? Never. So, I have to make these fake projects that are one-day projects where they see a beginning and then they see a result.	Administration asked us to give a 50% floor on grades [the lowest grade that can be given], which I don't do. We fought that and said no. We're not going to do that, I'm sorry.	I'm trying to ride the balance line between satisfying my administrator with my data, without losing the integrity of teaching art, and really what art is meant to be.
[The students] know its fake because I tell them. So, I tell them the day before that I'm having an observation and it's going to be the fakest day. We need to do all the things for the observation ... And they're like, okay.	All they want [is for] us to process the concept because administration says that's the most important thing. There is no "I didn't do a concept." We keep trying to tell administration because we're product-based it's completely different how we have to assess.	Now it's the most demanding it's ever been. The amount of work you have to do, you know, filling out stuff online, the amount of times we are observed, and [so] on, and just the amount of work we've got to do.
You need to know how to put on a show to get a good [teacher] evaluation.	They wanted us to do a multiple-choice and fill in the bubble and we were able to fight that and not have to do it.	This just doesn't make sense. But we have to do that for our evaluation. That's what we have to do to prove that were doing our jobs.
What's in the final in reality is worth 10% [of the student's grade], but in practice I just don't do it. Nobody checks up on that. Everyone's way too busy.	I'm not gonna test them on some vocabulary that doesn't really apply to the skill they're learning. Vocabulary is important, but my real job is to teach them how to draw.	We get directed, we have a model that we're supposed to be following ... and if we didn't get to what we're supposed to, that was fine.

(Continued)

TABLE 6.1 (Continued)
Abridged Table of High School Art Teachers' Statements about Student Art Assessment Requirements (Filbin, 2020)

Covert Resistance	Overt Resistance	Pragmatic Compliance
To be honest I could fudge all those numbers … this is taking the human component of teaching out of the equation on my evaluation, which I don't think is cool.	Did you ever see what subjects [are] at the top of Bloom's taxonomy? It says 'creative works'. … We're the ones at the top. But you're asking us to assess down at the bottom. … I can't reconcile those two, I can't. I can't make sense out of this; I don't know who they want me to be.	When we get evaluated, we have to show student growth using the rubrics we made. The way we do it is, because we're assessing the same thing from project one to the end of the year which is craftsmanship and composition. As long as the student has grown one number, we have met growth.
Until they really decide to crack down, and say "that's not reliable," I'm just [going] to do what works. I think what I'm doing is more valid than taking some stupid bubble test, you know.	I'm going to tell you something, this kind of taking charge of your own learning, this kind of self-sufficiency and learning, this is what it looks like, and it's learned in an art room. … [Students] just do it, so you keep that in mind next time [they] want us to quantify it and put it on a bubble sheet.	Those kinds of reflection things are included after the lesson has happened, although a lot of that is the feedback both to myself and [the students] – [administrators] only see a day of the lesson and usually our projects take a couple of weeks.

related to imagery. Such comments may be about participant reactions to familiar visual culture. For example, if a researcher seeks to gain information about social interactions in a home, they may interview participants by asking about social interactions around the television or ask participants to photograph important things in the home and explain why those objects were chosen. The researcher can include those images in their analysis to support and challenge comments made by participants as part of the process of triangulation to assess the validity and reliability of the methods used.

Analyzing Contexts

Participants may produce visual data within a research project: images that document an event or record a critical or emotional response that reveals information, which may be difficult to put into words. The analysis of participant visual commentaries (visual responses to research prompts) requires a determination of whether the response image is intended as a dispassionate fact, specific critique, or a more generally expressive or evocative reaction. Such images may be responses to a wide range of life experiences or specific, researcher-initiated experiences. So, it is important to give attention to both the visual and symbolic character of the response within the context that image was created.

A number of analytical approaches and procedures have been developed to analyze participants' visual commentaries. One approach is to use viewers' comments to determine the success of the visual commentary in convincing viewers to think, feel, or act during or after their viewing. For example, in a study of high school art student social commentaries, one of this text's authors (Freedman) asked participants to each create a visual commentary about a social issue of their choice intended to cause both participants and viewers to think about that issue. Participants and viewers demonstrated such thought through (a) research conducted by the participants, (b) care and length of time spent creating the artwork, (c) comments by creators and viewers, (d) viewing time, and (d) any action taken by viewers as a result of seeing the work. In another project, widespread participation and publicity about the project, and other projects emerging from the original project, demonstrated influence on a local and global scale, which may be considered as part of the analysis (e.g., Perez-Martin & Freedman, 2018).

As visual analytic methods become more sophisticated, contradictory approaches may seem to be recommended. In *Embodied Research Methods*, Thanem and Knights (2019) argue against exploring the visual through digital tools because digital technologies can change the material qualities of images. This is in contrast to Laura L. Ellingson's (2017) *Embodiment in Qualitative Research*, who suggests that digital methods create embodied experiences during the process of data analysis. Both approaches are valid, they simply exhibit different loci of analysis on the materiality of the visual. They are pursuing tacit knowledge from different directions. Therefore, a researcher should explain why they choose a specific visual analytic method.

Besides participants making visual images, participants may also respond visually to images provided by the researcher. When analyzing such response images, researcher comparison between the original image and the participant-created image is important. In this case, the comparison should include a formal analysis of the original image and the response image, as well as a symbolic analysis. Questions to ask include: What is the symbolic meaning suggested by the image content? Are the formal qualities different in the original and response images? What are the expressive or symbolic purposes of the formal qualities in the response image?

Individual responses are conditioned by social contexts. In his large-scale study, sociologist Pierre Bourdieu (1984) demonstrated that family art preferences begin early, are based on socioeconomic level, and stay with an individual until later in life. Similarly, youth make popular visual art choices based on visual preferences they believe represent them or are connected to something they seek to achieve, such as friends. Individuals become part of social groups by associating themselves with peers who have made similar choices and develop similar viewing and creation preferences, in part, to strengthen friendships (Freedman et al., 2013; Karpati et al., 2016). Even people who identify primarily as creatives—people who actively make their own images—are profoundly influenced by the cultural contexts within which they make their imagery. In studies of such communities (e.g., Manifold, 2009) that seek to analyze communal connections among young creators, researchers have found that the creation of imagery based on popular visual culture preferences requires an analysis of local and global community context and the ways these are internalized by participants. In such studies, the imagery made by the participants had similar stylistic qualities, and so required analyses of the source styles, the relationships among creators, and the influences of these on individuals' visual work considered to be data. Thus, an analysis of imagery may need to take global visual culture influences into account.

Using Rubrics for Scoring

To this point, our questions and interpretive examples have focused primarily on qualitative analysis. We turn now to translating qualitative analysis of images into quantitative data through rubrics. Quantitative data is data which can be counted; in other words, data that has an amount. Amounts of qualities can be seen in any visual image or form, for example, photographs, drawings, paintings, digital images, sculptures, landscape designs, or graphic novels. Since certain amounts of qualities are present in images, quantitative measures can be used to analyze an image. For example, one can determine the proportion of space in an image used to represent a human figure, the apparent distance seen in a photograph of a landscape, or the saturation level of a hue.

Analysis of these amounts of qualities can aid a researcher when comparing research participants' responses to images or choosing images for their visual qualities to ensure that the qualities per se do not confound viewers' responses to the content. This is not to say that amount will lead to a certain interpretation or that the same amount of qualities in different images will result in the same interpretation by different people. However, it does suggest that the same amount of qualities in images that are similar can confidently result in a similar interpretation by the same person.

As we discussed in Chapter 3, the three most typical criteria for assessment of images are technical use of media, use of formal qualities, and subject or concept. We discussed the ways that these criteria can be judged to assess the aesthetic quality of images made by research subjects of participants (as in the case of *Image as Data*) or imagery created by the researcher (as in the case of *Image as Presentation*). Analytic rubrics can be used to score these judgments.

Analytic rubrics

We now turn to ways that researchers can use rubrics to quantify the characteristics of qualities when aesthetic quality is not the emphasis of the analysis. For example, a research project may require that children draw narratives or adults take a series of photographs to convey something about their experience. A researcher can and should analyze such images qualitatively, which we discuss below, but a quantitative analysis can also be done.

Rubrics can help researchers quantify the qualities of images. Rather than starting with numbers as a data set and then interpreting them, we use rubrics to start with analytical interpretations, then attach a number to that analysis. This might be considered in opposition to looking at numbers and then interpreting them, but with regard to images, it makes sense to write levels of interpretation or descriptions of qualities, number the levels, and then decide which level is right for a particular image.

Analytic rubrics can be used as coding devices for images in research. The defining characteristic of an analytic rubric is that it is made up of levels of criteria, which describe selected qualities of an image. Such rubrics can be helpful in analyzing bodies of images in research. They enable a consistent and comparative coding of a set of images, which results in a quantitative data set, for comparison.

Below is an analytic rubric used to quantify the amount present of variables that can be seen in a work of art (Table 6.2). In the study of high school art students' visual commentaries mentioned above, Freedman's use of the rubric resulted in an inter-rater reliability score, determining the closeness of raters' judgments pertaining to the variables: (a) technical skills, (b) formal qualities, (c) conceptual complexity, and (d) interdisciplinary knowledge. The amount of each variable in evidence was determined by agreement of the judges for each of 120 works of high school student art.

The rubric describes the qualities present in the work and enabled raters to record to what degree those qualities are present. The raters' judgments revealed the degree to which each of those qualities are judged to be apparent by the rater. The inter-rater reliability score affirmed a moderate level of consistency of judgments about the qualities and demonstrated that a better than random agreement existed among the raters' assessments that the qualities exist in those amounts. In other words, the rubric enabled the raters to document their judgment of high school student knowledge and skills revealed through the artwork revealed through the visual qualities of the work.

Visual Methods of Inquiry

TABLE 6.2
Image Coding Rubric Example

Evidence of Technical Skills:		
☐	1	The artwork does not demonstrate a purposeful manipulation of the chosen media. The artwork is well below the basic skill potential for students of this age and experience. The work shows no evidence of media use to achieve a basic level of expression.
☐	2	The artwork demonstrates minimal purposeful manipulation of the chosen media. The artwork is below the basic skill potential for students of this age and experience. The work shows minimal evidence of media use to achieve a basic level of expression.
☐	3	The artwork demonstrates satisfactory manipulation of the chosen media with an average level of confidence and skill. The artwork meets the basic skill potential for students of this age and experience. Shows fundamental knowledge of the particular qualities of this media, which is applied to the content of the work to achieve a rudimentary level of expression.
☐	4	The artwork demonstrates the ability to manipulate the chosen media with an above average level of confidence and skill. Shows good knowledge of the particular qualities of this media and is applied to the content of the work in a reasonably effective way. The technical resolution in the artwork is above the typical skill potential for students of this age and experience.
☐	5	The artwork demonstrates the ability to manipulate the chosen media with an outstanding level of confidence and skill. Shows exceptional knowledge of the particular qualities of this media and is applied to the content of the work in a highly expressive manner. The technical resolution in the artwork well exceeds the typical skill potential for students of this age and educational experience
Evidence of Formal Qualities:		
☐	1	The elements and/or principles of design in the artwork do not achieve visual resolution or expressive outcome that support the content. The formal qualities of the work demonstrate no knowledge of composition and is well below expectations for students of this age and educational experience.
☐	2	The elements and/or principles of design in the artwork achieve a small degree of visual resolution and expressive outcome that support the content. The formal qualities of the work demonstrate little knowledge of composition and is below expectations for students of this age and educational experience.
☐	3	The elements and/or principles of design in the artwork achieve a basic level of visual resolution and expressive outcome that support the content. The formal qualities of the work demonstrate knowledge of composition that meets typical expectations for students of this age and educational experience.
☐	4	The elements and/or principles of design in the artwork achieve a good level of resolution and expressive outcome that support the content. The formal qualities of the work demonstrate knowledge of composition that is above typical expectations for students of this age and educational experience.

(Continued)

Making Judgments

TABLE 6.2 (Continued)
Image Coding Rubric Example

☐	5	The elements and/or principles of design in the artwork achieve a high level of visual resolution and expressive outcome that support the content. The formal qualities of the work demonstrate knowledge of composition that well exceeds the typical understanding for students of this age and educational experience.
Evidence of Conceptual Complexity:		
☐	1	The artwork illustrates no complexity of concept. It is derivative and no originality or research and/or experimentation is evident. The image and text are not mutually supportive to inform or convince through visual form. No conceptual knowledge of art is apparent in the handling of content, and the work is well below the typical understanding of art concepts revealed by students of this age and educational experience.
☐	2	The artwork illustrates a low level of complexity of concept. A minimal amount of originality is evident reflecting minimal research and/or experimentation. The image and text are fairly mutually supportive to inform or convince through visual form. Limited conceptual knowledge of art is apparent in the handling of content, and the work is below the typical understanding of art concepts revealed by students of this age and educational experience.
☐	3	The artwork illustrates a basic level of complexity of concept. A medium amount of originality is evident reflecting fundamental research and/or experimentation. The image and text are mutually supportive to inform or convince through visual form. Average conceptual knowledge of art is apparent in the handling of content, and the work shows a typical understanding of art concepts revealed by students of this age and educational experience.
☐	4	The work illustrates a high level of conceptual complexity. Sophisticated originality of thought is evident reflecting sophisticated research and/or experimentation. The image and text are strongly mutually supportive to inform or convince through visual form. A high level of conceptual knowledge of art is apparent in the handling of content, and the work shows a higher than typical understanding of art concepts revealed by students of this age and educational experience.
☐	5	The work illustrates an exceptional level of conceptual complexity. Outstanding originality of thought is evident reflecting extensive research and experimentation. The image and text are extremely mutually supportive to inform or convince through visual form. An extremely high level of conceptual knowledge of art is apparent in the handling of content, and the work well exceeds the typical understanding of art concepts revealed by students of this age and educational experience.
Evidence of Interdisciplinary Knowledge:		
☐	1	No apparent associative knowledge is referred to by the work. Formal, technical, and/or conceptual processes do not communicate knowledge beyond that of the visual arts. The content of the work demonstrates very few connections to other disciplines or school subjects.

(Continued)

TABLE 6.2 (Continued)
Image Coding Rubric Example

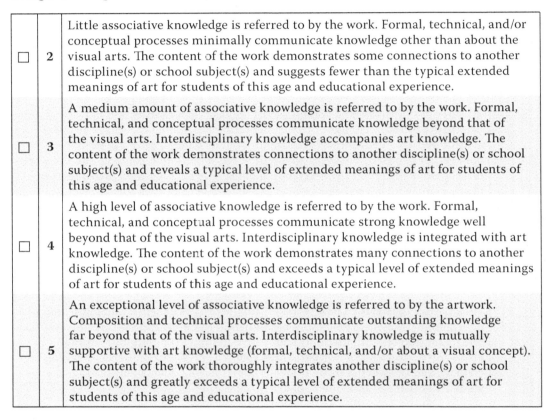

Holistic rubrics

As well as analytic rubrics, researchers can also use holistic rubrics to determine the characteristics of imagery based on criteria. A holistic rubric can be an effective means for analysis in situations where a breakdown of content or visual qualities is not necessary, but rather the purpose is to explore an overall conveyance of information, emotions, or learning through the viewing or production of an image. For example, holistic rubrics can be used to analyze the general impact of images collected in a study on viewers or to analyze participant artwork when judgments of skill-based quality would be inappropriate (Table 6.3).

We now turn to a matrix of visual examples we have developed to illustrate the ways images can be used and analyzed in research.

Making Judgments

TABLE 6.3
Rubric for Holistic Judgments

Select the descriptor below which best reflects the participant's submission of artwork. Enter a mark in the right-hand box which appropriately indicates the degree to which the participant's work has achieved the level described. Enter that mark multiplied by four for the percentage and enter the level at which the work is located based on the percentage (1=low, 2= medium, 3=high, 4=exceptional). A possible range of five marks is provided against each descriptor.

MARK RANGE	HOLISTIC DESCRIPTORS	MARK	MARK % /100	LEVEL /4
0–5	An inadequate amount of work has been completed and is lacking in evidence of technical skill or relevant knowledge of artistic expression.			
6–10	A small amount of work has been produced which demonstrates a limited understanding of the conceptual and/or technical underpinnings of artistic expression. The work illustrates a limited or diffused exploration of ideas appropriate to the visual arts, and a limited ability to resolve concept, media, and technical expression.			
11–15	A reasonable amount of work has been produced which demonstrates an adequate understanding of the conceptual and/or technical underpinnings of artistic expression representative of the cultural context and chosen artistic genre(s). The work illustrates a reasonably focused exploration of ideas appropriate to the visual arts, and a good resolution of concept, media, and technical expression in many works.			
16–20	A strong collection of work has been produced which demonstrates a very good understanding of the conceptual and technical underpinnings of artistic expression representative of the cultural context and chosen artistic genre(s). The work illustrates a comprehensive exploration of ideas appropriate to the visual arts, and a good resolution of concept, media, and technical expression in the majority of works.			
21–25	A very powerful collection of work has been produced which demonstrates an exceptional understanding of the conceptual and technical underpinnings of artistic expression representative of the cultural context and chosen artistic genre(s). The work overall illustrates a highly sophisticated exploration of ideas appropriate to the visual arts, and an outstanding resolution of concept, media, and technical expression.			

Visual Methods of Inquiry

The Image Analysis Matrix

The following is the Image Analysis Matrix (IAM). The IAM is based on the image use categories of the RIF. It explains the evidence that can be found connected to an image, why the image would be used in a research project, and how it can be analyzed. These characteristics of image handling can help researchers use images effectively in their work. The matrix includes examples of the types of imagery referred to in order to illustrate answers to three questions about an image: What is the evidence? Why is it used? How is it analyzed?

Making Judgments

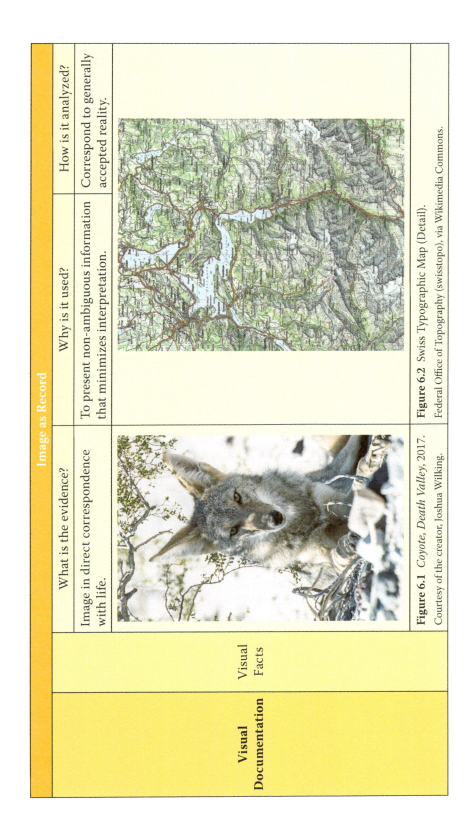

		Image as Record		
		What is the evidence?	Why is it used?	How is it analyzed?
Visual Documentation	Visual Facts	Image in direct correspondence with life.	To present non-ambiguous information that minimizes interpretation.	Correspond to generally accepted reality.

Figure 6.1 *Coyote, Death Valley*, 2017.
Courtesy of the creator, Joshua Wilking.

Figure 6.2 *Swiss Typographic Map* (Detail).
Federal Office of Topography (swisstopo), via Wikimedia Commons.

Visual Methods of Inquiry

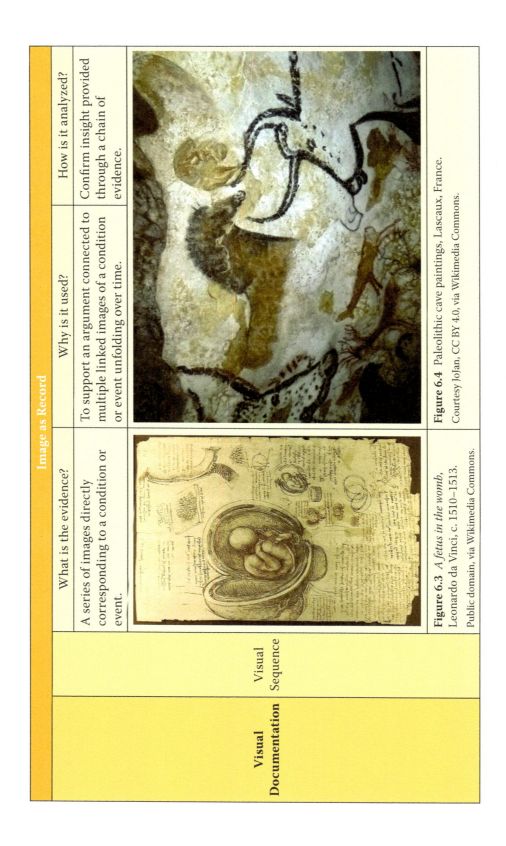

		Image as Record		
		What is the evidence?	Why is it used?	How is it analyzed?
Visual Documentation	Visual Sequence	A series of images directly corresponding to a condition or event.	To support an argument connected to multiple linked images of a condition or event unfolding over time.	Confirm insight provided through a chain of evidence.

Figure 6.3 *A fetus in the womb*, Leonardo da Vinci, c. 1510–1513. Public domain, via Wikimedia Commons.

Figure 6.4 Paleolithic cave paintings, Lascaux, France. Courtesy JoJan, CC BY 4.0, via Wikimedia Commons.

174

Making Judgments

Image as Record		
What is the evidence?	Why is it used?	How is it analyzed?
Visual substantiation of a particular point of view.	To support an individual account.	Confirm that the image is consistent with the researcher's or participant's point of view.

Figure 6.5 *Promised Land* by Willie Birch, 1985.
Courtesy Brandywine Workshop and Archives.

Figure 6.6 *Children sleeping in Mulberry Street* by Jacob Riis, 1890.
Public domain, via Wikimedia Commons.

Visual Authenticity — Visual Argument

175

Visual Methods of Inquiry

		Image as Record		
		What is the evidence?	Why is it used?	How is it analyzed?
Visual Authenticity	Visual Recording	Real-time, video, or film recording of an event.	To document communication mediated by non-human actors.	Analyze formal and symbolic meaning through mediated, recorded behaviors.
		Figure 6.7 Image from the video of the Think Tank Panel: "Renewing Education through Art Practices," coordinated by Kerry Freedman and Carlos Escaño, 2022. Courtesy Carlos Escaño, CC BY-NC-SA.		**Figure 6.8** President Nixon during an interview with network TV news anchors, 1971. Series: Nixon White House Photographs, 1/20/1969–8/9/1974, White House Photo Office Collection (Nixon Administration), 1/20/1969–8/9/1974. Public domain, via Wikimedia Commons.

176

Making Judgments

		Image as Data		
		What is the evidence?	Why is it used?	How is it analyzed?
Artifact Collection	Participant-made Art	Process and product resulting from participant manipulation of visual materials. 	To collect participant-made visual data. 	Identify participant intentions and tacit knowledge in response to a research question.

Figure 6.9 Student artwork from Kerry Freedman's professional archive of student work.

Figure 6.10 A Lolita model presents Elegant Gothic Lolita fashion, 2020.
Courtesy Toastchan, CC BY-SA 4.0, via Wikimedia Commons.

177

Visual Methods of Inquiry

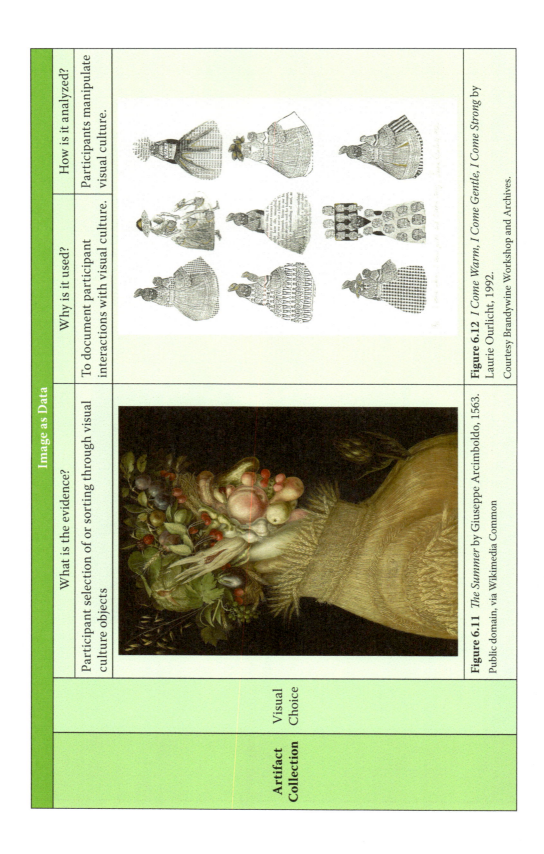

		Image as Data		
		What is the evidence?	Why is it used?	How is it analyzed?
Artifact Collection	Visual Choice	Participant selection of or sorting through visual culture objects	To document participant interactions with visual culture.	Participants manipulate visual culture.
		Figure 6.11 *The Summer* by Giuseppe Arcimboldo, 1563. Public domain, via Wikimedia Common	**Figure 6.12** *I Come Warm, I Come Gentle, I Come Strong* by Laurie Ourlicht, 1992. Courtesy Brandywine Workshop and Archives.	

178

Making Judgments

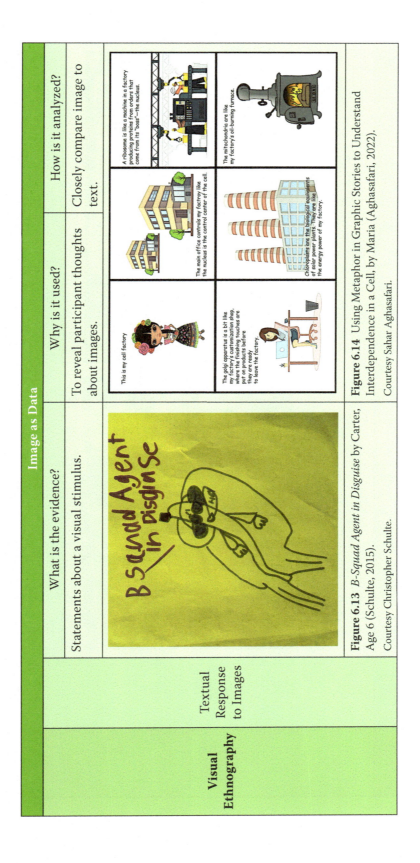

Image as Data			
	What is the evidence?	Why is it used?	How is it analyzed?
Visual Ethnography / Textual Response to Images	Statements about a visual stimulus.	To reveal participant thoughts about images.	Closely compare image to text.

Figure 6.13 *B-Squad Agent in Disguise* by Carter, Age 6 (Schulte, 2015).
Courtesy Christopher Schulte.

Figure 6.14 Using Metaphor in Graphic Stories to Understand Interdependence in a Cell, by Maria (Aghasafari, 2022).
Courtesy Sahar Aghasafari.

Visual Methods of Inquiry

		Image as Data		
		What is the evidence?	Why is it used?	How is it analyzed?
Visual Ethnography	Visual Field Notes	Snapshots taken or made during observation.	To create research documents through the use of visual journaling and recording.	Interpret the image to create a data stream for further analysis.
		Figure 6.15 Brooke Anne Hofsess & Mindi Rhoades (2022). Courtesy of the creators.	**Figure 6.16** *Stolen Moments*, Sara Scott Shields, COVID-19 ABR Consortium, 2020. Courtesy of the creator.	

Making Judgments

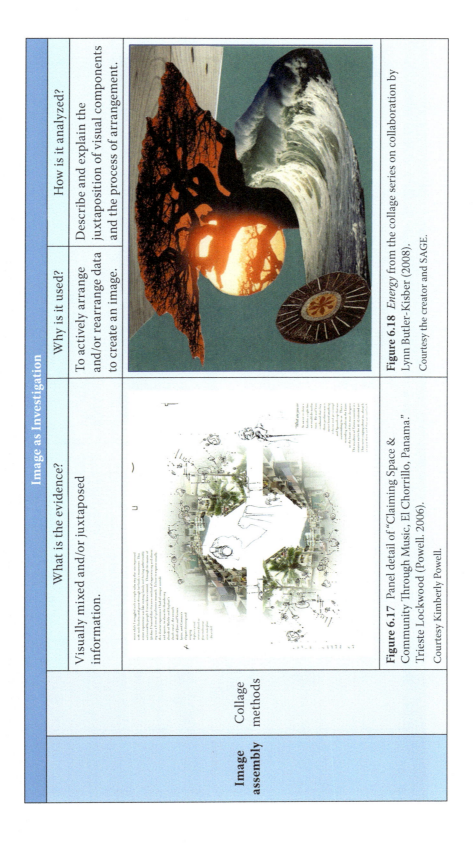

		Image as Investigation		
		What is the evidence?	Why is it used?	How is it analyzed?
Image assembly	Collage methods	Visually mixed and/or juxtaposed information.	To actively arrange and/or rearrange data to create an image.	Describe and explain the juxtaposition of visual components and the process of arrangement.

Figure 6.17 Panel detail of "Claiming Space & Community Through Music, El Chorrillo, Panama." Trieste Lockwood (Powell. 2006).
Courtesy Kimberly Powell.

Figure 6.18 *Energy* from the collage series on collaboration by Lynn Butler-Kisber (2008).
Courtesy the creator and SAGE.

Visual Methods of Inquiry

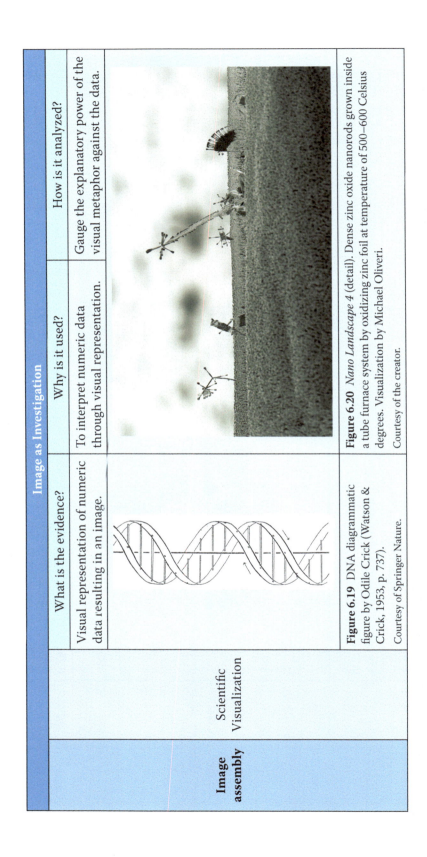

Image as Investigation

Image assembly		What is the evidence?	Why is it used?	How is it analyzed?
	Scientific Visualization	Visual representation of numeric data resulting in an image.	To interpret numeric data through visual representation.	Gauge the explanatory power of the visual metaphor against the data.
		Figure 6.19 DNA diagrammatic figure by Odile Crick (Watson & Crick, 1953, p. 737). Courtesy of Springer Nature.		**Figure 6.20** *Nano Landscape 4* (detail). Dense zinc oxide nanorods grown inside a tube furnace system by oxidizing zinc foil at temperature of 500–600 Celsius degrees. Visualization by Michael Oliveri. Courtesy of the creator.

Making Judgments

	Image as Investigation		
	What is the evidence?	Why is it used?	How is it analyzed?
	Image that is an investigation of a visual problem.	To represent complexity without essentializing.	Explain how formal qualities are used to create symbolic meaning.
Artistic Iteration	**Figure 6.21** *Sketching Entropy* by Nick Sousanis (2016). Courtesy of the creator.	**Figure 6.22** The abandoned school. Digital Photography by Natalie LeBlanc (2018). Courtesy of the creator.	
Studio inquiry			

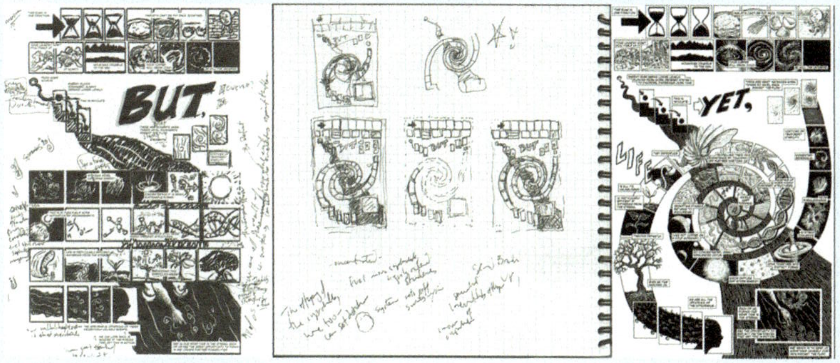

Visual Methods of Inquiry

Image as Investigation

	What is the evidence?	Why is it used?	How is it analyzed?
Studio inquiry — Visible Border Exploration	Image of a previously unseen or unimagined possibility.	To generate avant-garde art to disrupt form or accentuate complexity.	Suggest multiple imaginative and conflicting interpretations.

Figure 6.23 *Old Become New 0081-021* by Shei-Chau Wang, 1997+2021. Courtesy of the creator.

Figure 6.24 *English Learning Paradise*, Created in Virtual Commons for Education and Research (VCER) by Xinyi Wang. Courtesy of Sandrine Han.

184

Making Judgments

		Image as Theory		
		What is the evidence?	Why is it used?	How is it analyzed?
Reflexive Making	Therapeutic Expression	Intuitive, performative image creation.	To engage a process of participant or auto-ethnographic discovery or healing.	Theorize the relationship between creation process and mental state.
		Figure 6.25 *Untitled (Learning from That Person's Work)* (detail) by Matt Mullican, installation Museum of Modern Art, 2005. Courtesy MoMA.		**Figure 6.26** Walking the Dragon's Teeth Maze labyrinth on Makāluapuna Point, Kapalua, Maui, 2021. Larry D. Moore, CC BY-SA 4.0, via Wikimedia Commons.

185

Visual Methods of Inquiry

Image as Theory		
What is the evidence?	Why is it used?	How is it analyzed?
Original result from a pre-determined, systematic process.	To explore visual-kinesthetic experience to discover unconsidered possibilities.	Describe how the process enabled theory.

Reflexive Making — Embodied Practice

Figure 6.27 One collage from *Folded Collages* by Jorge Lucero, 2013–ongoing. Courtesy of the creator.

Figure 6.28 *Straw Box* by Sam Gilliam, 1997. Courtesy of the collector, Kerry Freedman.

186

Making Judgments

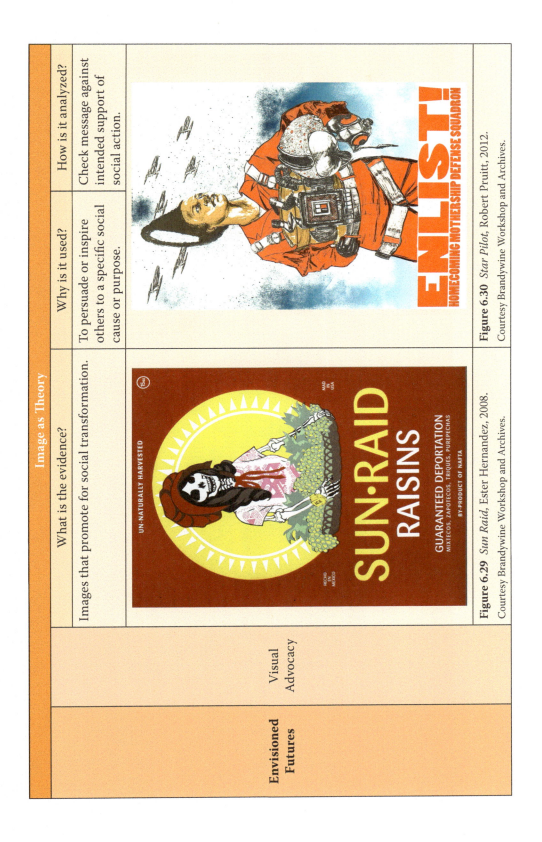

		Image as Theory		
		What is the evidence?	Why is it used?	How is it analyzed?
Envisioned Futures	Visual Advocacy	Images that promote for social transformation.	To persuade or inspire others to a specific social cause or purpose.	Check message against intended support of social action.

Figure 6.29 *Sun Raid*, Ester Hernandez, 2008. Courtesy Brandywine Workshop and Archives.

Figure 6.30 *Star Pilot*, Robert Pruitt, 2012. Courtesy Brandywine Workshop and Archives.

Visual Methods of Inquiry

		Image as Theory		
		What is the evidence?	Why is it used?	How is it analyzed?
Envisioned Futures	Social Art	Group-made images to disrupt or resist social conditions.	To promote social change through a group.	Explain how the image-making empowered participants.

Figure 6.31 Kryssi Staikidis and Paula Nicho Cúmez collaborate on an image (Staikidis, 2020).
Courtesy Kryssi Staikidis.

Figure 6.32 *Youth Climate Action Team Climate Strike Art Build*, researcher Kim Cosier (2019).
Courtesy Joe Brusky/Art Build Workers.

188

Making Judgments

		Image as Report		
		What is the evidence?	Why is it used?	How is it analyzed?
Research Illustration	Correspondent Figures	Full visual report in charts or graphs of one or more data sets.	To add clarity to a discursive analysis of findings.	Evaluate the accuracy of conclusions in the visual representation.
		Figure 6.33 *Mesh: Human Powered Outdoor Activity 2015* by Stephen Cartwright, 2018. Courtesy of the creator.		**Figure 6.34** *Norms and Anomalies Flatcap Forms* by Dan Barney, 2013 (Kalin & Barney, 2014). Courtesy of the creator

189

Visual Methods of Inquiry

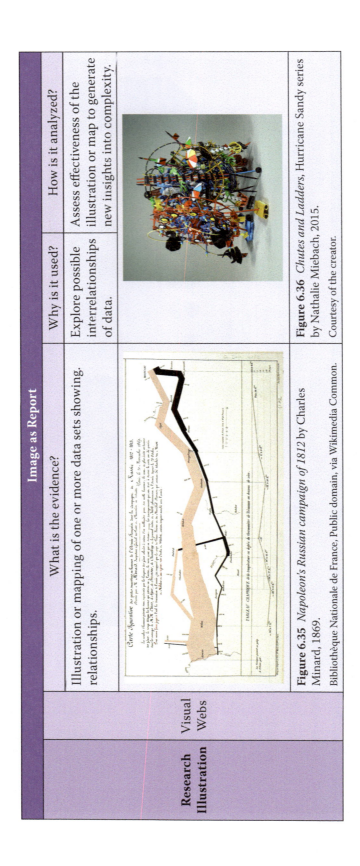

		Image as Report		
		What is the evidence?	Why is it used?	How is it analyzed?
Research Illustration	Visual Webs	Illustration or mapping of one or more data sets showing relationships.	Explore possible interrelationships of data.	Assess effectiveness of the illustration or map to generate new insights into complexity.
		Figure 6.35 *Napoleon's Russian campaign of 1812* by Charles Minard, 1869. Bibliothèque Nationale de France, Public domain, via Wikimedia Common.	**Figure 6.36** *Chutes and Ladders*, Hurricane Sandy series by Nathalie Miebach, 2015. Courtesy of the creator.	

Making Judgments

Image as Report

		What is the evidence?	Why is it used?	How is it analyzed?
Research Presentation	Visual Narrative	Sequential art that tells a complex story.	To narrate the researcher's exploration of a path of inquiry.	Appraise the success of the visual storytelling to bring into view the results of the study.

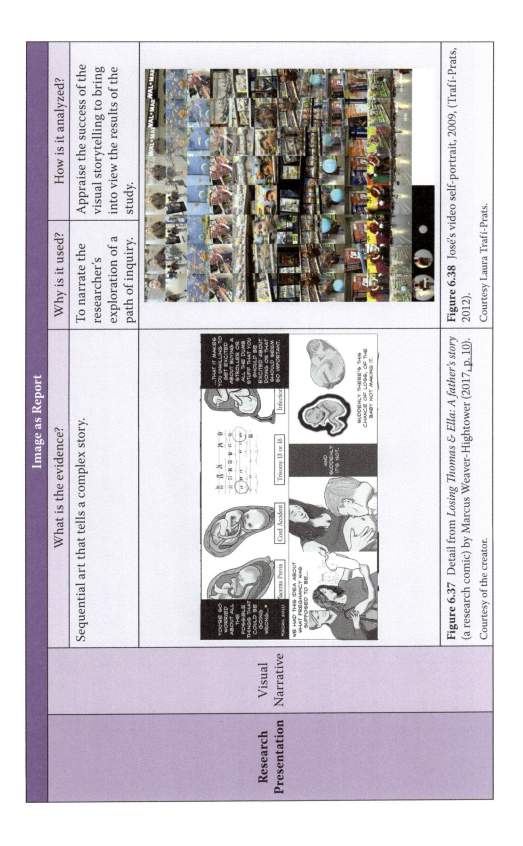

Figure 6.37 Detail from *Losing Thomas & Ella: A father's story* (a research comic) by Marcus Weaver-Hightower (2017, p. 10).
Courtesy of the creator.

Figure 6.38 José's video self-portrait, 2009, (Trafí-Prats, 2012).
Courtesy Laura Trafí-Prats.

191

Visual Methods of Inquiry

Image as Report

		What is the evidence?	Why is it used?	How is it analyzed?
Research Presentation	**Visual Exhibition**	Three-dimensional display of imagery in a space. 	To guide the audience through the researcher's process of inquiry. 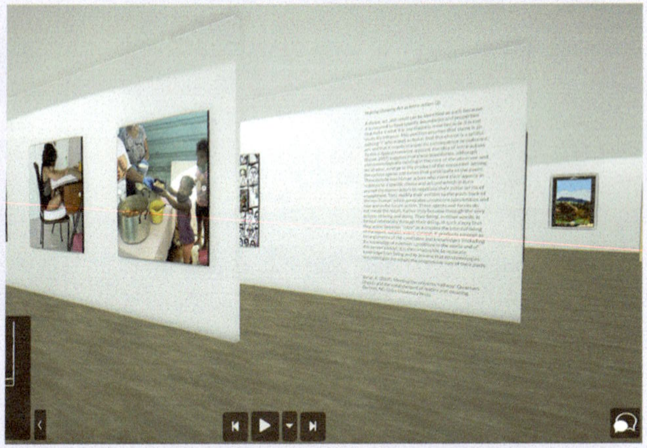	Judge the ability of the display to generate dialogue and/or multiple potential answers to a research question.

Figure 6.39 *Mining the Museum*, installation by artist Fred Wilson at the Maryland Historical Society, 1992–93, Cigar store Indians facing portraits of community members of American Indian descent. Courtesy Maryland Historical Society.

Figure 6.40 *Sustaining Life on Earth: Arts-Based Responses to the Lived Experience of COVID-19*, COVID-19 ABR Consortium, 2022. Courtesy COVID-19 ABR Consortium, Lynn Hendricks, Gioia Chilton, and Suzanne Crowley.

Conclusion

Images can be analyzed for both qualitative and quantitative information. Qualitative analyses are important not only in terms of the empirical, that is, what can be seen. They can also provide and reveal experiences that cannot be readily seen or measured. Quantitative analyses can be used to supplement qualitative analysis when applying visual research methods to the quantity of qualities. When analyzing images for inclusion in research or as a result of participant creation or selection of images, the formal visual qualities are as important as the symbolic qualities of content. The medium through which an image is made is also an important consideration because materials shape the ways they can be analyzed. The analysis of images in research must consider participants' level of artistic development and experience with imagery in order to take their visual, technical, and symbolic capabilities into account. Considerations of whether an image can and should be analyzed in and of itself or with regard to a context, and the breadth of that context, are also important considerations.

> When contemplating how to analyze images in research, consider the following questions:
>
> 1. How will the quality of images selected to be used in the study be judged?
> 2. Will participant art made before or during the research be assessed in terms of aesthetic quality or analyzed based on some other criterion or criteria?
> 3. What criteria will be used to analyze images created as part of the research?
> 4. Could imagery be used to help to theorize during or after the completion of the research?
> 5. How will the images be used in the presentation or reporting of research?

References

Archibald, M. M. (2022). Interweaving arts-based, qualitative, mixed methods research: Showcasing integration and knowledge translation through material and narrative reflection. *International Review of Qualitative Research*, *15*(2), 168–198. https://doi.org/10.1177/19408447221097063

Argott, D. (2009). The art of the steal *[Film]*. MAJ Productions.

Aghasafari, S. (2022, February 3). *Examining how bi/multilingual high schoolers construct meaning through the integration of visual art and biology* [on-line paper presentation]. European Congress of Qualitative Inquiry, European Network Qualitative Inquiry.

Barrett, T. (1988). A comparison of the goals of studio professors conducting critiques and art education goals for teaching criticism. *Studies in Art Education, 30*(1), 22–27. https://doi.org/10.2307/1320648

Berger, J. (1977). *Ways of seeing*. British Broadcasting Corporation; Penguin Books.

Bochner, A. P., & Ellis, C. (2016). *Evocative autoethnography: Writing lives and telling stories*. Routledge.

Bourdieu P. (1984). *Homo academicus*. Stanford University Press.

Brown, N. & Collins, J. (2021). Systematic visuo-textual analysis: A framework for analyzing visual and textual data. *The Qualitative Report, 26*(4), 1275–1290. https://doi.org/10.46743/2160-3715/2021.4838

Buckley, J., Seery, N., & Kimbell, R. (2022). A review of the valid methodological use of adaptive comparative judgment in technology education research. *Frontiers in Education, 7*(March), Article 787926. https://doi.org/10.3389/feduc.2022.787926

Buster, K., & Crawford, P. (2009). *The critique handbook: A sourcebook and survival guide* (2nd ed.). Prentice Hall.

Butler-Kisber, L. (2008). Collage as inquiry. In J. G. Knowles & A. L. Cole (Eds.), *Handbook of the arts in qualitative research: Perspectives, methodologies, examples, and issues* (pp. 265–277). SAGE.

Chapman, L. H. (1978). *Approaches to art in education*. Harcourt Brace Jovanovich.

Culshaw, S. (2019). The unspoken power of collage? Using an innovative arts-based research method to explore the experience of struggling as a teacher. *London Review of Education, 17*(3), 268–283. https://doi.org/10.18546/LRE.17.3.03

Dewey, J. (1989). *Art as experience* [The later works, 1925–1953] (J. Boydston, Ed.), (Vol. 10). Southern Illinois University Press. (Original work published 1934)

Eisner, E. W. (1991). *The enlightened eye: Qualitative inquiry and the enhancement of educational practice*. Macmillan.

Ellingson, L. L. (2017). *Embodiment in qualitative research*. Routledge.

Feldman, E. B. (1970). *Becoming human through art: Aesthetic experience in the school*. Prentice Hall.

Feldman, E. B. (1994). *Practical art criticism*. Prentice Hall.

Filbin, D. N. (2020). *Art assessment policy and practice at the high school level: Validity, reliability, and resistance* [Doctoral dissertation]. Northern Illinois University.

Freedman, K. (2003). *Teaching visual culture: Curriculum, aesthetics, and the social life of art*. Teachers College Press.

Freedman, K. (2015). Learning as a condition of creativity: The relationship between knowing and making art. In E. Zimmerman & F. Bastos (Eds.), *Creativity in art education*. National Art Education Association.

Freedman, K., Heijnen, E., Kallio-Tavin, M., Karpati, A., & Papp, L. (2013). Visual culture learning communities: How and what students come to know in informal art groups. *Studies in Art Education, 53*(2), 103–115. https://doi.org/10.1080/00393541.2013.11518886

Gerstenblatt, P. (2013). Collage portraits as a method of analysis in qualitative research. *International Journal of Qualitative Methods, 12*(1), 294–309. https://doi.org/10.1177/160940691301200114

Hannes, K., & Siegesmund, R. (2022). An analytical apparatus for analyzing visual imagery applied in a socio-behavioral research. *International Review of Qualitative Research, 15*(2), 278–302. https://doi.org/10.1177/19408447221097061

Hofsess, B. A., & Rhoades, M. (2022). P(l)aying attention: Wilding correspondence as methodological possibility. *International Review of Qualitative Research, 15*(2), 216–247. https://doi.org/10.1177/19408447221090650

Isaacson, W. (2017). *Leonardo Da Vinci*. Simon & Schuster.

Kalin, N. M., & Barney, D. T. (2014). Inoperative art education. *Journal of Social Theory in Art Education, 34*(68), 63–75.

Karpati, A., Freedman, K., Kallio-Tavin, M. Heijnen, E., & Castro, J. C. (2016). Collaboration in visual culture learning communities: Towards a synergy of individual and collective creative practice. *International Journal of Art and Design Education, 36*(2), 164–175. https://doi.org/10.1111/jade.12099

Kopatich, R. D., Steciuch, C. C., Feller, D. P., Millis, K., & Siegesmund, R. (2021). Development and Validation of the Aesthetic Processing Preference Scale (APPS). *Psychology of Aesthetics, Creativity, and the Arts*, 1–15. http://dx.doi.org/10.1037/aca0000449

LeBlanc, N. (2018). The abandoned school as an anomalous place of learning: A practice-led approach to doctoral research. In M. Cahnmann-Taylor & R. Siegesmund (Eds.), *Arts-based research in education: Foundations for practice* (2nd ed., pp. 174–189). Routledge.

Manifold, M. (2009). What art educators can learn from the fan-based art-making of adolescents and young adults. *Studies in Art Education, 50*(3), 257–271. https://doi.org/10.1080/00393541.2009.11518772

Perez-Martin, F. & Freedman, K. (2018). Social justice in art and design education: An example from Africa's last colony. *The international encyclopedia of art and design education. Curriculum*, (Vol 2). Wiley. https://doi.org/10.1002/9781118978061.ead103

Schulte, C. M. (2015). Intergalactic encounters: Desire and the political immediacy of children's drawing. *Studies in Art Education*, *56*(3), 241–256. https://doi.org/10.1080/00393541.2015.11518966

Sousanis, N. (2016, June 22) *Sketching Entropy*. Spin Weave & Cut. https://spinweaveandcut.com/sketching-entropy/

Thanem, T., & Knights, D. (2019). *Embodied research methods*. SAGE.

Trafí-Prats, L. (2012). Urban children and intellectual emancipation: Video narratives of self and place in the City of Milwaukee. *Studies in Art Education*, *53*(2), 125–138. https://doi.org/10.1080/00393541.2012.11518857

Tufte, E. R. (1990). *Envisioning information*. Graphics Press.

Vivirito, J. A. (2012). Confronting "difficult knowledge:" Critical aesthetics and war in the classroom [Doctoral dissertation, Northern Illinois University]. ProQuest Dissertations and Theses Global.

Watson, J. & Crick, F. (1953). Molecular structure of nucleic acids: A structure for deoxyribose nucleic acid. *Nature* 171, 737–738. https://doi.org/10.1038/171737a0

Weaver-Hightower, M. B. (2017). Losing Thomas & Ella: A father's story (a research comic). *Journal of Medical Humanities*, *38*, 215–230. https://doi.org/10.1007/s10912-015-9359-z

CHAPTER 7

Ethics of Practice for Visual Research Methods

Ethical issues are important in any discussion of research. Appropriate use of materials, language, and processes are critical to the safety of research participants and other stakeholders in the conduct of all social science inquiry. This includes conduct that influences both short-term and long-term effects on participants. Since images can be remembered for decades, the long term can be very long indeed when it comes to the use of visual research methods.

We have touched on several issues concerning the ethics of visual research methods in previous chapters of this book. In this chapter, we revisit those issues and highlight practices of ethical creation, acquisition, and use of images in research. We do this not as a coda, but as the restatement of a theme that has guided this book: researchers must be extremely attentive to their ethical stance when making, adopting, analyzing, and audiencing images. As we have discussed, the power of images makes researcher positionality perhaps even more important when using visual methods compared with other methods. A commitment to visual theory and an awareness and exposure of the researcher's positionality are ethical actions (Metcalf, 2016). We start by summarizing five major points: responsibility in social science research, the agency of imagery, images and truth, interpretation and rationality, and the moral obligation of creation.

Responsibility in Social Science Research

Standards of ethics change over time and ideas about ethical uses of imagery have as well. Since their formal origins in the 19th century, the social sciences have been plagued with what scholars now see as unethical uses of images, from cultural appropriation to conscious visual distortion and psychological manipulation. For example, early anthropologists manipulated indigenous people through images that aligned with Western prejudices (Banks & Ruby, 2011). At times, researchers' visual records have been ethically insensitive (even if technically accurate), and violated cultural beliefs about privacy, representation, and the acceptability of public viewing outside their original, cultural context. Visual deception resulting in emotional harm to participants was a feature of notorious psychological studies, such as the Milgram Shock Experiment (Milgram, 1962) and the Stanford Prison Experiment (Haney et al., 1973).

Out of concern for the ethical treatment of human beings during scientific research, the Declaration of Helsinki (World Medical Organization, 2013), first formalized in 1964 and most recently revised in 2013, established recommendations for the protection of research participants. The Declaration guidelines stress the protection of vulnerable groups, the responsibility of professionals to not only shield participants from harm, but to serve the participants' best interests, and most importantly, calls on individual nations to institute review boards to monitor the ethical conduct of research. In the United States, this call led to the Belmont Report (National Commission for the Protection of Human Subjects of Biomedical and Behavioral Research, 1979). The European Union follows protocols established by the Oviedo Convention on Human Rights and Biomedicine (1977). While national guidance for the ethical conduct of social science research may vary, the Belmont Report is typical in establishing three areas of concern: respect for persons, beneficence, and justice. These three areas are critical for the ethical conduct of image use in social science.

Respect for Persons

Informed consent and confidentiality are foundational ethical principles to social science research. Participants must understand their role in research and agree to how the visual imagery they make, or the imagery that records their likeness, will be used. Some strategies can ensure full agreement, for example, when individuals either actively respond to pictures in which they appear or to actively collaborate in the making of imagery.

However, conventional informed consent may not be sufficient. Does the participant understand potential implications of carrying a frightening research image in their iconic store? Is the participant conscious of how they will feel after a negative public reaction to an image they have created, even if presented anonymously? The researcher's responsibility is greater than confirming that a participant understands and is willing to comply.

We have discussed at great length the importance of attending to bias when selecting images to use in research because they can carry long histories of prejudice. Issues of cultural and other forms of identity require particularly careful attention when it comes to making choices about imagery. However, it is not only the images themselves that must be considered. The researcher must act in a way that is in the best interest of individual participants and groups with regard to at least two antecedents that carry bias in the research process: (a) assumptions about image-based results that come from past research; and (b) historical antecedents of visual culture that lead to assumptions about the contemporary impact of images.

Assumptions Based on Past Research

For any research method, the way resources are selected or created will influence data collection and expectations about what will be seen in the data. Therefore, decisions about not only the images chosen, but also how they will be used, should be incorporated into any original plan for research. This includes a plan for analyzing images and not assuming that participant response to an image is self-evident. For example, an extensive literature in human drawing development exists. Educator Rhoda Kellogg (1970) and others have created detailed taxonomies of children's drawing after decades of research and viewing experience (Figure 7.1). The taxonomies carry with them the assumption that if a researcher asks children to spontaneously draw images as part of a study, the researcher can reasonably expect to see drawings generally assumed to look like those created by children at a given developmental level. If a large number of drawings look dramatically different from that assumption, the researcher might have cause for doing additional research into what is influencing those differences. For example, the study itself could be introducing bias because the lack of diversity in those early studies promotes assumptions that would be inappropriately applied to the analysis of drawings by a diverse group of participants. Alternatively, an adult may have influenced the students' drawings to such an extent that they cannot be considered authentically spontaneous.

Assumptions About the Contemporary Impact of Historical Antecedents

Historical information related to visual evidence might need to be interrogated before conducting the study. Although humans have a large number of images

Visual Methods of Inquiry

Figure 7.1 Rhoda Kellogg at the Golden Gate Kindergarten in San Francisco (1967).
Billybgrant, CC BY-SA 4.0 via Wikimedia Commons.

in our iconic stores, we frequently do not know the history behind each of those images, which can carry a variety of meanings and influence interpretation differently for different people. Images can carry or elicit racial, gender, and other biases that can influence interpretation, in part, through what the authors of this book have referred to as intergraphicality. Through these interconnections, direct or indirect historical associations shape participant conscious and unconscious responses to imagery. For example, few people might be aware of the ways that American film director George Lucas drew on the imagery of Nazi film director Leni Riefenstahl in his first *Star Wars* movie, but the impact of her early Nazi films has been felt through the aesthetic of dozens of movies that seek to evoke authority and grandeur.

As another case, consider weather mapping. Weather maps have long tended to include a popular culture rainbow intensity of hues representing differences in weather (Figure 7.2). This decision to use color to indicate different weather patterns, such as temperature, originated in the early 1800s in the early days of modern meteorology. When weather mapping began to be shown on television, television continued the tradition and the rainbow increased in intensity

Ethics of Practice for Visual Research Methods

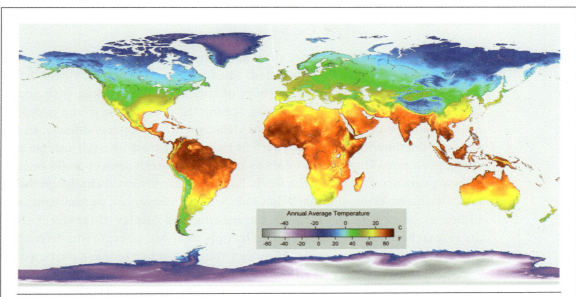

Figure 7.2 Estimated average temperature over land from 1951 to 1980, based on the interpolation of ground-level weather station data by Berkeley Earth, 2014. Robert A. Rohde/Berkeley Earth, CC BY 4.0, via Wikimedia Commons.

as visual technologies increased in sophistication. As discussed in Chapter 3, people tend to be attracted to bright colors, like the primary and secondary colors of a rainbow, and these colors have been a default palette since the early days of color, digital technologies. However, the limitations of rainbow colors make it difficult to perceive for example, subtle complexities of weather that are important to understand, particularly in a time of climate change. Recently, as the color capabilities of technology have advanced, changes have been made in weather map color schemes, making them more accessible and easier to interpret.

In some cases, art historical study related to the images that will be used in research might be appropriate. One of the authors of this book did a study of stylistic preferences that involved using historical and contemporary still lifes (Freedman, 1988). Extensive searches of still life reproductions were required to find images that were similar in content and composition, but different in style. As well as reviews of many painting reproductions, literature reviews had to be conducted about 17th-Century Dutch still life painting, the origin of Western still life, and contemporary still life styles. From these reviews, images were chosen that best suited the study. So, the act of finding evidence for the study came as a process of not only reading literature, but also viewing images, only some of which would be able to provide visual evidence relevant to the study.

Beneficence

When proposing, conducting, or evaluating research with images, a risk/benefit analysis should be conducted. Multiple types of risk may exist when making an image. One of the authors of this book has worked with young graffiti artists in her research. Photographing the art of these young people in action could be documenting a felony defacement of property offense, so the research documents could put youth at risk. In contrast, the self-esteem of a young person making a work of art as part of a research project could be hurt if their peers see and reject the work. So, researchers should challenge themselves with questions, such as: What risks will the researcher, participants, and audiences be exposed to through the making and display of imagery? Does the researcher need to adjust data collection, analysis, or reporting to protect human or non-human actors? How can the researcher prepare participants to reduce the possibility of risk? The researcher must make ethical decisions regarding the overarching good.

One argument for an aesthetic education is that aesthetics, inherently, is a search for goodness. Historically, the term aesthetics has been connected to the concept of beauty, and the definition of beauty in an aesthetic sense has been tied to goodness, enlightenment, and elevation of spirit. The philosopher Nelson Goodman (1978) argued that any task engaged with the production of a coherent form required the maker to discern "goodness of fit." This is one conception of aesthetics that can apply to research—the form of research is shaped in continual reflexive praxis requiring judgment in pursuit of the good, imbued with an attentiveness to an ethical sense of care. At its most fundamental, aesthetics is the rational exercise of such subjective judgments (Shusterman, 2006). Aesthetic judgments are made whenever imagery is created or applied to research. However, the "goodness" conception of aesthetics is complex. Sometimes images act as if they are "good" merely because their formal qualities seduce, and at times creators deliberately work against the notion of goodness in aesthetics to challenge the tradition.

The ethics of imagery includes environmental ethics, which is a social issue. Even photographs of animals and other wildlife have been manipulated to show a particular perspective or prejudice, such as to weaken arguments in support of endangered species. Production of the visual arts has long involved debates about appropriate uses of material, and specifically, whether materials have been used in environmentally responsible ways. Even photographs, which have a relatively small carbon footprint on a phone, raise environmental questions when large numbers of photographs are stored online. So, consideration of global concerns may need to be taken into account when using images in social science research.

Justice

Qualitative research has been distinguished in its concern for social justice (Denzin & Lincoln, 2018), which can involve the positionality of the researcher. For example, research may be motivated by the researcher's indignation over social injustice. As well as a general disclosing of researcher position that could influence interpretation, a statement about the goal of social justice, or a position against a particular social agenda may be appropriate in the reporting of research because it can influence the images made and selected.

However, the creators of images also speak for themselves through their work. Lewis Hine's child labor photographs, discussed in Chapter 2, sought to bring a moral outrage to the attention of a nation. Hine showed his anger at an economic system that exploited children and he created imagery that led others to feel that anger as well. A thin line exists between works that bring a moral issue into view and images that attempt to close down discussion by excluding potentially mitigating evidence. Arts-based researcher Susan Finley (2018) argues that a researcher should not shy away from a morally worthy cause. Finley suggests that to be agents of change, researchers should take on that challenge and be strident when necessary. An ethical test of an image is its power to bring human and non-human participants into broader discussion with a standard of achieving greater justice for all.

Images and Truth

It is natural to think that the creation of an image is the recording of truth. The image corresponds to something that is real, or it documents an event that happened, even if that event is the creation of the image itself. The image is not merely an illustration; it is an event. However, the visual image simultaneously erases other aspects of reality through selection and attention. Fine artist Robert Rauschenberg's erasure of a pencil drawing by Wilhelm DeKooning, and his exhibition of the almost blank piece of paper as a work of art, is a comment about this phenomenon. All images to some degree traffic in acts of disappearance that both support and disrupt our existing schematic blinders (Tervo, 2020). What an image erases and occludes is as much a point of analysis as that which the image reveals.

This may seem counter-intuitive to the idea that images correspond to truth. Seeing is supposed to be believing, as long as we can be confident that what we are seeing has not been manipulated. This is the epistemological foundation of digital technologies, such as facial recognition software; however, face recognition software has been shown to demonstrate the cultural prejudices of its initial programmers. The creation of any image depends on a process of manipulation through the use of technology, whether pencil, paint and brush, camera, or computer. Since the invention of photography, documentary photographs have been staged. Even the simple act of framing a shot includes and excludes information; smiling for the camera is an attempt to influence a data point.

In addition to being manipulated, images shift according to the contexts in which they are seen. Audiences can change the truth of an image. As an image becomes distributed through visual culture, its ethical interpretation—the truth that it reveals—may change. For example, the Italian fashion company The Colors of Benneton launched its first foray into the United States market in the 1980s with a vibrant advertising campaign that promoted the brand as inclusive across gender, race, and age. The pictures first initiated ethical praise for the representation of "truthful" images of human beings that challenged the highly stylized body images normally promoted by the fashion industry. However, the images of children (some naked) and adolescents were later scrutinized as a fetishizing of vulnerable populations (Innovative Design History, 2014). This shifting ethical reading of the advertising campaign was accentuated as Benetton introduced new and increasingly shocking images.

Social scientists who use visual imagery must be sensitive to audience interpretation and respect a broader perspective of truth than an image may seem to represent. How the audience ethically reads an image may not have a relation to the creator's initial aim. As we have discussed in earlier chapters, when an audience's interpretation of an image is divergent from the creator's intention in the context of research, an image creator cannot attempt to dismiss the audience reaction by a claiming "That is not what I meant." From a research perspective, the superior interpretation is supported by the most visual evidence—not the most impassioned exhortations or intricate philosophical calisthenics. While image creators might appeal to personal aesthetic license and personal vision, social scientists need to acknowledge visual empiricism. As in the law and medicine, empirical data may be ambiguous. In these cases, a dialogic circle is the best way for arriving at the most trustworthy interpretation.

A dialogic circle is a process through which meaning can be established through interactive discussion within a group of people. In the case of viewing images, a dialogic circle can act as a form of critique where people (perhaps the researcher and a focus group) discuss individual interpretations of an image or set of images to find an interpretive range. Members of the group are asked to generate their own interpretations, providing reasons for those interpretations from the image itself. The group should use inductive argument by assembling the evidence and making a case. In this process, there are no "right" or "wrong" answers; rather there are interpretations more or less supported by evidence. This emphasis on objective, visual evidence is a process of demonstrating deep appreciation for the form and complexity of images. It honors the image's agency.

Ethics of Practice for Visual Research Methods

In data analysis, researchers need to demonstrate an awareness of the ways the images in their projects could have worked at various levels of interpretation. Kearny and Hyde (2004) argued that images can at least confirm research participants' verbal data. However, as Sharafizad et al. (2020) demonstrate in their study of female academics, participant drawings showed more information (more openness and honesty) than participant verbal statements in interviews alone. Therefore, researchers need to consider what images might mean beyond what participants claim.

However, the ethical practices of honesty with regard to image use include creator ownership of an image of their making (even as interpretations of that image may vary by viewer), and ethical treatment of creators is imperative in research. Contemporary creators can hold copyrights on their images and seek financial remuneration if the image is reproduced. As a result, researchers must ask permission to use some contemporary images, such as fine art images less than 75 years old. As with the use of other research methods, when working with minors, researchers need to obtain written *consent* from the minor's guardian and written *assent* from the minor. When working with very young children, assent forms may incorporate visual images, such as emojis, to help assure that children understand the data collection process.

The Agency of Imagery

The information provided by an image is often dependent on the way a person encounters, experiences, or lives with the image. In such cases, the effect of an image can be like that of operatic tenor Luciano Pavarotti's rendition of the *Nessun Dorma* aria from Puccini's (1926/2002) *Turandot*, which is close to a universal, visceral response. While meaningful information about Pavarotti's performance can be counted (e.g. his album released with this aria became the best-selling classical album of all time and Pavarotti was invited to perform the aria at four FIFA World Cup Finals), what is enduring is the performance's somatic quality. The music and the specific way that Pavarotti performs it is a tacit experience; it affects people's bodies. Even if people cannot describe their response in language, they feel it. The work communicates in the space in-between words. The tune has enchanted audiences in many visual culture venues. For example, in 2007, a Welsh cell phone salesman, Paul Potts, auditioned for Simon Cowell's television variety show *Britain's Got Talent*. Utterly prosaic, awkward, and poorly dressed, he brought the audience to its feet with a rendition of *Nessun Dorma*, which carefully mimicked Pavarotti's. The YouTube video of Potts' performance shows members of the audience wiping their eyes as the initially cynical judges glance nervously at the enthusiastic crowd cheering behind them. The Hollywood movie *One Chance* tells Potts' story of how one song, in one instant, can communicate (Frankel, 2013). The tacit knowledge of that visual culture experience worked in the incredibly powerful way that much visual culture does—it can be highly emotional.

Images live on in individuals' iconic store, often continuing to influence a viewer for the rest of their life. Perhaps you remember the first original masterpiece you saw in a museum, an ancestor in an old photograph that led you to search for their life story, or a character you enjoyed watching on television as a child that you emulated in your appearance. Expand this experience to the impact of images of war, poverty, ecological disaster, and other disturbing crises. In the broadest sense, images can be thought of as actors, in both personal and cultural contexts, because they can influence people who then may act in response to that influence.

Because images are so powerful—because they can change people's minds—care is required when using them. For example, careful consideration of unconscious, as well as conscious responses to images, must be taken when research participants act as creators and viewers. That care should be taken not only in terms of the controlled environment of the research project, and the overt impact of the images related to a research question, but also with regard to potential long-term effects that may not be apparent to the participants at the time of the project.

A contemporary perspective of image viewing is that the agency of an image comes as part of a partnership among creator, image, and viewer (with experts just one set of many possible viewers). A viewer might be thought of as having an obligation to attend to and try to ascertain the intended meaning—the meaning the creator wants viewers to see—but the power of images suggests many possibilities to viewers as viewers make their own meanings.

This contemporary perspective has the advantage of pushing against the use of images that are manufactured with the intent to deceive. It invites challenges to declared or received meanings by acknowledging that images have a life of their own. However, as we have discussed, not all interpretations are equally valid. Evidence in the picture itself, and evidence drawn from the cultural context in which the picture exists, demonstrates that "some interpretations are better than others" (Barrett, 1992, p.116). Perhaps the best, most credible interpretations draw from the broadest sources of evidence (Elster, 2009).

An ethical viewer (and by extension, researcher) of images not only uses the evidence in the image and its contexts in constructing meaning but also works with that evidence to avoid attaching inappropriate, exploitative, and de-contextualized meanings. Visual evidence may exceed, indeed even conflict with, the creator's intent, demanding careful reflection. For once an image becomes attached to a lie and is embedded in an iconic store, it becomes difficult to detach the lie from it.

At the same time, this ability to become attached to a variety of meanings is what makes images so attractive in the formation of entertaining stories, myths, and other fictions where creators determine the lines of ethics. In an

Ethics of Practice for Visual Research Methods

international study, youth and young adults worked together as creators in visual culture learning communities (groups that focus on the creation of visual culture forms), such as graffiti, fanart, conceptual art, manga, and video (Freedman et al., 2013). Each of these groups had rules about appropriate behavior when members created the visual culture form. For example, among a group of fan artists, the group established rules about the appropriate interpretation of characters when they created fan art. Members of the group were not allowed to create fan art in which a character behaved in a way inconsistent with their original story. For instance, they could not show a character behaving badly who was intended by the original creator to be good.

Because the many influences on viewing make it difficult to predict precisely how viewers may respond to even a simple image, piloting images before their use in research is imperative. Images carry general associations, but new meanings are attached and interpretation is renewed over time and place. Consider the example of certain fine art masterpieces, such as Grant Wood's (1930) *American Gothic*. This work of art has been recycled over generations and used and edited in advertising, popular culture, and other fine arts. It is often used to suggest rural America. However, each time the image is used, potential new meanings become attached to it (Figures 7.3–7.5).

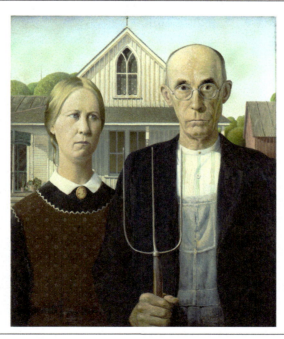

Figure 7.3 American Gothic by Grant Wood, 1930.
Public domain, via Wikimedia Commons.

Visual Methods of Inquiry

Figure 7.4 American Gothic by Gordon Parks, 1942.
Public domain, via Wikimedia Commons.

Figure 7.5 Mural Short North Arts District, Columbus, Ohio by Steve Galgas and Mike Altman, 2002.
Courtesy Carol M. Highsmith, Public domain, via Wikimedia Commons.

Interpretation and Rationality

Perhaps the most important issue of ethics related to imagery is that social scientists have avoided the use of images because their interpretation seems difficult to trust. We have discussed the variability of image interpretation as being one of the reasons that visual culture in general has not been given appropriate attention in social science research. Greater visual literacy through education can help with image interpretation, but responsible researchers must check their interpretations against logic—the interpretation of images requires the application of sense. Through a systematic analysis of visual, qualitative relationships, the use of images in research becomes a reflective, rational process of interpretation that takes the tacit into account.

Researchers may intend that participants in their studies interpret images as widely as possible. The images could have been made specifically to be used as a prompt within the context of the study to deliberately broaden interpretation by providing viewers with a variety of choices of meaning. However, images might be used to narrow interpretation as well. In either case, the researcher should test the images in a pilot study to ensure that the range of interpretation is appropriate for the study.

Because humans have both rational and impulsive responses to images, the researcher must explore interpretation as a dynamic. Often, humans respond to images emotionally because of preferences instilled in our youth (Bourdieu, 1980). Take the example of face recognition and preference. Capacities for facial recognition are based on genetic variation. In contrast, although facial preferences are based to some degree on biological considerations of attractiveness (such as symmetry), the main influence is that of environments, which are uniquely individual (Germine et al., 2015). This intuitive, emotional reaction is worth exploring for individual bias.

Another example is the response in the human brain to images of violence. Researchers at Columbia University's Functional Magnetic Resonance Imaging Research Center found that viewers have a strong emotional response to images of violence, but that response seems to be less strong when people are exposed to violent imagery on a regular basis (Kelly et al., 2007). It has long been understood that the amygdala is the part of the brain that sets off an alarm when humans see a violent image; then other parts of the brain relay this alarm to the body. Given this understanding, the researchers were not surprised to find that violent images set off both the amygdala and the orbital frontal cortex. What interested them was that with repeated exposure to the violent imagery, the inhibitory signal from the orbital frontal cortex to the amygdala—which essentially conveys the message "cool off!"—gradually grew weaker. In commenting on this study, co-author and director of the Center, Joy Hirsch noted that "This did not happen with the other control stimuli (i.e., the images showing sports action or frightened faces)... It is specific to violence" (Jacobs, 2018, para. 16).

The fact that the brain's de-escalation response gradually weakened and the aggressive response strengthened during the Columbia study points to the relevance of raising ethical questions about the use of violent imagery in research. As we have discussed in previous chapters, images teach viewers how to look at them, and in this case, they can tacitly influence the way the brain functions over time. This influence can shape reaction to images in subtle ways not necessarily apparent to viewers.

Skillful image creators know this and exploit the opportunity to their advantage. They can bait an unsuspecting viewer into traps, which could flirt with a line of ethical practice. Contemporary creators from fine artists to illustrators, designers, and advertisers intentionally engage viewers' tacit visual understanding by luring them into experiences where the viewer mentally fills in the blanks. They purposively provoke the viewer to complete the composition or finish the thought. There is a long historical tradition of artists provoking the viewer. For example, the 17th-century Flemish painter Anthony Van Dyck, for his documentary portfolio titled *The Iconography*, created over 100 individual portraits of noteworthy figures of his day and etched his own self-portrait print in which his face was fully rendered but the body was left as contours. Van Dyck stares haughtily directly into the eyes of the viewer, while the rest of his own image remains unfinished. The startling contrast of fine-grained realism against an expansive emptiness invites the viewer to psychologically fill the void surrounding this mysterious and elusive artist. Yet the artist will never be captured by the viewer's gaze, even as his portfolio presents a hundred completed images of very important people and Van Dyck places himself as a peer. We attend to his portrait among the other depictions of luminaries because of its difference, and yet, he taunts us. He will show us his world, but we will not see him (Figure 7.6).

Researchers Sara Lawrence-Lightfoot and Jessica Hoffman Davis (1997) call their method of qualitative inquiry *portraiture* as it draws on this artistic tradition of representation. They point to the portrait artist's intentional removal of detail and softening edges that draw the viewer in so that the viewer will dwell with the image. Traditionally, good portraiture reveals the character of the subject. It helps the viewer know the subject deeply. The artist, through the beauty of their medium, lures the viewer into contemplation. Lawrence-Lightfoot and Hoffman Davis contend that qualitative inquiry should ensnare its audiences in conversation. This is not done through propaganda, but instead through the craft of aesthetic forming that draws forth deep engagement with the subject. The researcher, like the portrait artist, carries an ethical responsibility in formation.

Ethics of Practice for Visual Research Methods

Figure 7.6 Self-Portrait by Sir Anthony van Dyck (c. 1626). National Gallery of Art, CC0, via Wikimedia Commons.

Images can be manipulative and the creators who make them may intend them to be so for a number of reasons: as inquiry, deception for the purpose of financial gain, flattery, or personal aggrandizement. Contemporary professional creators are aware of the power of images and the ethical implications of the power that comes from both image-making and exhibition. Creators in advertising, the sex industry, politics, and other professional fields may be hired specifically to use the power of images in an unethical manner. It is the researcher's responsibility to be aware of such uses of imagery and to either avoid manipulative images in their research or have a valid reason for using them.

The Moral Obligation of Creation

The images research participants create can have a powerful impact on them personally and socially. Because art-making is expressive as well as creative, it can be therapeutic by enabling a cathartic experience, or raise long buried, painful memories. As well as requesting a typical IRB approval for conducting human subjects research, you may be asked to include a consent or assent form specific to imagery. Video recording of participants requires a separate consent or assent form.

Generally, the moral obligations of avant-garde art creators and research creators are different. Members of those two professional communities have different expectations and make different types of judgments when it comes to their own work and the work of their peers. In contrast to the social science credo of "do no harm," art can be intentionally disruptive and include an expectation that artists and audiences bear witness and respond to uncomfortable truths. In this context, to use visual research methods, the researcher may be obligated to produce visual images that provoke.

For example, if a photojournalist were seeking to capture a telling image of a person or animal in distress, the photographer might not consider themselves obliged to drop the camera and provide aid or comfort to the afflicted individual. The question of whether journalists should help individuals in crisis or tell the wider story about the crisis is highly debated in their professional community. If the logic of the autonomy of art were followed, the researcher, when producing or applying visual images to research, would not be responsible for mitigating the pain of others as long as the research itself achieves some greater good. However, the position of social science is clear: put down the camera, stop data collection, and render aid.

The line between clear, ethical behaviors when handling the making and presenting of visual images is further blurred through the rise of doctoral programs in visual art studio practice and the advancement of arts-based methods in the social science. One area of study in these degrees is the ethics of art. Art educator Donal O'Donoghue (2009) has argued that difficult, ethically questionable visual art forces audiences and students to make their own authentic, ethical choices. Thus, a potentially unethical image could serve to bring ethical clarity when studied. The study of art autonomy unhindered by ethical restraint raises questions about whether creators should force audiences to grapple with ethical problems and think for themselves, rather than expect others to censor unpleasantness and disturbance. Art historian Claire Bishop (2012) is critical of fine artists who reject the ethical implications of their work by hiding behind a shield of aesthetic autonomy. If, as O'Donoghue suggests, a visual image's ethical ambiguity is designed to provoke engagement with an overarching ethical issue, then the researcher should state that clearly and justify the beneficence at play in the study. The spectacle of the visual cannot substitute for purposeful inquiry.

Professional communities make judgments about the quality of their work. As with other research, the work of using visual research methods is, in part, to conduct our own oversight through editorial boards, personnel committees, research commissions, doctoral student committees, and so on. As a community, researchers have common ground; one aspect of that common ground is the intention to achieve rigor in our work. Differences in defining and teaching rigor exist, but authors think of rigor as the struggle to achieve qualities of goodness. Our continuing struggle to put tacit knowledge into language makes the care we take when doing that work even more important.

Conclusion

Researchers must consider and address the five dimensions of ethical concern that have guided the discussion throughout this book: responsibility in social science research, the agency of imagery, images and truth, interpretation and rationality, and the moral obligation of creation. These dimensions are parameters for responsible action on the part of researchers when engaged in the visual. We have argued that as the visual becomes an integral part of social science research across disciplines, these parameters act as guidelines that all qualitative researchers should know.

The rise of arts-based methods in the social sciences combined with the increasing acceptance of the Ph.D. in arts practice has blurred the traditional lines that established guidelines of ethics in the social sciences and aesthetics in the fine arts. Post-structural, qualitative researchers work without guardrails, jumping lanes and breaking boundaries. The complexity of these boundaries demands that researchers take responsibility for their actions, including possible repercussions of their inquiry with regard to participants.

The generation of images that allows the researcher the ability to bring data into visuality where it can be analyzed and enter hermeneutic cycles of interpretation and fractal expansions of meaning is an immense responsibility. The ethical stance of the researcher when using the power of the visual is critical to maintaining the integrity, relevance, and trustworthiness of the research. An awareness of the generative and potentially abusive power of the visual needs to be a foundation of social science disciplines.

Research slows down those emergent processes so one can see them. This benefit of visual methods of research is apparent in the study of a hummingbird. When a hummingbird flaps its wings, they go so fast that humans cannot see them with the naked eye. But, slowing a video of the wings down enables one to visually study their construction and function. Yes, we are imposing a human technology on the seeing, but at the same time, the technology becomes a prosthetic to enhance our abilities to come to know, appreciate, and protect. The ethics of visual methods use is a way of coming to understand the critical responsibility of a community to look carefully at its own criteria for assessment and make judgments based on that care.

References

Banks, M., & Ruby, J. (Eds.) (2011). *Made to be seen: Perspectives on the history of visual anthropology.* University of Chicago Press.

Barrett, T. M. (1992). Criticizing art with children. In A. Johnson (Ed.), *Art education: Elementary* (pp. 115–129). National Art Education Association.

Bishop, C. (2012). *Artificial hells: Participatory art and the politics of spectatorship.* Verso Books.

Bourdieu, P. (1980). *The logic of practice.* Stanford University Press.

Declaration of Helsinki. (2013). World Medical Organization.

Denzin, N. K., & Lincoln, Y. S. (Eds.) (2018). *The SAGE handbook of qualitative research* (5th ed.). SAGE.

Elster, J. (2009). Interpretation and rational choice. *Rationality and Society* (21), 5–33. https://doi.org/10.1177/1043463108099347

Finley, S. (2018). Critical arts-based inquiry: Performances of resistance politics. In N. K. Denzin & Y. S. Lincoln (Eds.), *The SAGE handbook of qualitative research* (5th ed., pp. 561–575). SAGE.

Frankel, D. (2013) *One Chance* [film]. The Weinstein Company.

Freedman, K. (1988). Judgments of painting abstraction, complexity, preference and recognition by three adult educational groups, *Visual Arts Research*, *14*(2), 68–78.

Freedman, K., Heijnen, E., Kallio-Tavin, M., Karpati, A., & Papp, L. (2013). Visual culture learning communities: How and what students come to know in informal art groups. *Studies in Art Education*, *53*(2), 103–115. https://doi.org/10.1080/00393541.2013.11518886

Germine, L., Russell, R., Bronstad, P. W., Blokland, G. A. M., Smoller, J. W., Kwok, H., Anthony, S. E., Kakayama, K., Rhodes, G., & Wilmer, J. B. (2015) Individual aesthetic preferences are shaped mostly by environments, not genes. *Current Biology*, *25*(20), 2684–2689. https://doi.org/10.1016/j.cub.2015.08.048

Goodman, N. (1978). *Ways of worldmaking.* Hackett Publishing.

Haney, C., Banks, C., & Zimbardo, P. (1973). Interpersonal dynamics in a simulated prison. *International Journal of Criminology and Penology*, *1*(1), 69–97.

Innovative Design History (2014, April 8). *The United Colors of Benetton Campaign History.* https://innovativedesignhistory.wordpress.com/2014/04/08/the-united-colors-of-benetton-campaign-history/

Jacobs, T. (2018, June 4). This is your brain on violence. *Pacific Standard.* https://psmag.com/social-justice/this-is-your-brain-on-violence-4779

Kearny, K. S. & Hyde, A. E. (2004). Drawing out emotions: The use of participant-produced drawings in qualitative inquiry. *Qualitative Research 4*(3), 361–382. https://doi.org/10.1177/1468794104047234

Kellogg, R. (1970). *Analyzing children's art*. National Press Books.

Kelly, C. R., Grinband, J., & Hirsch, J. (2007). Repeated exposure to media violence is associated with diminished response in an inhibitory frontolimbic network. *PLoS ONE, e1268*(12). https://doi.org/10.1371/journal.pone.0001268

Lawrence-Lightfoot, S., & Davis, J. H. (1997). *The art and science of portraiture*. Jossey-Bass.

Metcalf, A. S. (2016). Educational research and the sight of inquiry: Visual methodologies before visual methods. *Research in Education, 96*(1), 78–86. https://doi.org/10.1177/0034523716664577

Milgram, S. (1962). *Obedience* [Film]. Alexander Street.

National Commission for the Protection of Human Subjects of Biomedical and Behavioral Research (1979). *The Belmont report*. United States Department of Health, Education, and Welfare.

O'Donoghue, D. (2009). Are we asking the wrong questions in arts-based research? *Studies in Art Education, 50*(4), 352–368. https://doi.org/10.1080/00393541.2009.11518781

Oviedo Convention on Human Rights and Biomedicine. (1977). *Convention for the protection of human rights and dignity of the human being with regard to the application of biology and medicine*. Council of Europe.

Puccini, G. (2002). Nessun dorma [audio recording]. In *The voice of Puccini*. UMG Recordings. (Original work published 1926)

Sharafizad, F., Brown, K., Jogulu, U., & Omari, M. (2020). Letting a picture speak a thousand words: Arts-based research in a study of the careers of female academics. *Sociological Research and Methods*. https://doi.org/10.1177/0049124120926206

Shusterman, R. (2006). The aesthetic. *Theory, Culture & Society, 23*(2–3), 237–252. https://doi.org/10.1177/0263276406062680

Tervo, J. (2020). Not in the name of: Time and disappearance in ethics of art education. In C.-P. Buschkühle, D. Atkinson, & R. Vella (Eds.), *Art – ethics – education*. Brill Sense.

Wood, G. (1930). American gothic *[Painting]*. Chicago Art Institute.

World Medical Organization (2013). World Medical Association Declaration of Helsinki: Ethical principles for medical research involving human subjects. *Journal of the American Medical Association, 310*(20), 2191–2194. https://doi.org/10.1001/jama.2013.281053

Index

Note: Page references in *italics* denote figures, in **bold** tables and with "n" endnotes.

abduction 122
Aboriginal: groups 51; paintings 8, *8*, 12, *13*
Abstract Expressionism 137
Adaptive Comparative Judgment (ACJ) 151
Adorno, Theodor 89
advertisements 76, 106, 123
advertisers 36, 130, 210
advertising 70, 77, 105–106; campaigns 105, 204; creators in 211; images 105; and youth identity 18
aesthetics 103; autonomy 212; cognitive aesthetics 37, 53, 55n1; dimension 89; discipline of 48; education 202; empirical 47–48; engagement 62; experience 79, 91, 98; imagery 22–24; judgments 202; learning 18; Modernism 86–90, *87–88*, *87–88*, *87–88*, *90*; new materialism 50–52; qualities 85, 92, 167; response 91; visual aesthetics 91–92
agency: agency of images 205–208; agential realism 51; human agency 35, 125; material agency 21–22; non-human 28, 125; personal agency 99–100
Albers, Josef 38
All Star Comics 119
Altman, Mike *208*
American Civil War 11
American Gothic 119, 207, *207, 208*
The Americans (Frank) 103
amygdala *see* brain
analysis: analysis of images 156–171; of data 20, 31, 67, 165, 205; formal analysis 157, 159, 165; qualitative 159, 193; quantitative 147, 149, 167, 193; in research 158; symbolic 159; textual 101, 161; visual 101–102, 150–151
analytic precision 45
analytic rubrics 167
Angkor Wat 10, *10*
animation 14, 73
anthropocentric: attitude 48; foundations of modern philosophy 69; intent 50
anthropologist(s) 102, 103, 117, 130, 132, 198
anthropology 102–103
archeologist(s) 78, 131
Archibald, Mandy 160
architecture 8, 66
Arcimboldo, Giuseppe 130, *178*
Arnheim, Rudolph 40
art(s): avant-garde 87; education 108–109; educators 108; fine art 150, 158, 205, 207; participant-made 129; representational 128; school 151; therapy 107; visual arts (*see* visual arts)
Art as Experience (Dewey) 64, 79, 152
art assessment requirements **163–164**
art critic 49, 64, 150, 159
art criticism 40, 63, 80, 91, 159; *see also* criticism
art education 16, 28, 61, 70, 74, 108–109; art and design education 32, 38; art teaching 19
art educator(s) 47–48, 107–109, 120, 138–139
artifact(s) 8, 17, 21, 61, 63, 127–128, 130–131
Artifact Collection 129–130, *177, 178*

Index

artificial intelligence 25
artist(s): avant-garde 28, 87; Chinese 15; contemporary 138; court 10; European 12–13; historic 76; Modernist 89–90; postmodern 69; Shoujo manga 67; social 93; visual 99
Artistic Iteration 134, *183*
art materials *see* materials
a/r/tography 108
arts-based research 159; *see also* visual research
arts-based research methods 1, 21, 24, 67, 108, 117, 121, 159–160, 212
assent form(s) 205, 212; *see also* Institutional Review Board
assessment 65, 108, 151, 162, 166
assumptions: based on past research 199; and historical antecedents 199–201
audience(s): of images 204, 205; of research 138–139
audience-created art 19
audience interpretation 104, 204; *see also* interpretation
Australian Aboriginals 51
authoritarianism 40
avant-garde art 87

Baldacchino, John 101
Bang, Molly 65
Banks, M. 103
Barad, Karen 35, 51
Barnes, Albert C. 151–152
Barney, Daniel 139, *189*
Barone, Tom 54
Baroque 89
Barnett, Michael *8*
Barrett, Terry 61
Baudrillard, Jean 105–106
Bauhaus 38
becoming 49, 94, 108, 135
behavior: ethical 212; human 4, 19; social 4–5
behavioral patterns 20
beliefs 2, 4, 75–76, 87, 91, 103, 120, 123, 162, 198
Belmont Report 198
benchmark(s) 32, 66, 123, 125, 126, 152; *see also* visual benchmarking
beneficence 202
Benjamin, Walter 89
Berger, John 49, 63–64
Berkeley Earth *201*
Berlyne, Daniel 79
bias(es) 120

Bible 8
Birch, Willie 128, *175*
Bishop, Claire 212
Black Lives Matter movement 19
Bohr, Niels 35
Bonaparte, Napoleon 87, 139, *190*
Boughton, George Henry 107
Bourdieu, Pierre 64, 165
brain 4, 11, 24, 26–28, 37–38, 42–45, 68–70, 91, 120, 122–125, 133, 159, 209–210
brain research 4
Breton, Jules Adolphe 107
bricolage, vision as process of 45–47
Britain's Got Talent 205
Brown, Nicole 160
Brusky, Joe *188*
Bunjil Shelter *8*
business 105–106
Butler, Judith 106
Butler-Kisber, Lynn 133, *181*

Calvin Klein 106
camera(s) 3, 14–16, 37, 62, 94, 102, 105, 121, 127–128, 136, 161, 204, 212
cartography 110, 132
cartoon(s) 59, 73; *see also* comics
Cartwright, Stephen 139, *189*
Catelazo, Tomas 53
cave paintings 8, 78–79, 127
Chambers, David 19–20
children's drawing(s) 19–20, 46–47, 77, 199
Čižek, Franz 108
Classical period 89
Clifford, J. 102
climate: change 201; justice 138; *see also* global warming
cognitive: aesthetics 37, 53, 55n1; development 47; psychologist 45; vision 38, 45, 46; vision scientist(s) 45–46
Cohen-Evron, Nurit 75
collage 132–133, 136
collage methods 132–133, *181*
color(s) 16, 23, 26, 28–29, 36, 53, 66–70, 73, 78, 90, 137, 148–150, 155–159, 200–201; *see also* hue
Color Field painting 137
Colors of Benneton 204
Comenius, John Amos 15
comic(s) 18, 59, 67, 69; cartoon 59, 73; manga 67, 207
Comic-Con *18*
communication 104–105; visual communication 21, 46, 66, 98

Index

communities of agreement 31, 60, 93, 102, 149; *see also* expert community
computer 20, 62, 121, 204
computer-manipulated photograph 150
conceptual art 207
conceptual framework(s) 36–37, 55, 59, *60*, 85–86, 107, 118, *118*, 125
confidentiality 198; *see also* Institutional Review Board (IRB)
confirmation bias 120
connoisseurship 151
conscious 32, 35–38, 45, 94
consciously 26, 64, 73, 75, 106
consciousness 47, 70, 72, 122–123
consent 101, 198, 205, 212; *see also* Institutional Review Board (IRB)
constructionist theorists 69
constructivism 37; perceptual 45–47
constructivists 45, 47, 50, 89
consumer(s) 36, 105–106, 110
contemporary: art therapy practitioners 107; images 86–90, *87–88*, *90*; perceptual constructivism 45–47; popular visual culture 109
content: expressive 60, 62–64; of the image 165, 201; symbolic 62, 90, 129, 193; visual 7
context(s): analysis 164–166; creation 158; viewer 158
Cooke, Ebenezer 19
core knowledge 21, 46–47
Correspondent Figures 139, *189*
Cosier, Kim 138, *188*
cosplay 129
covert resistance **163–164**
COVID-19 ABR Consortium *180*, *192*
Cowell, Simon 205
create 154–155
creation 154–155; context 158; moral obligation of 211–213
Creative and Mental Growth (Lowenfeld) 107
creativity 106–107
creator(s): co-creator(s) 93, 128; creator-researchers 140
Crick, Francis 124
Crick, Odile 133, *182*
criteria 30, 80, 147, 154, 155–158, 166–167, 213
critical analysis 32, 65, 94
critical moment 128
critical pedagogy 162
critical theories 51, 89; *see also* theory
criticism: art 40, 63, 80, 91, 159; cultural 137; visual 86, 90–93

critique 150–151
cross-disciplinary 85, 104
Csikszentmihalyi, Mihaly 77
Culshaw, Susan 159–160
cultural: appropriation 198; capital 64; contexts 30, 74, 166, 198, 206; critique 137; groups 19, 60, 79, 92; issues 29; knowledge 64, 91; meanings 90; observation 47; traditions 99; understandings 35
cultures: and images 88, *88*; international youth 89; visual 18–21, 109; *see also* visual culture, popular culture
curriculum 16, 32, 54, 63, 107

data: empirical 101, 204; image as 123, 129–130, 153, 155; manipulation of 43; numerical/quantitative 93, 132–133, 139, 149, 166–167; raw 130, 139; verbal 205; visual 2, 4, 21, 31, 52, 71, 94, 129, 161, 164
data analysis 20, 31, 67, 165, 205
data collection 21, 25, 30, 129, 135, 161, 199, 202, 205
data visualization 32, 38, 133
Da Vinci, Leonardo 13–14, 20, 128, 148, *174*
Declaration of Helsinki 198
deconstruction 52
deduction 29
Deleuze, G. 40, 49–50, 94, 100, 135
Delso, Diego *10*
Derrida, Jacques 40
design: elements of 65–69; principles of 65–69
designers 19, 38, 106, 156, 210
development 46, 47–48; *see also* children's drawings
Dewey, John 49, 52, 54, 55n1, 63–64, 79, 80, 93, 117, 152
dialogic circle 204
didactic: images 78–79; instruction 47; power of visual form 30
difficult knowledge 75, 124, 136, 162
digital: art 131; design 70; drawing 131; fabrication 130; images 2, 19, 166; media 7, 62, 64; methods 165; technologies 17, 79, 130, 134, 165, 201, 203; tools 165; visual culture 151; visual imaging 120
dissensus 93
documentation 25, 123, 127
double-coding 66–67; *see also* dual coding
Dow, Arthur Wesley 66
Drake, Sarah 15
Draw-a-Man Test 20

219

Index

Draw-A-Scientist Test 20
drawing: as artistic process 51; as artwork 124; children's 19–20, 46–47, 77, 199; digital 131; gesture 131; implements 158, 160
Dretske, Fred 45
dual coding 24
Duchamp, Marcel 101
Duck Soup (McCarey) 107
Dürer, Albrecht 14

Eastern Zhou period 8
ecological optics 42–45
education 107–109; aesthetics 202; art 108–109; researchers 3, 117, 156; visual research methods 107–109; *see also* art and design education
educational psychologists 48
educational researchers 91, 117, 130
Efland, Arthur 66
Einstein, Albert 122
Eisner, Elliot 91, 110, 159
elaboration 49, 106–107
elementary school 20, 46; *see also* school
elements and principles of design 65–69
Ellingson, Laura L. 165
embodied analysis 85
embodied practice 136–137, *186*
Embodied Research Methods (Thanem and Knights) 160, 165
Embodiment in Qualitative Research (Ellingson) 165
emojis 59, 205
emotions: and colors 90; and knowledge 90–93
empirical: aesthetics 47–48; data 101, 204; empirical aesthetics 47–48; evidence 69–71; research 49, 61–62; structure 99–100
empirical evidence: objectivity and subjectivity 70–71; validity and reliability 71; visual qualities and new materialism 69–71
empiricism 69, 204
empiricist 37, 99
endogenous *see* eye movements
Enlightenment 10, 150, 202
environment: complex 43; controlled 206; dingy 53; educational 162; ethics 202; exhibition 140, 159; on-line gallery 140; virtual 140; visual 91
environmental ethics 202
envisioned futures 137–138, *187*, *188*; Social Art 138; visual advocacy 137–138
Envisioned Futures 135, 137–138

epistemological humility 54
epistemology 4
Erased de Kooning Drawing (Rauschenberg) 101
erasure 101
ethical viewer 206
ethics: of art 212; environmental 202; issues 197, 209; of practice for visual research methods 197–213; in social sciences 213; *see also* Institutional Review Board
ethnographic: art-making 138; studies 88, 102, 130
ethnography: defined 130; visual 130–132
European Congress of Qualitative Inquiry (ECQI) 2
European Union 198
evidence: within the context 73–74; of creator intent 74–75; empirical 69–71; formal 158; image as 132–133; measurement 149; within the object 72–73; objective 70; qualitative 149; sensory 72–73; symbolic 158; of viewer association 75–76; visual 119–120, 147–193
Experience and Nature (Dewey) 64
expert community 71, 147; *see also* communities of agreement
expertise 31, 64–65, 71, 74, 149, 151–152
expressive content 60, 62–64
eye: 'eye is a camera' 37; movements 23, 26, 39, 73, 78

facial recognition 203, 209
facial recognition software 203
factual knowledge *see* knowledge
Fairey, Shepard 137
Fallis, S. W. *17*
falsified images 120
fanart 207
fashion 110, 129–130, 151, 159
fashion industry 204
Fechner, Gustav Theodor 55n1
Federal Office of Topography, Switzerland (swisstopo) *173*
feeling, and knowing 92
feminist: ideals 119; researchers and theoreticians 50; studies 103
fiction 52–54
field notes 131, 160
figure: figure and ground 68–69; human figure 77, 166
Filbin, Deborah 162
film 104, 107–108, 128, 140, 200
Filo, John 104

Index

fine art 150, 158, 205, 207; *see also* art
fine artist(s) 152–153, 203, 210, 212
Finley, Susan 203
flexibility 27, 106–107; phenomenological 86, 93–94
flow 77
Floyd, George 19
fluency 106–107
focal point 68
focus group 204
formal evidence 158
formal qualities 24, 72, 74, 76, 129, 153, 155, 157, 161, 165–169; *see also* formal visual qualities; visual qualities
formal visual qualities: elements and principles of design **65**, 65–69; visual elements 67–68; visual principles 68–69; *see also* formal qualities; visual qualities
formative: critique 102; feedback loops 134
Foucault, Michel 51, 89–90
framework(s) 36–37, 55, 59, *60*, 85–86, 107, 118, *118*, 125
Framework for Visual Arts Research 99, *99*
Frank, Robert 103
Frankfurt School 89
Freedman, Kerry 66, 159, 167
Freire, Paulo 138
Freitas, Elizabeth de 133
French Post-Impressionism 152
Froebel, Friedrich 20

Galgas, Steve *208*
Galileo Galilei 14–15
games; *see also* popular culture 18, 73
Garza, Carmen Lopez 128
Gauguin, Paul 152–153
gaze 102, 210; male gaze 49, 76; Western gaze 102
generalizability 134
genre 156–157; in visual arts 157
geography 109–110
Gerstenblatt, Paula 136, 160
Gertz, Clifford 40
Gestalt 23, 26; psychologists 38, 43, 46; psychology 37, 38–42, 45; vision theory 38, *39*
Gestaltists 40, 42
Gibson, James J. 42–45
Gilliam, Sam 137, *186*
Glackens, William 151–152
Glasser, Barney 135
global warming 128; *see also* climate
Goodenough, Florence 20

Goodenough-Harris Drawing Test 20
Goodman, Nelson 22, 202
goodness of fit 202
Goya, Francisco de 87–88, *87*
graffiti 202, 207
graphic design(s) 38, 43
graphic novel(s) 128, 134, 140, 166; *see also* comics; sequential art
Greenberg, Clement 63
grounded theory 135; *see also* theory
Guatemala 53, 138
Guattari, Félix 49–50, 94, 100, 135
Gude, Olivia 67

Hallowell, John K. *17*
Hannes, Karin 161
Harper, Donald 103
Harvard University 151
Heidegger, Martin 80
Helmholtz, Herman 45
Henry VIII (King of England) 10, *12*
hermeneutic 93, 101, 110, 213
Hernandez, Ester 137, *187*
higher order thinking 47–48
high school 20; art student social commentaries 165, 167; art teachers 162, **163**, **164**; *see also* education
high vision 46–47
Hine, Lewis 41–43, *42*, *43*, 53, 128
Hirsch, Joy 209
historical materialism analysis 85
historical record 10, 11, 16
Hoffman Davis, Jessica 210
Hofsess, Brooke 94, *180*
Hokusai, Katsushika 88, *88*
Holbein, Hans 10, *12*
holistic 23; rubrics 170, **171**
hue 22, 68, 70, 166
human agency 35
human brain 11, 28, 69, 133, 209
human sensory system 48
Hyde, A. E. 205
hyper-real 17
hyper-reality 61

I Come Warm, I Come Gentle, I Come Strong (Ourlicht) 130
iconic store 31, 71, 75, 94, 117, 156, 200, 206; building 119–120; common 152
The Iconography (Van Dyck) 210
"I have a dream" speech 119
illustrate: images 117–118, **170–171**; religious manuscripts 8; visual records 128

Index

image(s): agency of 205–208; and culture 88, *88*; interpretation of 3–4, 54, 155–156, 209–211; maker 92; making of 94, 108, 198; meaning of 27; and social change 89; and symbol systems 89; textual response to 130–131, *179*; viewer 92; visual 1, 7, 32, 37–38, 40, 49–50, 54, 62, 72, 78, 86–87, 103, 106–108, 129–130, 133–140, 148–149, 165–166, 212
Image Analysis Matrix (IAM) 31–32, 127, 147, 172–192
Image as Data 123, 129–130, 153. 155
Image as Investigation 124, 125, 132–135, 154
Image as Record 123, 127–128, 153–155
Image as Report 138–140, 154–155; Research Illustration 139; Research Presentation 139–140
Image as Reporting 124–125
Image Assembly 132–133, *181*, *182*; collage methods 132–133; scientific visualization 132, 133
Image as Theorizing 124, 135–138, 154; envisioned futures 137–138; reflexive making 135–137
images function: attention and focus thought 76–77; didactic and convince 78–79; images are information 77–78; past influencing future 79
Impressionist 12, 158
Independencia, Lima, Peru *14*
Indigenous: knowledge systems 48, 69; people 102, 198
inductively 29
industrial work 16
infant 46, 130; cognitive psychological research 23; participants 20; pre-verbal 45
inferential 52; reasoning of interpretation 61–62; visual 133; *see also* reasoning
inferential reasoning 61–62
informed consent 198 *see* consent
inquiry: Studio Inquiry 133–135; and visual culture 21
Institutional Review Board (IRB) 211
integration 4, 29
intent: anthropocentric 50; artist 27; creator 72, 74–75, 159, 206
intention: artist 27, 158; creator 27, 31, 204; of research 162; *see also* intent
intentional phenomena 93
interdisciplinary: cultural theory 50; knowledge 167, **169–170**
intergraphicality 24, 200

International Baccalaureate 124, 149
International Congress of Qualitative Inquiry (ICQI) 2
international youth culture 89
interpretation(s) 149, 156, 209–211; audience 104, 204; of images 3–4, 54, 155–156, 209–211; inferential reasoning of 61–62; range of 41, 72, 119, 123, 209; subjective 102; viewer 75
interpretivist 61, 99
intertextuality 24
interview/interviewing 3, 21, 124, 130, 141, 160–161, 205
intuitive reaction 40, 43, 209
Ishikawa, Katsuhiko 129

Jameson, Fredric 66
Jenks, Charles 66
Jesse Window 9
journalism 104–105
judge 28, 45, 71, 148, 150, 153
judgment 147–193; analysis of research images 156–171; criteria 155–156; Image Analysis Matrix (IAM) 172–192; qualitative analyses 148–153; of quality 147–148, 151; quantitative analyses 148–153; reliable 153–155; *vs.* taste 151–153; zone of image interpretation 156
junior high school 20
justice 75, 203; climate 138; social 99, 137, 203; *see also* social justice

Kearny, K. S. 205
Kekulé, August 122
Kellogg, Rhoda 199, *200*
Kent State University 104
Kerschensteiner, Georg 19
King, Martin Luther 119
Klein, Calvin 106
Knights, David 105, 160, 165
knowing, and feeling 92
knowledge: core 21, 46–47; cultural 64, 91; difficult 75, 124, 136, 162; and emotion 90–93; factual 25; new 14, 30–31, 87, 106; qualitative 93; tacit 25–26, 40, 46–47, 80, 123–124, 129, 133–134, 162, 165, 206; visual 24, 31, 46, 60, 62, 65
Kooning, Wilhelm de 101, 203

labyrinth 136
La Mujer de los Siete Nombres movie 77–78
language 50, 59; academic 70; appropriate way to use 69; and images 134;

Index

metaphorical use of 22; Polanyi on 40; spoken 23–24; traditional 25; and visuality 107
Languages of Art (Goodman) 22
Lannenranta, Markus 22
Lascaux, France 127, *174*
Latinx 89
Lawrence, Jacob 128
Lawrence-Lightfoot, Sara 210
LeBlanc, Natalie 134, *183*
Leuba, Namsa 153
Limbourg brothers *11*
limitations: of interpretation 27; of language 69; of textual interpretation 124
lines of flight 49, 94
linguistic 46; explanation 40; imperialism 24; mental processes 136; postmodern 50; pre-linguistic 45, 131; theorists 50
literacy: text-based 22; visual (*see* visual literacy)
Little Red Riding Hood (Grimm) 65
Liu Cai 9
Lockwood, Trieste *181*
logo(s) 119
logocentric 69
Loika, Pat *18*
Lolita 129, *177*
Lowenfeld, Victor 107
Lucas, George 200
Lucero, Jorge 136, *186*
Luquet, Georges-Henri 19

Magritte, René 150
male gaze 49, 76; *see also* gaze
manga 67, 207; *see also* comics
manipulated 17, 25, 104, 120, 203–204; digitally images 154; environmental ethics 202
manipulation: of clay 100; of data 43; opportunistic 20; problem of 25; psychological 198; of symbols 64; of symbols and visual elements 134
manipulative: images 211; practices of commercial marketing 131
Mannay, Dawn 104, 110
map 12, *14*, 100, 127, 132, 133, 139, 201
mapping 106, 132, 139, *190*, 200
Marcus, G. E. 102
Marcuse, Herbert 89
Marx, Karl 150
Marxist historical materialism 51
Maryland Historical Society 140, *192*
mass produced 15–17

material(s) 63–65, 67, 69, 100, 103, 161, 202; influences 62; monumental 11; natural 51; objects 22; qualitative 63; thinking with 79–80; visual 30, 61; world 50
materiality 62, 110; contextual 103; of images 158; nomadic 63
Materia Medica (Dioscoride) 8
Matisse, Henri 152
McCloud, Scott 140
McNiff, Shaun 107
meaning: attached 119, 123; construction 47–48; cultural 90; divergence of 26–27; of image(s) 27; intended 68, 149, 206; levels of 41, 62–63; multiple 27, 148; tacit 47–48
media: digital 7, 60, 62, 64–65; traditional 103; visual 2–3, 103
media arts 19, 131
media studies 21, 70
medium 98, 156–158, 210; visual 74
Meisel, Steven 105
memes 119
Merian, Maria Sibylla 15, *16*
metaphor 37, 44, 46, 134; text-based 85; visual 122–123
metaphorical thinking 134
methodology/ies: emergent 100; photo-voice 44; research 31, 67, 108, 110; visual a/r/tographic 108
Michelangelo 51, 67
Middle Ages 8, 12
Miebach, Natalie 139, *190*
Milgram Shock Experiment 198
Miller, David 20
mimesis 150
Minard, Charles Joseph 139, *190*
Mining the Museum exhibition 140
Mirabella 130
model(s) 52–53; in advertising 130; DNA 124; rhetorical 157; textual 156; theoretical 53
Modernism: aesthetic 86–90, *87–88, 90*; *The Third of May 1808* 87, *87–88*
Modernist 66, 86–87, 89–90, 92
Mona Lisa 119, 148
Monet, Claude 158–159
monumental materials 11
moral obligation of creation 211–213
morals 8, 16, 107, 203, 211–213
motion 49–50, 100; continuous 39; function of 46; pictures 17; repetitive 41
Mullican, Matt 136, *185*

223

Index

Mural Short North Arts District, Columbus, Ohio *208*
museum(s) 27, 61, 72–74, 150, 153, 206; *see also* Museum of Modern Art
Museum of Modern Art 17, 136, 159, *185*

narrative(s) 11, 54, 90, 106, 138; defined 140; visual 140, *191*
Native Americans 74, 119
nature: artists 15; of images 86; traditional approach 52; visual facts 127; visual imagery 37
negative space 38, 69
neo-colonial studies 102
neo-Marxist Frankfurt School 89
Nessun Dorma (Pavarotti) 205
new materialisms 69–71; aesthetic foundations of 50–52
Nixon, Richard *176*
nomadic materiality 63
non-human: communities 107; interactions 128; participants 203
non-human agencies 28, 125
non-linear 107, 132, 160
nonlinguistic 43
non-objective art 90
non-visual 24, 132
Norman, Don 43
numeric: data 133, 149; explanation 40; expression of probability 52; information 133; symbol systems 46
numerical data 132–133, 139, 149; *see also* data

Obama, Barack 137
objectivity 70–71
observation: behavioral 124; cultural 47; as visual criticism 91–92
O'Donoghue, Donal 44, *212*
Oliveri, Michael 133, *182*
One Chance (movie) 205–206
online: images accessible 120, 154; photographs stored 202
On Quality in Art (Rosenberg) 62
ontological: concern regarding humans 49–50; creator's, presence 107
ontological turn 49–50
ontology 4
optics: ecological 37, 42–45
originality 106–107
Ourlicht, Laurie 130, *178*
overt resistance **163–164**
Oviedo Convention on Human Rights and Biomedicine 198

painting(s): Australian Aboriginal rock art 8, 12; cave 8, 78–79; dreamtime 12, *13*; emotional 88; Gauguin's 153; landscape 29; of Shei-Chau Wang 135; Tahitian 152
Palmer, Stephen 45
paradigm 32, 37, 43, 46
Parks, Gordon *208*
participant-made art 129, *177*
participant-made photographs 124
participants: infant 20; non-human 203; textual comments about imagery 161–164
participant textual response to images 130–131
pattern(s) 46, 66, 68, 80, 103, 133; behavioral 20; visual 14, 39, 41
pattern recognition 41
Pauwels, Luc 104, 110, 125
Pavarotti, Luciano 205
peer review 27
perception 48–54; cognitive 40–41, 45; critical 38; embodied 48; empiricist interpretation of 37; enlargement of 101, 110; gestalt 41; sensory 48; unconscious 38; visual (*see* visual perception)
perceptual: array 38, 46; constructivism 45–47; experience 40; knowledge and experience 37; scientists 26; system 26, 45; world 41
performativity 105–106
personal agency 100
perspective: multiple 100; research 77, 204; scientific 13; social science 89, 150
phenomenological: analysis 150; flexibility 86, 93–94
philosophers 45, 48–49, 55, 76, 93, 105–106, 202
philosophical speculation 36
phone, mobile 1, 121
photodocuments 127
photo elicitation 21, 94, 104, 130, 153
photograph(s) 17, 19, 21, 202; computer-manipulated 150; as data 123; documentary 25, 204; as evidence 120; and memory 120; participant-made 124, 155; snapshot 154; stimuli 155
photographer(s) 16, 75, 103, 105, 130–131, 134, 212
photographic images 48, 120
photography 7, 17, 89, 103, 160, 204
photojournalism 104–105, 128
photojournalists 104–105, 128, 130, 212
photovoice 94, 105, 131
photowalk 94

224

Index

physical sciences 25
physiologists 45
Picasso, Pablo 152
picture(s) 41–42, 45, 49, 52, 130, 156, 204, 206; categorizing 101; historical 105; and meanings 66; motion 17; photojournalistic 104; unadulterated 105; *see also* image(s); photograph(s)
Picture Study Movement 107
Picture This: How Pictures Work (Bang) 65
Pilgrims Going to Church (Boughton) 107
pilot study 71, 76, 209
plane of immanence 49
Plato 150
point of view 100, 103, 128; *see also* perspective
Polanyi, Michael 38, 40
political: advertisements 123; manipulators 40; power 10; pressure for social change 89; reformers 128; statement 139
politics 211
popular arts 89
popular culture 18, 79, 91, 125, 200, 207
portfolio 149, 151, 210
portrait(s) 10, *17*, 210; collage 160; fashioned 136; photographed 101
portraiture 157, 210
positionality 197, 203
posthuman 69
posthumanism 51
Post-Impressionism 152
postindustrial countries 18
post-intentional phenomena 93
postmodern: art and architecture 66; considerations 70; linguistic theorists 50; principles 66
postmodernist 69
post-qualitative research 33, 70, 122, 135
post-structural 33, 70, 85, 89, 213
Potts, Paul 205–206
Powell, Kimberly 132
pragmatic compliance **163–164**
pre-12 school 46
pre-conscious 131
prejudice(s) 61, 198, 199, 202, 203
pre-linguistic 30, 45, 131
pre-symbolic thinking 63–64
principles of design 60, 65–69, 70, 90, 120
producer(s) 50, 108, 130
professional communities 70–71, 122, 149, 212; *see also* communities of agreement
propaganda 40, 108, 210
Prosser, Jon 103

prosthetics 53, 135–136, 213
provenance 103, 153–154
Pruitt, Robert, 187
psychoanalysis 85
psychobiological: functions 92; responses 149; visual systems 70
psychobiology 30, 69–70
psychological: cognitive research 23; concepts 36; integration of images 4; manipulation 198; studies 108, 198; theory of perception 37; visual perception 35
psychologists 38, 40, 42–43, 45–48
psychology 106–107; art therapy 107; creativity 106–107
publishers 24, 121
Puccini, Giacomo 205

qualitative: analyses 148–153, 193; evidence 149; inquiry 110, 210; knowledge 93; methods 25, 27, 30, 110; post- 33, 70, 122, 135; relationships 55, 150, 152, 209; research 25, 137, 203; researchers 1–2, 110, 122, 131, 141, 213; research methods 1, 21, 32; studies 29; thought 80
quality 147–148; aesthetic 167; of images 147–148, 153, 167; line 14, 67; visual 18, 23, 24–25, 28, 51, 53, 61, 65–70, 79, 92, 151
quantifiable 107
quantitative: analyses 93, 148–153, 166–167; information 193; knowledge 30; measures 52, 166; thought 80
queering 100, 101, 108, 154

Rancière, Jacques 93
rationality 209–211
Rauschenberg, Robert 101, 203
realism: agential realism 51; social realism 125
reality: hyper-reality 61; virtual reality 1
reasoning: deductive 52; inferential 52, 61–62
record(s): visual 54, 79, 94, 102, 128, 132, 136, 150, *176*; *see also* Image as Record
reflexive 202; analysis 101; consumers of art 110; dialogue 102; manner 36; process of gathering 132
reflexive making 135–137, *185*, *186*; embodied practice 136–137; therapeutic expression 136
reliability 25, 31, 52, 60, 69, 134, 151; determinations of 71; empirical evidence 71

Index

reliable judgment 153–155
Renaissance 8, 12, 14, *15*, 37, 86, 89, 128
representational art 128
representation(s): visual 8, 12, 36, 46, 89, 124, *182*, *189*
reproduction(s) 49, 66, 89, 101, 103, 119, 159, 201
research: as acts of fiction 52–54; arts-based 159; creation 121; educational 67, 85, 91; empirical 49, 61, 62; feminist 50; functions of images in 59–80; images function in 76–79; processes 21, 24; project 30, 74, 100, 110, 123–125, 139, 148, 154, 156, 158, 161, 164, 167, 172, 202, 206; questions 2, 21, 31, 32, 80, 117, 121–122, 125, 132, 157–158; scientific 60, 198; social science 198–203; sociological 64; therapeutic 107; visual (*see* visual research); as visual criticism 90–93; *see also* arts-based research methods; qualitative; quantitative; social science research; visual research
research creation 121
researcher(s): arts-based 1, 22, 139, 203; brain 4; education 3, 117, 156; qualitative 1–2, 110, 122, 131, 141, 213; social 2, 32; social science 2, 60, 140, 161; visual 2, 31, 50, 52, 102, 138–139, 156
Research Illustration 139, *189*, *190*
research image analysis 156–171; contexts 164–166; participants' textual comments about imagery 161–164; relevant qualities and contexts 158–159; research questions and purposes 157–158; through deep study 159–160
Research Image Framework (RIF) 31, *118*, 123–125; defined 117–118; expanding 125–140, **126**; Image as Data 123, 129–130; Image as Investigation 124; Image as Record 123, 127–128; Image as Reporting 124–125; Image as Theorizing 124, 135–138
Research Presentation 139–140, *191*, *192*; visual exhibition 140; visual narrative 140
research questions 121–122, 157–158
retina 43, 45
revisions 19, 110, 134
rhetorical situation 156–157
Rhoades, Mindi, *180*
Ricci, Carrado 19
Riefenstahl, Leni 108, 200
rigor 30, 213

Riis, Jacob 89, 128, *175*
risk(s) 54, 69, 202; *see also* Institutional Review Board (IRB)
Rivera, Diego 128
robot 45–46; design 1; laundry 45
robotics 46
Rolling, James 22, *23*, 100, 110
Roosevelt, Theodore 128
Rose, Gillian 61–63, 109–110, 138–139
Rosenberg, Harold 63
Rosenberg, Jakob 62
rubrics: analytic 167; holistic 170, **171**; image coding example **168–170**; for scoring 166–171
Rumpelstiltskin effect 11

Saint Louis Art Museum 9
schema(s) 4, 41, 50, 77, 203
school: elementary 20, 46; high 20, 91, 124, 138, 162, **163–164**, 165, 167; pre-12 46; public 16, 19; secondary 28, 107
science 29, 32, 35, 37–48, 52–53, 85, 122
scientific: experiments 38; knowledge 37
scientific visualization **96**, 123, 132, 133, *182*; *see also* visualization
scientist(s) 2, 3, 12, 14–15, 19–20, 25, 26, 37, 45–47, 55, 73, 89, 92, 102, 103, 105, 130, 133, 204
sculptures 8, 10, 17, 51, 138–139, 148, 166
self-expression 129
selfie 148, 153
semiotic: analysis 3, 49; code 49; imagery 22–24; markings 101; rules 80; signs 85; systems 3, 45
sense impressions 37
sensory: experience 55; information 80; perception 48; systems 48
sequential: art 128, 134, 140, *191*; drawings 14; movement 14; process 101
Shahn, Ben 128
Sharafizad, F. 205
Shields, Sara Scott 132, *180*
Shooting Back 105
Shusterman, Richard 63
Siegesmund, Richard 161
signs 38, 45, 49, 62, 85, 89
simulacrum 106
sketch(es) 102, 131, 132, 154, 155
sketching 100–101, 154–155
social: action 100; behaviors 4–5; contexts 3, 62, 64, 91, 101, 165; control 10; critique 89; issues 93, 109
Social Art 92–93, 138, *188*

Index

social change 89, 128, 137; and images 89; *see also* justice; social justice
social justice 99, 137, 203; *see also* justice
social life, and visual culture 18–21
Socially Engaged Art *see* Social Art
Social Realism 128
social research and visual arts 29–30
social science: assumptions 199–201; beneficence 202; discipline(s) 21, 31, 65, 85, 89, 94, 198–203; field(s) 25, 31, 102; inquiry 33, 137, 197; investigation 19–20; issues 117; justice 203; methods 1–2, 5, 31, 32, 60, 85, 94, 108; perspective 150; publications 124; research 2–4, 15, 20, 21, 24, 50, 60, 61, 70–71, 80, 86, 110, 117, 121, 141, 153, 197, 198, 202, 213; researcher 2, 60, 140, 161; respect for persons 198–199; theorists 89; visuality in 85–110
social science research 198–203; assumptions 199–201; beneficence 202; justice 203; respect for persons 198–199; visuality in 85–110
social scientists 2–3, 19, 25, 89, 102, 103, 105, 117, 122, 130, 204, 209
sociological 4, 35, 64, 104
sociologist 41, 103–104, 131, 165
sociology 3, 21, 85, 102, 103–104
software 14, 203; *see also* computer(s)
somatic: clues 54; quality 205
The Song of the Lark (Breton) 107
Sousanis, Nick 134, *183*
spectacle 108, 133, 212
Spelke, Elizabeth 45–47
Staikidis, Kryssi 138, *188*
Stanford Prison Experiment 198
Star Wars (movie) 200
statistics 139, 149
Statue of Liberty 119
stereotypes 20
Stern, Robert 66
still life *90*, 157, 201
stimuli 20, 35, 55, 153, 210
Strauss, Anselm 135
structuralism: Gestalt psychologists on 38; vision as linked chain of individual moments 37–38
structuralist analysis 85
structuralists 42, 45
studio art: artistic domains 99–100; visual research methods 98–102; *see also* fine art
studio inquiry 133–135, *183*, *184*
subjective 31, 53, 64, 70, 102
subjectivity 70–71

Sullivan, Graeme 99, 99–100
summative 49, 53, 102
Sun Raid (Hernandez) 137, *187*
surveys 3, 30–31, 85, 103, 161
sustainability 138
symbolic: analysis 159, 165; evidence 158; meaning 165, *176*, *183*; qualities 88, **95**, 193
symbolism 22
symbols(s) 4, 22, 45, 46, 49, 53, 59, 64, 80, 89, 134; visual 8, 59, 79
symbol system(s) 8, 46, 49, 89
systematic analysis of visual relationships 209

tacit: dimension 25, 40, 47, 49, 85; evidence 108; experiences 103, 205; information 27, 31, 38, 40, 67–68, 76, 157; knowing 108; knowledge 25–26, 40, 46–47, 80, 123–124, 129, 133–134, 162, 165, 206; learning 46, 47; levels 38, 41, 54, 62–63, 107; meaning 47–48; power 24, 85; qualitative meaning 100; relationships 49, 79; thinking 136; understanding 40
taste 25, 28, 51, 140, 147, 151–153
technique(s) 2, 14, 21, 24, 31–32, 50, 63, 86, 103, 120, 130, 135, 147, 159
technology(ies): digital 17, 79, 130, 134, 165, 201, 203; nano 133; new(er) 15, 61, 89, 110, 121, 129; visual 20, 70, 193, 201
television 12, 19, 49, 73, 77, 164, 205–206
text 24; based literacy 22; based metaphors 85; based theories 23; content analyses 25; illustration of 3; interpretive 103; as mechanism 50; participant-written 124
textbooks 15, 22
textual: analysis **97**, 101–102, 161; literacy 28; model(s) 156; response to images 130–131, *179*
Thanem, Torkild 105, 160, 165
theater 129
theoretical: constructs 21, 31, 70; foundations 7; framework 22–24; ideas 124; models 53; point of view 100; vision 137
theory: of abduction 122; constructivist 45; critical 89; critical education 138; cultural 50; Dewey's 63; of ecological optics 43; of emergent properties 38; Gestalt vision 38; grounded 135; literary 22; new materialism 51; of perception 37, 38, 45; of relativity 122; social 137; visual 197; visual culture 22; *see also* Image as Theory
therapeutic: approaches 106; expression 99, 135, 136, *185*; perspective 136; research 107

Index

thick description 40
thinking: abstract 122–123; higher order 47–48; with materials 79–80; metaphorical 134; paradigmatic 54; pre-linguistic 45; pre-symbolic 63; tacit 136; visual 23–24, 160
The Third of May 1808 (Goya) *87*, 87–88
three-dimensional: display of imagery *192*; objects and space 13, 68, 133, 140; surface 133
time arts 140
Torrance, Paul 106
Trafi-Prats, Laura 140, *191*
transcripts 25
transduction 4
transferability 25
transformation 19, 61, 91, 93, 100–102, 153
transmission 4, 136
The Treachery of Images (Magritte) 150
Très Riches Heures 10, *11*
triangulation 25, 30, 164
Trinidad and Tobago *109*
Triumph of the Will (film) 108
truth(s) 102, 137, 197, 203–205, 212
Tufte, Edward 38, 127, 139, 149
two-dimensional: art forms 68; representation of animal 127; surface 13

unconscious 20, 37–38; brain 122; careful consideration of 206; choices 35–36; inaccessible 46; luck 63; perception 38; responses to imagery 200; tacit information 38; use of images 94
unconsciously 46, 75, 149, 150
Understanding Comics: The Invisible Art (McCloud) 140
unethical: image 212; manner 211; uses of images 198
unlearning 101, 110

Vagle, Mark 93
validity 25, 31, 52, 60, 69, 134, 151; determinations of 71; empirical evidence 71
Van Dyck, Anthony 210, *211*
Van Hoogstraten, Samuel *90*
variable 99, 167
Vecchio, Mary Ann 104
Venus and Mars (Botticelli) 49
videos 19, 78, 103, 120, 140, 205, 207, 212, 213
Vietnam Veterans Memorial (Washington D.C.) 119

viewer: association(s) 75–76; context(s) 158; ethical 206; experience 70; eyes 73; feelings 76; image 92; intentions 75; interpretation(s) 75; response(s) 63, 123; understanding 210
visceral experiences 105
visibility 93, 100, 103
Visible Border Crossing 134
Visible Border Exploration *184*
vision: aesthetic foundations of new materialisms 50–52; cognitive 38, 45, 46; deconstructing visual making 52; high 46–47; and humans 49–50; imaginative 79; as linked chain of individual moments 37–38; ontological turn 49–50; peripheral 79; personal 204; philosophy of 48–54; as process of bricolage 45–47; research as acts of fiction 52–54; theoretical 137
visual: as evidence 119–120, 147–193; systematic analysis of 209
visual advocacy 137–138, *187*
visual analysis 101–102, 150–151
visual analytic method(s) 165
visual analytic technique(s) 159
visual anthropology 21; *see also* anthropology
visual argument 128, *175*
visual arts 2, 10, 150; communities 51, 149; and critique 101–102, 150; genre in 157; production of 202; professionals 27, 119; and social research 29–30; two-dimensional objects in 68–69
visual authenticity **97**, 127, 128, *175*, *176*
visual benchmarking framework **126**
visual border exploration 134–135
visual characteristics 24, 29, 92; *see also* visual qualities
visual choice 129–130, *178*
visual commentary(ies) 137, 165, 167
visual criticism 86; observation as 91–92; reporting as 92; research as 90–93
visual culture: importance of 21; influence of, on social life 18–21; learning communities 207; social science investigation 19–20
visual data 2, 4, 21, 31, 52, 71, 94, 129, 161, 164; *see also* data
visual documentation 127–128, *173*, *174*
visual elements: color 67–68; contrast 67–68; line 67–68; shape 67–68
visual ethnography 130–132, *179*, *180*
visual evidence 28, 53, 71–72, 119–120, 147–193, 204, 206; *see also* evidence
visual exhibition **98**, 140, *192*

228

Index

visual experience(s) 37, 44, 47, 91, 140, 150
visual facts 127, *173*
visual field notes 131–132, *180*
visual form 22, 47, 76, 78, 105–106, 133, **169**; of analysis 160; conditions of 2; of expression and communication 7; humanly created 7, 18; qualities of 28; range of 18
visual gestalts 23, 61; *see also* gestalt
visual imagery 136; *see also* imagery
visual images *see* image(s)
visual information 2, 7, 20, 23, 26, 28, 45, 151; assessment of 65; features of 60; qualities of 14–15; seductive and immediate character of 29; in social science publications 124; symbolic and tacit 59; types of 59
visual interpretation: within the context 73–74; of creator intent 74–75; within the object 72–73; of viewer association 75–76
visual investigation 7–18
visuality: in social science research 85–110
visualization 20, 122; of categorical quantities 40; data 38, 133; of imaginative idea 134; nanoscience 133; scientific **96**, 123, 132, 133, *182*; of three-dimensional objects 133; *see also* data visualization
visual journal 132
visual journaling **98**, *180*
visual knowledge 24, 31, 46, 60, 62, 65
visual literacy 209; building 64–65; of expressive content 62–64; inferential reasoning of interpretation 61–62; and power of image 61–65; visual culture and social science 64–65; *see also* literacy
visual making: approaches to 100–101; deconstructing 52
visual methodologies 31, 86, 93–94
Visual Methodologies: An Introduction to Researching with Visual Materials (Rose) 110
visual methods 117–141; choosing right 121–123; Research Image Framework (*see* Research Image Framework (RIF)); visual evidence 119–120; *see also* arts-based resarch methods
visual narrative **98**, 140, *191*
visual perception: cognitive development 47; contemporary perceptual constructivism 45–47; ecological optics 42–45; Gestalt psychology 38–40, *39*, 40–42; implications for empirical aesthetics 47–48; overview 35–37; perceptual constructivism 47; philosophy of vision and perception 48–54; science of 37–48; structuralism 37–38; tacit meaning 47–48; vision as process of bricolage 45–47
visual principles 68–69
visual properties 38
visual qualities: amounts of qualities 80; elements and principles of design 65–69; empirical evidence 69–71; formal visual qualities 65–69; images function in research 76–79; materials 79–80; new materialism 69–71; and new materialism 69–71; overview 59–60; power of image 61–65; qualitative thought 80; quantitative thought 80; relationships 80; visual interpretation 71–76; visual literacy 61–65
visual recording 94, 128, *176*
visual records 54, 79, 102, 128, 132, 136, 150, 198
visual representations 8, 12, 36, 46, 89, 124, 139, *182*, *189*
visual research 3–4, 14, 69, 99, 103; analyses of 158; conceptions of 35–55; data article 27; dimensions of 99; divergence of meaning in 26–27; participant-made art 129; post-intentional phenomenal 94; social research and visual arts 29–30; strategies **96**; taste *vs.* judgments 28–29; verifiable/tacit knowledge 25–26; visual as verifiable, tacit knowledge 25–26; visual choice 129; visual perception and conceptions of 35–55; *see also* arts-based research methods
visual researcher 2, 31, 50, 52, 102, 138–139, 156
visual research methods **95–98**, 197–213; agency of images 205–208; anthropology 102–103; business, advertising and performativity 105–106; choosing right 121–123; communications/journalism 104–105; disciplinary approaches to use 98–110; education 107–109; geography 109–110; images and truth 203–205; interpretation 209–211; moral obligation of creation 211–213; overview 7; psychology 106–107; rationality 209–211; social science research 198–203; sociology 103–104; studio art 98–102; visual culture and social life 18–21; and visual investigation 7–18; *see also* arts-based research methods; visual methods
Visual Sequence **98**, 127–128, *174*

Index

visual sources 21, 25, 31, 148–153, 159
visual technologies 20, 70, 201; *see also* technology(ies)
Visual Webs 139, *190*
Vitruvian Man (DaVinci) 148
Vivirito, Jessica 162
Vogue Italia 106
Volkman, Alfred Wilhelm 20
vulnerable: groups 198; populations 204; *see also* Institutional Review Board (IRB)

walking 132, 136
Wang, Shei-Chau 135, *184*
Watson, James 124, 133
Ways of Seeing 49
Weaver-Hightower, Marcus 140, *191*
Wells Cathedral, *9*

Western: culture 90; fine art 49, 158; gaze 102; imagery benchmarks 66; prejudices 198; still life 201; thought 48; traditions 37
Where Do We Go from Here? (Rolling) 22, *23*
Wiley, Kehinde 138, 153
Wilking, Joshua 127, *173*
Wilson, Fred 140, *192*
Wood, Grant 119, 207, *207*
World War II 20
Writing Culture (Clifford and Marcus) 102

Yoshida, Hatsusaburō *13*
Yoshinaga, Masayuki 129
YouTube 205

zone of image interpretation 156; *see also* interpretation(s)